EDUCATIONAL ISSUES IN THE LEARNING AGE

edited by

Catherine Matheson and David Matheson

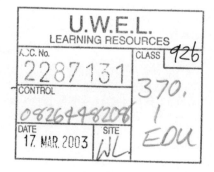
CONTINUUM

London and New York

Continuum
Wellington House
125 Strand
London WC2R 0BB

370 Lexington Avenue
New York
NY 10017–6503

First published 2000

British Library Cataloguing-in-Publication Data
A catalogue record for this book is available from the British Library.

ISBN 0–8264–4820–8 (hb)
    0–8264–4803–8 (pb)

Typeset by York House Typographic Ltd
Printed and bound in Great Britain by Biddles Ltd, Guildford and King's Lynn

Contents

Preface

In 1996, the UNESCO commission chaired by Jacques Delors published its report on lifelong learning entitled *Learning: The Treasure Within* in an apparent attempt to synthesize the state of the issue in the world today and to give us examples of what might count as 'good practice'. This represented a major step in the development of the debate on lifelong learning which, in modern times, owes much to the earlier UNESCO report *Learning To Be* (Faure *et al.*, 1972), in its own way a synthesis of much thought then current. Governments, private and public bodies have all made their contributions. Commentators, academic and otherwise, have questioned just what the hypothesis that was becoming known as 'The Learning Society' might look like.

The world of 1996 was not the world of 1972, however. The sense of hope in the future that seems to imbue much of the literature of the 1970s had gradually been overtaken by events which shook what was perhaps the complacent optimism that marked that earlier era. Oil crises, new epidemics, economic crises and many other events conspired to shift thoughts from one of never-ending expansion and development, where tomorrow would inevitably be better than today, to one more cynical. A realization set in that many of yesterday's promises were simply not coming true. Predictions of shorter working weeks for the many gave way to longer working weeks for the few. Unemployment in developed countries became such an apparently fixed part of the landscape that at least one writer questioned whether formal education should continue to be posited on the notion that one might get a job at all (White, 1997). Others pointed to the dearth of permanent, decent jobs (Aronowitz and de Fazio, 1997). Differing conceptions of lifelong learning, such as lifelong training, were increasingly voiced. Training was described as 'the great palliative of our time' (*Observer*, 1996), cheaper than creating jobs and with no need to ask what work there was for the students at the end of it. In the developing world, grand investment schemes, such as dam-building, were increasingly seen as lacking a lasting, positive impact on ordinary people. Additionally, the shock realization in the developed world that many of the world's poorest nations were paying more in debt interest charges than they were receiving in aid, stirred more than one conscience into questioning not just the text of what was going on but the sub-text also.

In 1998, the UK government published its Green Paper *The Learning Age: A Renaissance for a New Britain* (DfEE, 1998) and a new term entered common parlance. What the term actually meant was discussed and debated. In the UK and elsewhere it was becoming ever more common to hear mention in the media of Learning Ages, Learning Societies, Lifelong Learning and so on. Generally, these more public references created an impression of unalloyed good. However, the background against which this was operating was one where governments were redefining their role in relation to their citizens' lives. And it is against this changing background that we engage in the discussions that comprise this book. It is a background where The Market has grown and entered territory which, in the post-war years, in much of the developed world, had been closed to it. Education, previously a public good, began to be mixed with ideas that, even in the public sector, it might become, to some degree, a private service. Life in the 1990s certainly seemed to lack the simplicity (or naïvety?) of life in the 1970s.

So it is, at the dawn of a new century, with the *fin de siècle* self-evaluation taken to new heights by millenarianism, that we find ourselves in an apparent Learning Age where questions are raised ever more frequently over not just what education *does* or can do but also over what education *is*, what it is *for*; what it should contain, to whom educators should be answerable and in what terms. The purpose of this book is to examine some of these educational issues in the Learning Age.

Our list of issues is clearly not exhaustive and it goes without saying that different editors would have identified different issues (or the same issues in different terms) and that different writers would have tackled these issues in a different manner. But such is the nature of academic writing, or any other writing for that matter. What we have endeavoured to do is to present the reader with a wide range of educational issues across a variety of educational spaces from contributors who demonstrate a wide range of styles and preferences.

We hope that the reader will appreciate this diversity; that his/her understanding will be deepened, and that at least some of his/her preconceptions will be challenged.

CATHERINE MATHESON
DAVID MATHESON
JANUARY 2000

References

Aronowitz, S. and de Fazio, W. (1997) 'The new knowledge work', in A. H. Halsey, H. Lauder, P. Brown, and A. Stuart Wells (eds) *Education, Culture, Economy and Society*. Oxford: Oxford University Press.

Department for Education and Employment (DfEE) (1998) *The Learning Age: A Renaissance for a New Britain*. London: The Stationery Office.

Faure, E., Horrera, F., Kaddoura, A.-R., Lopes, H., Petrovsky, R. and Ward, F. (1972) *Learning To Be*. Paris: UNESCO.

Observer (1996) 'On your unicycle', 21 July.

Report to UNESCO of the International Commission on Education for the Twenty-first Century (chaired by Jacques Delors) (1996) *Learning: The Treasure Within*. Paris and London: UNESCO and HMSO.

White, J. (1997) *Education and the End of Work*. London: Kogan Page.

Contributors

Abdeljalil Akkari	Senior Lecturer in Education, University of Fribourg, Switzerland
James Arthur	Professor of Education, Canterbury Christchurch University College, UK
Stephen Brookfield	Professor of Education, University of St Thomas, St Paul, Minnesota, USA
Trevor Corner	Professor of Comparative and International Education, University of Middlesex, UK
Jon Davison	Professor of Teacher Education and Head of School of Education, University College Northampton, UK
Joanne Dillow	Researcher in Education, Canterbury Christchurch University College, UK
David Limond	Lecturer in Education, University College Northampton, UK
Catherine Matheson	Researcher in Education, City University, London, UK
David Matheson	Field Chair Education, University College Northampton, UK
Soledad Perez	Senior Lecturer in Education, University of Geneva, Switzerland

Tim Peskett   Lecturer in Education, University College Northampton, UK

Martyn Roebuck   Visiting Professor of Education, University of Glasgow, UK

Christopher Winch   Professor of Philosophy of Education, University College Northampton, UK

Acknowledgements

The editors would like to thank, first and foremost, the authors for their contributions. An earlier version of *Education and Training* appeared as 'Education Needs Training', *Oxford Review of Education* 21 (3), 1995, 315–25. We thank the publisher Taylor & Francis Ltd for permission to reproduce excerpts from this paper in the present volume.

Educational Spaces and Discourses

Catherine Matheson and David Matheson

Discourse, language and power

It is self-evident that language is the vehicle of education. Without language, education (and this can take multiple forms) simply could not happen.

> For most everyday human purposes, power is exerted through verbal channels: language is the vehicle for identifying, manipulating and changing power relations between people. (Corson, 1998, p. 5)

As Gramsci (in Mayo, 1999, p. 51) puts it, 'every language contains the elements of a conception of the world'. But Gramsci goes on to say that language is in effect a situational construct and that the situation will determine to a large extent the things the speaker is capable of saying and hence thinking. Therefore the conception of the world that one has is determined, at least in part, by the words one has at one's disposal. The number of Inuit words for snow exemplifies how the situation can affect the language available.

Language is not static; it evolves, it changes with the times, new words are created, old ones discarded or their meanings are changed. One such new word is 'discourse' and the aim of this chapter is to examine the term and relate it to the gaps which arguably exist in education, between the rulers and the ruled, the rich and the poor and so on.

Discourse is much more than just exchanging words. Consider, for example, the manner in which a teacher might speak to a learner. This consists of far more than simply passing information. The tone the teacher employs, the sentence construction and so on convey notions to do with the teacher's authority, the teacher's power and the power, or lack of it, that the learner has.

Discourse theory is associated principally with the work of Michel Foucault

(1926–84) who uses discourse as a conceptual framework to explain ways of thinking about the world that are so deeply embedded in practice that we are unconscious of their existence and yet they inform our internalized expectations, values and behaviour. Discourses are articulations of ideologies (sets of beliefs) and of power equated to knowledge. As Winch and Gingell (1999) state, 'discourses are articulations of power and domination' (p. 66) and this is so to such an extent that Foucault stated 'you do not speak the discourse, the discourse speaks you!' (*ibid.*, p. 66). Discourses legitimize power relations (which may be the unintended consequences of the intentions of those engaged in the practice).

> Power is not an object. It is not a thing that can be held on to and used for political purposes. Rather power is a force acting upon the body, through a series of relations, relays, modes of connection. It is transmitted, it cannot be possessed because it is constantly in play, acting on individuals who are its conduits, its subjects. (Barker, 1993, p. 78)[1]

Power and power relations are part of the key to understanding discourse but we must be careful not to read too much into the manner in which power is wielded. We cannot assume that power in discourse implies the conscious attempt to exert one person's will over another. Discourses have historical roots and, as we try to demonstrate below, within any discourse there is an acquiescence to the dominant or a resistance to it. In other words, one cannot have a discourse on one's own. Historically, though, are we ever alone? In other words, does solitude exempt one from the discourses within which one grew up?

It is questionable whether discourses are entirely deterministic or whether they can be authentically resisted. The latter might be attempted by manipulating discourses, or offering an alternative discourse, or by mounting resistance in the intellectual space outside the discourse. Resistance to discourses and manipulation of them are themes returned to at several points throughout this book. For the moment, let us draw on the examples given by Mansfield (1992) who considers both Freire and Rogers as advocates of means of liberating oneself from the dominance of the dominant discourse. Mansfield tells us that these two writers are comparable in their approach to some of the ideas that underpinned consciousness-raising groups in the women's movement, an excellent example of resisting the dominant discourse. As an introduction to her argument, Mansfield states that 'implicit in the work of Freire and Rogers is the idea that true freedom is only gained once one is free from the fear of freedom itself' (p. 14). This obviously can lead us to wonder just what this 'true' freedom might consist of and the two writers considered by Mansfield are somewhat vague on the issue. However, we are told that for Rogers, the aim of this liberation is for 'the individual to become a fully functioning person' (Mansfield, 1992, p. 14) and that this will signify a change in the way the person behaves and relates to others. In other words, the patterns of thought of the individual will appear to have altered. Whether this might be qualified as *resistance* to the discourse is open to question, but changing the manner in which one behaves implies at least a reinterpretation of one's relation to the discourse.

For Freire the group is paramount and 'individual freedom which is not translated into collective action for the liberation of both the oppressor and the oppressed is not freedom at all' (Freire and Shor quoted in Mansfield, 1992, p. 14).

Discourses become internalized (and, as far as Rogers and Freire are concerned, one is not free) by the internalization of the values of others. To become free, one must discover for oneself one's own sense of self-worth and value. This comes about through reflecting upon and taking ownership of one's own experiences and feelings which entails, for Rogers, the discovery of denied attitudes whereby one develops awareness of attitudes experienced but not acknowledged (Mansfield, 1992). Thus one must reappraise how one feels and reacts to events in order to (re)discover what one really feels and to realize that these are authentic and valid feelings. Take, for example, the manner in which the crude sexist and racist 'jokes' of various comedians were previously deemed to be of sufficiently broad appeal to mainstream society that they were displayed on television, regardless of the offence that the objects of this 'humour' might have felt. The dominant discourse of humour of the time deemed these comedians funny. Therefore anyone who found them offensive, as opposed to simply unfunny, appeared as deficient in some way, 'unable to get the joke'. However, notable is the extent to which women would laugh at sexist jokes, non-whites would laugh at racist jokes. In other words, they had internalized the discourse which showed them as objects to be mocked, which had reduced them to the level of stereotypes whose traits were in themselves targets of mockery. Notable among sexist and racist jokes is that they make fun of persons not for what they do but for what they are. Therefore, by laughing at such comedians, the objects were collaborating in the denial of their individuality and it was upon this denial that the humour was posited.

The first step in resistance to such discourse is the recognition that there is denial of attitudes on the part of the objects. That this did not occur sooner is simply testimony to the internalization of the discourse. However, through the demand by growing numbers of them that previously denied attitudes be acknowledged, the objects of these comedians began to recognize their feelings, to question why they were subject to such attacks and then, finally, saw their feelings recognized as valid. The discourse was resisted and was eventually altered, at least as far as such public displays were concerned. Gratuitous offence has mercifully been declared unfunny. What would be interesting to ascertain is the extent to which those who protested against this humour acted as individuals who felt offended or as offended members of a group. In other words, were they acting in a Rogerian individualistic style or in a Freirean collective style?

The educational implications of what humour is deemed 'mainstream' are multiple especially as regards televisual humour, as this puts a stamp of general acceptability on a way of discussing others. Of course, in these days of 'watersheds' whereby material can become more *risqué* after 9 p.m. (in the UK), this requires some nuancing. Notable is that the comedians referred to above tended to perform at peak viewing times when material broadcast is supposed to have the widest appeal. The perception held by television chiefs would appear to have been that of living in an overtly racist and sexist society and that this was not to be questioned. Indeed, it was to be praised through humour.

However, if discourses are indeed deterministic, then they might well be all-pervading. They might, as Gramsci famously suggests that hegemony does, allow apparent counter-discourse. For Gramsci, hegemony 'acts to allow the appearance of liberty in order to absorb dissenting elements' (Matheson and Wells, 1999, p. 11). As we shall see, discourses can take this notion much further. Discourses influence the very manner in which we are capable of thinking about an issue by influencing the meanings attached to the words we have at our disposal. None the less Foucault insists that 'there are no relations of power without resistances' (Barker, 1993, p. 78). However, we must bear in mind the role of language itself and its capabilities for constructing or diminishing the means of resistance.

We need only examine the sub-discourse of gender and educational achievement for an illustration of a manner in which dissent can be side-tracked or even hijacked. From the 1970s onwards (if not before), there was a growing awareness that the school system in the UK was biased in many respects against girls. From this grew various initiatives to equalize opportunity between boys and girls. An unintended consequence was that girls' achievement at post-16 external examinations began to outstrip that of boys. This is not to say that boys' performance actually declined. Indeed, quite the opposite. Both boys' and girls' performance at post-16 improved but girls improved faster than did boys. The manner in which the focus of attention shifted is quite remarkable. Within a very short space with time, we were regaled in media of all sorts with tales of boys' underachieving, even to the extent of loss of male identity. Girls' remarkable progress in a short space of time slipped down the agenda. In effect, what occurred was that the resistance to the discourse of male educational superiority was momentarily acknowledged before the very motivations behind it (equality of opportunity, social justice etc.) were being used in an attempt to re-establish male supremacy in formal education. That girls' under-achievement never caused the same furore is seldom mentioned, at least not in the popular media, and is remarkable since it suggests that the discourse of male educational superiority never went away. It merely looked around for modern tools to maintain itself. In the manner of hegemony, it required and allowed some dissent in order to revitalize itself. That girls were underachieving since the invention of state schooling until just a few years ago is conveniently overlooked in the light of just a few years of statistical evidence of boys apparently falling behind (Martin, 1999). Notable throughout the discourse of male educational superiority is the reduction of the school-age population to the level of two objects: boys and girls. We return shortly to the issue of objectification.

With the hijacking of the gender sub-discourse, many of the questions arising from gender have been supplanted by questions arising from social class. Social class, rather than gender, is increasingly presented as the 'cause' of educational underachievement and so the tools of one sub-discourse are employed by another while the first gradually loses its prominence.

The discourse of educational achievement is remarkable not only for its capacity to absorb dissent but also for its capacity to evolve only slowly. A rose blooming in

Table 1.1 Parallel educational discourses

Historical period	Prevalent discourses of education	Prevalent discourses of gender and education
1940s, 1950s	Equality of opportunity: IQ testing (focus on access)	Weak (emphasis on equality according to 'intelligence'
1960s, 1970s	Equality of opportunity: progressivism/mixed ability (focus on process)	Weak (emphasis on working-class, male disadvantage)
1970s to early 1980s	Equality of opportunity: gender, race, disability, sexuality (focus on outcome)	Equal opportunities/anti-sexism (emphasis on female disadvantage)
Late 1980s, early 1990s	Choice, vocationalism and marketization (focus on competition)	Identity politics and feminisms (emphasis on femininities and masculinities)
Mid-1990s	School effectiveness and improvement (focus on standards)	Performance and achievement (focus on male disadvantage)

Source: Weiner, Arnott and David (1997, p. 622)

January does not make it a month of spring. Neither does a little amount of attention given to one sub-discourse rather than another change the overall direction of the main discourse which declaims quite clearly that males should achieve better than females and if they do not then there is cause for alarm.

Weiner, Arnott and David (1997) chart the development in the UK of the prevalent discourses of education which they set in parallel with the prevalent discourses of gender and education. 'From the 1940s to the early 1960s there was relatively little discussion of gender and education, or of gender issues more widely' (p. 623). As we see from Table 1.1, while the prevalent discourse of education evolved through various notions of equality of opportunity to arrive at the current discourse of effectiveness and school improvement (which arguably are simply part of the discourse of the market), the prevalent discourse of gender and education had a brief flirtation with female disadvantage before returning its focus to male disadvantage.

For a fictional example of an extreme case of language being used to determine reality we suggest George Orwell's *1984*. Here we are presented with a revised form of English, 'Newspeak', wherein it becomes impossible to even *think* dissenting thoughts. Orwell's Newspeak is accompanied by a mode of thinking termed 'double-think', the capacity to hold two opposing opinions simultaneously without feeling any contradiction. In many social and educational discourses we may claim to do one thing and, indeed, even be entirely convinced that we are doing it whilst also doing another. If we are aware of both then we are engaged in double-think. Double-think within a discourse allows us not to see the contradictions within it. It allows us to deny evidence as invalid simply because it does not tie in with our personal internalization of the discourse, and to be convinced of the rationality of an irrational position. In this, we move into the realm of discourse as a modifier of meaning.

Discourse as a modifier of meaning

Discourse can be determinant of what is judged true and what is judged false, what is deemed good and what is deemed bad. '(The) effects of truth are produced within discourses which in themselves are neither true nor false' (Foucault, 1986, p. 60). As an example of this, Schrag examines the role of examinations in the lives of American school students.

> The examination ... illustrates a prominent way in which power and truth ... are connected in modern society. Without power over students, examinations could not yield 'truths' about them and these 'truths' could not be used for purposes of 'placing' them in social hierarchies and shaping their expectations of themselves and others. (Schrag, 1999, p. 377)

The examination is derived from the discourse within which it exists. The examination wields power and determines 'truth'. Therefore the discourse itself is determinant of the 'truth' surrounding the examinees or is at least determinant of the mechanisms whereby 'truth' is ascertained.

Another example of this determination of truth concerns the effective school. Just how is a school deemed *effective*? In itself, the term 'effective' is to all intents and purposes devoid of meaning since it is such a personal value judgement. On the other hand, if we situate the effective school within a particular discourse then we can arrive at various meanings for the term. Within the discourse of the market an effective school may be one which scores well in external examinations or which sends a substantial part of its leavers into higher education (and hence figures quite highly in any relevant league tables of results or leavers' destinations). It may achieve this high score partly through divesting itself of those pupils whose performance risks lowering the average examination score. Such a school would hardly be termed effective in the discourse of inclusion (which has superseded the discourse of equity). The 'truth' of the effectiveness of a school is thus determined by the discourse within which we measure that effectiveness.

It is not just major concepts that are subject to shifting meaning. Take, for example, the word 'more'. In the discourse of selectivity, more (as in more students) means *worse*. In the discourse of inclusion, more means *different* and selectivity has become *exclusion*. The discourse employed will determine whether the cup is half full or half empty.

Ryan (in Sokal and Bricmont, 1998) sounds a cautionary note regarding Foucault's ideas on truth:

> It is, for example, pretty suicidal for embattled minorities to embrace Michel Foucault ... The minority view was always that power could be undermined by

truth ... Once you've read Foucault as saying that truth is simply an effect of power, you've had it. (*Ibid.*, p. 250)

So, we have to take care with just how far we take this notion of truth being determined by the discourse. There is the question of objective truths (as opposed to our interpretation of them which may be far from objective). From an ontological perspective it makes perfect sense to ask 'what objects exist in the world? What statements about these objects are true?' (Sokal and Bricmont, 1998, p. 251). On the other hand, as Sokal and Bricmont seem to overlook, the discourse may well be determinant of the questions that we ask. The truth may be out there but what we find, and whether we find it at all, will in large measure depend on what we are looking for and the questions we ask. This is, of course, in addition to how we interpret what we find.

Discourse as a determinant of what is valuable and what is not is seen very clearly in the subjects which appear in the school curriculum. Where, for example, is hair care? Why is science deemed important? And so on. The answer, according to Barrow and Woods (1995), lies in the relative sophistication of the latter topic at its highest levels. Science is deemed more sophisticated than hair care. We could follow this up by examining what is entailed in school science in comparison with some (imaginary) school course on hair care. This potentially interesting tangent would be missing the point: the discourse which is dominant in determining the content of the curriculum deems some knowledge (both in the sense of *knowing how* and *knowing that*) to be more worthwhile than other knowledge. This division of knowledge can, of course, be related to notions of cultural capital *à la* Pierre Bourdieu and there are all sorts of concomitant notions related to social class. One might wonder whether it is coincidental that Barrow and Woods (and they are far from alone in this) attach greater value to learning which *might* be associated with middle-class pursuits than they do to that associated with working-class pursuits. However, let us not lose sight of one of the fundamental ideas in discourse: that one may not even be aware of its effects. As Preece (1999) puts it, 'people can be so embedded in their societal belief systems that they neither question the dominant values nor realise how much they themselves are naturalised into them' (p. 17). Could it be, therefore, that Barrow and Woods's disparagement and even dismissal of certain types of knowledge is simply witness to their internalization of the dominant discourse?

On a more subtle level, the dominant discourse will determine what counts as 'proper' language, what counts as dialect and what counts as slang. This is a live and relevant feature of the daily lives of many young people with knock-on effects into their adulthood and hence into the lives of their children.

A term which occurs in several places in this book, and whose meaning has shifted according to the discourse that is employing it, is 'empowerment'. Chapter 10, for example, demonstrates that for Paolo Freire empowerment consists to a large extent in encouraging and facilitating people to take their destiny into their own hands and to do something with it. Freire's work focuses on communities, rather than on individuals. His teaching on learning, his pedagogy, is posited on gaining a better understanding of one's own environment and learning to exert an influence on it. Contrast this with consumer empowerment which uses the same term to describe the idea that consumers might influence what is on offer to them. The difference is quite stark: on the one hand, we have Freire arguing in favour of a more equitable society, made more equitable by enhancing the humanity of humans; and on the other hand, we have consumerism locked firmly into capitalism and the accompanying, very unequal, distribution of wealth. Same word, different meanings.

A word of warning is needed here: the 'usage [of the word 'discourse'] varies according to the discourse in which it is situated' (Fiske, 1990, p. 14).

Objectification of the subject

> There are two meanings of the word *subject*: subject to someone else by control and dependence, and tied to his[/her] own identity by a conscience or self-knowledge. Both suggest a form of power which subjugates and makes subject to. (Foucault, quoted in Barker, 1993, p. 77)

Within the discourse of power, subjects are commonly treated as if they were devoid of all humanity and had become objects. Medicine is notorious for this, although it is to some extent understandable when dealing with critically ill persons that one might not wish to get too close to them. None the less, that easy shorthand which reduces the person with renal problems to the 'kidney in bed 13' reconstitutes the human being in bed 13 as a problem, rather than as an individual. Personal experience of a hospital in 1997 does show that this attitude is attacked even from within medicine and nursing. One of the present writers overheard a nurse referring to him as the 'thyroglossal cyst'! To his relief, the nurse in charge immediately told off the offender, insisting to her that not only had the patient a name but to call him the 'thyroglossal cyst' was ridiculous since it had been removed the previous day. This apparently tangential mention of medicine is, we feel, important since it is often in hospitals that we are at our physically weakest and hence in greatest need of having our humanity reinforced. How awful it can be to learn that we have ceased to be human and have become an ailment.

In discourses surrounding education, similar objectification of the subject occurs. Indeed, it may be difficult or even impossible to avoid. How might a classroom teacher learn about learning strategies if s/he could not refer to 'the pupil'? The problems arise, however, when an entire set of norms and behaviours are ascribed to 'the pupil' with insufficient room for individuality. The notion of 'the pupil' can be taken to mean that in a given context there is only one kind of young learner. So, what if a young person is not learning, is s/he still a pupil? Are all pupils cast in the same mould?

Pupils are just one example of objectification of the subject which occurs in education and sociology. It is easy to make a lengthy list of these. Take, for example, 'the poor'. This is used as if it were an amorphous mass. 'The truant' appears similarly. We could go on and include in this list of objectified subjects boys, females, ethnic minorities. All these, and more, appear as if they were composed of one kind of person. How often do we hear, from educationists, from the media, from politicians, about 'ethnic minority pupils'? There are many suppositions hidden in this apparently bland statement such as that we actually know what constitutes an ethnic minority, and that all ethnic minority persons have certain common traits. It would be enlightening to know what these are.

Terms like these certainly can be a shorthand and might usefully be used, though with care and sensitivity, but even then there is an element of objectification. And the problem with objectifying a subject is that it makes it easier for a person who is not part of this objectification to speak for the subject rather than inviting the subject to speak for him/herself. And it goes further than that, because if you take whatever discourse is actually dominant, then that influences not only what is said about the subject but how it is said. Much more important, though, is that the discourse is determinant of how what is said about the subject is heard by others.

Discourses, education and spaces

Discourse and education are effectively inseparable. Discourse involves power relations and knowledge. Education involves power relations and knowledge. However, from what we have seen above it is the discourse which determines the power relations and knowledge in education. Discourse further involves learning and reconstituting knowledge to fit in with the appropriate paradigm. Education is thus subservient, or subsidiary, to the discourse within which it is situated. Meanwhile the existence of power relations implies that one person has more power than another. There is a gap, a space between the wielder of power and the object of the power. In Freirean terms, this might refer to the oppressor and the oppressed. We need not employ such extreme language, but it is worth bearing in mind that oppression and being oppressed are not absolute states and much that we couch in more comfortable (i.e. less strong) terms might well fit under these ones.

Much of discourse in education is dependent on notions such as cultural distance and cultural capital. Cultural capital refers to both *knowing how* and *knowing that*. Bourdieu states three forms for cultural capital:

1. the embodied state, or the long lasting dispositions of the mind and the body;
2. the objectified state: cultural goods such as pictures, books, instruments, machines etc;
3. the institutionalized state 'which must be set apart because . . . in the case of educational qualifications, it confers entirely original properties on the cultural capital which it is presumed to guarantee'. (Bourdieu, 1997, p. 47)

Knowing how to address teachers, for example, fits under the heading of the embodied state. Knowing how to use books etc. refers to the objectified state whereas the institutionalized state bears testament to a particular knowing that. Spaces appear where the cultural capital of one group does not coincide with that of another. In this respect, the distribution of cultural capital assumes the nature of a power relation and is subject to the discourse within which it operates. The space which exists between one set of cultural capital and another may be termed the 'cultural distance' which separates them. In this respect, the less one has of cultural distance from the dominant discourse then the greater the value that one's cultural capital possesses. For Bourdieu, 'modern society no longer maintains its position by transmitting material property to its children, but more through its transmission of cultural capital' (Bullock, Stallybrass and Troubley, 1988, p. 194).

The cultural distance one possesses from the dominant discourse will, in this vision of things, be highly influential on how we react both towards that discourse and within it. Indeed, Bourdieu (1973) and Bourdieu and Passeron (1980) have highlighted that educational achievement, and hence participation in higher education, is linked to the level of cultural capital that an individual or a group of individuals have. Thus in the discourse of inclusion in higher education, it is not sufficient simply to make more places available in higher education if one wants to increase participation by under-represented groups. One must take steps to reduce the cultural distance which the potential students perceive between themselves and the institutions of higher education. In the UK, expansion and structural change and even the recognition of alternative routes have, however, seemingly failed to change the culture of élitism and consequently how higher education is perceived especially among non-participants (Williams, 1997). Permission is insufficient to overcome the previously élitist discourse. Power is required and, indeed, more than that: one needs to be aware that one has the power *and* that one can use it.

We find similar tones in the discourses of exclusion, inclusion and marginalization. None of these notions could exist without the precursor of cultural distance. If my cultural capital is aligned with that of the educational provider then, assuming no other discrimination (for example, on ethnic grounds), my chances of educational success are enhanced. I am a fish swimming in a familiar pond. On the other hand, the less my cultural capital is aligned with that of the educational institution then either my chances of success drop or I am forced to assume a new and different load of cultural capital. In other words, if I cannot act to decrease my cultural distance then I am effectively doomed from the outset. But consider the price at which this *rapprochement* may come. I might well be educated, if not out of my social class, then out of my social group. I could be forced to increase one cultural distance in order to decrease another, that is, unless I could become bicultural which is, in itself, a tall order. The lack of success in becoming bicultural is neatly illustrated by Gottraux (1986) who suggests that working-class students in higher education tend to internalize blame for examination failure while their bourgeois peers put the blame on to anything and everything but themselves. One view is clearly as faulty as the other but when we consider which one has the greater chance of recovery and subsequent success then we might see which student has the lesser cultural distance from higher education.

Marginalization (and exclusion and inclusion) can, of course, have a more physical aspect of space applied to it, in the sense that the educational opportunities may simply not be available in certain geographical areas. The rapidity, or otherwise, with which geographical factors are overcome or are compensated for may be explained not only in terms of available technology but also in terms of the importance attached to the persons involved by those who have decision-making powers in such matters. Again, we return to power relations, this time as a means for confirming, denying or compensating for spaces in education.

Conclusion

In many respects, space is perhaps a key to understanding the effects of discourse. This space is to be understood in the multiple varieties in which it is to be found. Gray (1999) tells us that 'Lefebvre alone refers to at least ninety' (p. 120). He argues that

> Space is not a thing among other things, nor a product among other products: rather it subsumes things produced and encompasses their interrelationships in their co-existence and simultaneity – their (relative) order and/or (relative) disorder. (Lefebvre, quoted in Davidson, 1999, p. 57)

Discourses modify or confirm spaces. The two are intimately bound. In this light, only by understanding space (in appropriate senses), and concomitant notions such as cultural capital and cultural distance, can we understand the how and the why of discourses and their impacts on individuals and groups and their educational experiences. Discourses exist in social space. Their effects transcend all boundaries.

Note

[1.] The reader familiar with physics will notice the evidently partial knowledge of the subject that Barker and Foucault possess. Power is not a force. It is the rate of transfer (or transformation) of energy. Power has no direction in a physics sense although it does in a sociological sense, while force does in both cases. The analogy to physics in this quote from Barker does come through very strongly in his use of terms such as 'relays', 'modes of connection'. He and Foucault are correct in a physics sense to state that power cannot be stored. Energy can be stored and what is often referred to as storing power in fact means storing energy. Barker and Foucault's errors are minor and pale into insignificance beside a number of others. For a deconstruction of several of France's better known misusers of scientific notions, see Sokal and Bricmont (1998).

References

Barker, P. (1993) *Michel Foucault*. New York: Harvester.
Barrow, R. and Woods, R. (1995) *An Introduction to the Philosophy of Education*. London: Routledge.

Bourdieu, P. (1973) *Sociology in Question*. London: Sage.

Bourdieu, P. (1997) 'The forms of capital', in A. Halsey, H. Lauder, P. Brown and A. Stuart Wells (eds) *Education, Culture, Economy and Society*. Oxford: Oxford University Press.

Bourdieu, P. and Passeron, J.-C. (1980) *Reproduction in Education, Society and Culture*. London: Sage.

Bullock, A., Stallybrass, O. and Trombley, S. (1988) *The Fontana Dictionary of Modern Thought*. London: Fontana.

Corson, D. (1998) *Changing Education for Diversity*. Buckingham: Open University Press.

Davidson, I. (1999) 'Space, place and subversion in university adult and continuing education', in B. Merril (ed.) *The Final Frontier: Exploring Spaces in the Education of Adults*. Proceedings of the 29th Annual Conference of the Standing Conference on University Teaching and Research in the Education of Adults. Warwick: University of Warwick and National Institute for Adult Learning.

Fiske, J. (1990) *Television Culture*. London: Routledge.

Foucault, M. (1986) *The Foucault Reader* (P. Rabinow (ed.)). London: Peregrine Books.

Gottraux, P. (1986) *Quelques disparités en matière d'accès aux études supérieures*. Berne: Conseil suisse de la science.

Gray, P. (1999) 'Dis-stanced learning: adult learners, Heidegger and spatiality', in B. Merril, (ed.) *The Final Frontier: Exploring Spaces in the Education of Adults*. Proceedings of the 29th Annual Conference of the Standing Conference on University Teaching and Research in the Education of Adults. Warwick: University of Warwick and National Institute for Adult Learning.

Mansfield, S. (1992) 'Consciousness-raising in women's groups'. *International Journal of Community Education*, 1 (4), 12–16.

Martin, J. (1999) 'Gender and education', in D. Matheson and I. Grosvenor (eds) *An Introduction to the Study of Education*. London: David Fulton.

Matheson, D. and Wells, P. (1999) 'What is education?', in D. Matheson and I. Grosvenor (eds) *An Introduction to the Study of Education*. London: David Fulton.

Mayo, P. (1999) *Gramsci, Freire and Adult Education*. London: Zed.

Preece, J. (1999) 'Difference and the discourse of inclusion'. *Widening Participation and Lifelong Learning*, 1 (2), 16–23.

Schrag, F. (1999) 'Why Foucault now?' *Journal of Curriculum Studies*, 31 (4), 375–83.

Sokal, A. and Bricmont, J. (1998) *Intellectual Impostures*. London: Profile Books.

Weiner, G., Arnott, M. and David, M. (1997) 'Is the future female? Female success, male disadvantage and changing gender patterns in education', in A. Halsey, H. Lauder, P. Brown and A. Stuart Wells (eds) *Education, Culture, Economy, and Society*. Oxford: Oxford University Press.

Williams, J. (1997) 'The discourse of access: the legitimation of selectivity statistics', in J. Williams (ed.) *Negotiating Access to Higher Education: The Discourse of Selectivity and Equity*. Buckingham: SRHE and Open University Press.

Winch, C. and Gingell, J. (1999) *Key Concepts in the Philosophy of Education*. London: Routledge.

Education and Cultural Identity

Catherine Matheson and David Matheson

Introduction

Arguably one of the effects of the growth of the supranational state (such as the European Union) and the globalization of so many aspects of our lives, from the economy to communications, is that in many parts of the world there is greater attention being paid to what makes one feel to be what one is. In other words, greater attention is being focused on the notion of cultural identity and, in view of the role played by it in the development of this notion, education. Education can of course be construed in a wide variety of fashions and it is useful for the present if we do not dwell on these. Suffice to say that the type of education which acts in the development of one's sense of cultural identity will not be limited to formal education, although it is difficult to imagine it not being influenced by the latter.

The object of this chapter is to examine the evolving nature of cultural identity and the response to this evolution made by education. In order to give some direction to the discussion we shall concentrate on comparing the situation in two apparently very different contexts: Scotland and French Switzerland.

At first glance, it may appear a little odd to want to compare Scotland and French Switzerland. After all, these are on the surface two rather different part of Europe with different geographies, languages and so on. The first is very much on the edge and the second is at (one of) the traditional heart(s) of Europe. As we see below, these last notions are very much relative. In terms of power relations to central government, French Switzerland shares with Scotland an important aspect: each is in hegemonical subordination to the rest of the country. In Switzerland, this is demonstrated by the manner in which a small number of Germanic Cantons can impose their intransigence over the rest of the country (since proposals in votations have to be accepted by a majority both of those who vote *and* of the 26 Cantons and Half-Cantons). Germann (1991) demonstrates just how a small minority can cause an effective standstill in Federal votations. Unfortunately as he also shows, this minority tends to be located in German Switzerland. With a few rare exceptions, the French Swiss can vote as they like in Federal referenda: it is the German Swiss who will decide (Chérix 1997). In Scotland, even with the advent of the Scottish Parliament, most substantive political decisions affecting Scotland are taken in Westminster. The Scottish Secretary may refer many of those who seek to question him at Scottish Questions to the Scottish Parliament but the fact remains that the UK national government in Westminster controls most of what goes on in Scotland, not least because it controls almost all the Scottish budget. The Scottish Parliament for its part has minimal tax-varying powers to the tune of ± 3 per cent.

In both cases, people who are linguistically, culturally and/or legally distinct have the will of what are effectively outsiders imposed upon them in multiple domains (see, for example, Mitchison, 1993).

In historical terms, there are many similarities between Scotland and French Switzerland. The French Swiss long ago adopted French in the towns but maintained the indigenous patois in the villages (Favre, 1981). Gaelic in Scotland receded into the Highlands and Islands and was eventually seen as a language of barbarity.[1] The Scots had, however, an added complication in the form of Scots, a language which had grown in parallel with English but which was definitely distinct from English in much the same way as German and Dutch or Czech and Slovak are distinct (Corbett, 1997). In other words, they were and are mutually comprehensible but with varying efforts on the parts of the interlocutors. Scots in its turn was assimilated into the role of barbarity and general uncouthness (Matheson and Matheson, 1998). In both French Switzerland and Scotland (as in many other countries), the schools were recruited to extirpate the indigenous languages and the parlous state of both the Patois and the Gaelic is testament to the success of this endeavour. As for Scots, it managed to lose its status as a language and is frequently seen just as bad English. Both Scotland and French Switzerland became plurilingual regions in which one language was seen as that of civilization and progress, and the other(s) not. In each case, only the 'language of civilization' was deemed official. So it was and is that Patois, Gaelic and Scots have no official status.

Going further back in history we see the links between the Scottish Lowlands and Geneva in the Reformation. It was no coincidence that Knox referred to the Geneva Bible, nor that there is an ancient Church of Scotland in Geneva. Just as in Scotland, the progress of the Reformation in Switzerland effectively limited itself to the non-mountainous areas (though in Scotland there was a second wave of Reforming at the end of the eighteenth and into the nineteenth centuries in the wake of the infamous Clearances). Within the Reformed areas, universal primary school was established and, arguably, it was these areas which had Europe's first school systems although, at least in the case of Scotland, the quality of the provision waxed and waned over the centuries (Bell and Grant, 1977).

Both areas had Christianity introduced into them by Columba or his followers (such as Gallus). In the mountainous areas of each, for centuries the main, and sometimes only, source of hard cash was the exportation of mercenaries (Antonietta, 1991; Cassini, 1991; Matheson, 1989; Steffen, 1991)

They are both, incidentally, very adept at misnaming or misunderstanding each other's countries. The Scots are remarkable at confusing Switzerland with Sweden, even to the extent that a renowned Scottish university for whom Catherine Matheson worked asked her to translate writing in Swedish into English. Despite her having given her languages as English, French and German, the university person concerned who read Catherine's details *assumed* that all the Swiss spoke Swedish. Perhaps it is the *Sw*-sound at the start which confuses. This, incidentally, was merely an extreme version but not an isolated incident. The alternative is the universal germanophonie. The Scots (and many other Britons), as we have found, all too frequently assume either that if they are in fact not Swedish then the Swiss all speak German as their first language or some unknown tongue called *Swiss*. For their part the French Swiss tend to assume that Scotland is simply part of England and that England, Great Britain and the United Kingdom are the same thing. David Matheson had enormous difficulty when he had a Swiss work permit of getting his nationality listed as *Britannique* or *Ecossais*. As he explained to the officials concerned, it was not that he had anything against the English, simply that he was not one. Finally it was only by asking an official in Lausanne in the Canton of Vaud if she would appreciate being termed *Fribourgeoise* (from Fribourg, a neighbouring Canton) that the error was changed.

On the nature of identity

To give any sense to a discussion on the evolving nature of any identity, it is useful to attempt to define the term. Grant (1996) refers to identity as being composed of markers such as religion, 'race', language and simply *feeling* that one belongs to one group rather than another. To this must be added the sense of *place*. It is remarkable, as Anderson (1983) has noted, that peoples of all sorts associate themselves with a place. These writers treat identity as if it were in some ways akin to the layers of an onion, or to a series of concentric circles. In effect, for Grant (1996) the further one moves from one's personal epicentre then the more layers one brings into view. In this respect, one might be Catholic in Glasgow, Glaswegian in Scotland, Scottish in England and so on. Notable in this scenario is that potential layers may be omitted. Depending on the attitude one has to the official nation-state one may or may include it in one's layers of definition. In this way, it is commonplace for English (and Scottish) persons to describe themselves as English (or Scottish) in any circumstances which refer to nationality. The English are accused of doing so for reasons of assimilating the whole of the UK into England (Breitenbach, Brown and Myers, 1998) or for equating England with Great Britain with the UK (White, 1996). The Scots do so for reasons of asserting that they are not English, given the English equation noted above. Matheson (1992) adapts this model by suggesting, in looking at French Switzerland, that there can also be an overlaying of another culture. In the case in question he proposes concentric rings but with an oval of

French culture which interacts with the French Swiss culture at all levels. This relates in many respects to the metaphor of the web.

Identity in the form of self-identity may be understood using the metaphor of the web. Self-identity is constructed partly under guidance from the self, though not in its overall control. Competing circumstances, influences and constraints overlap and fuse since the creation of identity is a collective affair. Politics are inseparable from the construction and maintenance of the self. The experience of acceptance and rejection, near the centre and at the edge of the centre, is closely related to the structures of power in the society in which the self finds itself. The self is 'constrained by overlapping, various communities, each of which is itself changing' (gender, social class, family, school, region, nation etc.) (Griffiths, 1995, p. 93). The metaphor of the web allows the possibility of emphasizing some parts of one's identity whilst momentarily diminishing others *but* without implying a change in their value, merely in the momentary perception of them. In this respect it is perhaps a more complete metaphor for how one considers oneself than the concentric ring theory.

Brock and Tulasiewicz (1985), for their part, consider the aspect of identification and repudiation in the construction of identity. Their image ties in very much with that of Griffiths above.

> Since an act of separation involves a contest or agreement, identity can only be formed in a system of relations which crystallises into commitment. Politics – indeed educational policies – can be used to further transform or destroy a social, cultural or national identity and does affect individuals in different levels of scale of change. (Brock and Tulasiewicz, 1985, p. 1)

The notion that assimilation and repudiation are at the root of much of identity is a theme which we shall return to but it is one which, as Gikandi (1996) makes clear, has been at the heart of the constructions of many cultures whom the British, and especially the English, have touched in their various ways. There is the fundamental question of defining oneself (and hence one's culture) with respect to the *Other*. In this, the distance, be it political, geographical or cultural, from the Other becomes important. As we shall see, in the case studies that follow, the perception of the Other has been evolving. In this light, let us consider notions of centrality and peripherality.

Relative terms: the centre and the edge

> Let us call for the blessing of the Lord upon the people of our isle [Skye], not also forgetting the people of the neighbouring islands of Raasay, Lewis and Harris, Uist and Barra, Britain and Ireland. (Grant, 1988, p. 155)

So is quoted a Presbyterian minister on the Isle of Skye. The centre for that minister was clearly where he stood. He demonstrated a clear sense of self and his relation to the world and was not afraid to declare that he and his island were at the centre of *their own worlds.* There is incidentally no irony or humour in the minister's pronouncement, for as Grant comments: 'Calvinist ministers do not joke with the Almighty' (*ibid.*). When we move into the abstraction which is politics, life becomes less straightforward. All attempts at finding the centre of Europe, for example, are doomed from the outset. They are doomed on a globe since there is no agreement as to where the edges of Europe lie. They are doubly doomed on a map since not only is there no agreement over where the edges lie, there is the distortion due to transposing features from a spheroid on to a flat surface. With this in mind, let us proceed to plot the centre of Europe.

The geography text which Catherine Matheson used while at primary school is unequivocal in putting the centre of Europe in Berne (Rébaud 1963). This literal self-centring reminded us of when we lived in Madrid and had occasion to risk life and limb to cross part of the bus station at Puerta del Sol. There, crass with dirt and diesel, on the floor, driven over every few seconds by yet another bus was a plaque about the size of a dinner plate. Inscribed on this brass plate were the words *El centro del mundo*. Clearly the Swiss placing the centre of Europe on their own capital pales beside this Spanish example. When David Matheson was at school, there was no such centring on any part of Scotland. However, if we borrow some ideas from Nigel Grant[2] (1999) we do come up with some interesting responses as to where the centre of Europe lies.

We could, for example, join the capitals of the countries of the European Union and find the centre of Europe in Belgium, a notion which fits in neatly with the idea so prevalent in many European Union (EU) countries that the centre of Europe is indeed in Brussels.

Mind you, no matter how much the UK media discuss the EU as if it were synonymous with Europe, it clearly is not and so perhaps we should enlarge our Europe to include Russia to the east and even Turkey to the south and then join the capitals. This places the centre of Europe in eastern Germany.

We could go further and link the edges of land masses whose inhabitants consider themselves European. In this way, we join the north-western tip of Iceland to the eastern tip of Crete, the Azores to Franz Josef Land. This centres Europe on Glasgow, an observation which might well come as a surprise to the inhabitants of that city.

Unfortunately, the real centre is not to be found through some game with maps and lines. The real centre is where the political and economic power lies. In this respect, both the Scots and the French Swiss share a major attribute: in neither case do they control the main parts of their own economies and this in itself cannot help but influence their perceptions of themselves. Economics and its hard realities can be more educative than those means more commonly thought of as education.

Wha's like us? Gie few an ther aa deid: defining the Scots and the French Swiss

The Scots tend to define themselves very frequently by opposition to the English (known as the Auld Enemy). However, they also have various heritages of literature and since probably the 1950s with the arrival of the present queen, the first Elizabeth of the UK, are undergoing a cultural revival which is still gaining pace. Few Scots refer to themselves as British and certainly none (any more) as English. Terms such as 'The North' serve as major irritants to Scots when The North is south of where they are. The often synonymous use of English and British by writers who often should know better also rubs in the wrong direction. This is frequently found in modern writings on education and it is doubly ironical in, for example, texts on intercultural education (see Verma, 1997 – critiqued in Matheson, 1999).

Religion used to be a major marker of Scots identity but this is declining (except in certain parts of the Central Lowlands). Indeed attempts at expanding the Troubles in Northern Ireland into Central Scotland failed despite various bombings of pubs in Glasgow in the early 1970s. In recent years those erstwhile bastions of bigotry, Rangers and Celtic football clubs,[3] have tried to put sectarianism behind them and have undertaken various initiatives which have included soccer coaching by Rangers players in schools near their stadium and this with no regard as to whether the schools were denominational (i.e. Catholic) or not. An incidental irony in this apparent growth in tolerance concerns the Orange Walks in Glasgow which used to be seen as an occasion for the whole community to watch the bands, regardless of religious affiliation. Now, as the rest of society appears more tolerant, there is less tolerance of those very Orangemen and Orangewomen whose marches David Matheson's very Catholic mother used to take him to see several times every summer.

The Scots tend to be *perceived* as more tolerant of difference than their southern neighbours and this has resulted in many families of Indian and Pakistani origin moving north from England. The extreme right-wing National Front has made few inroads into Scotland. But, how much this perceived tolerance is reflected in behaviour is very much open to question. Accounts from members of visible ethnic minorities tend to support this hypothesis but it should not be assumed that racist behaviour is absent from the Scottish scene. Indeed there have been numerous accounts of English immigrants into Scotland being racially abused. Interesting, however, is that in the run-up to the elections to the Scottish Parliament there were numerous reports in the media of support given to the Scottish National Party (SNP) by first and second generation immigrants.

Like Scotland, French Switzerland has been subject to various waves of both emigration and immigration, and for much the same reasons: economic and social (see, for example Papilloud *et al.*, 1992; *Valais d'Emigration*, 1991). It is associated with notions of tolerance but this is on condition that incomers make some minor effort to fit in with the ways of the place they are coming to. This compares with attitudes in the Highland and Islands of Scotland to immigrants from anywhere (see Matheson and Matheson, 1998). French Switzerland is culturally divided into Protestant and Catholic Cantons but as the impact of religion declines then so does the importance of this marker. The former Protestant Rome, Geneva, is now majority Catholic (*c.* 52 per cent practising Catholic and less than 20 per cent identify themselves as Protestant *at all*). Even the very Catholic Canton of Valais has seen its church attendance plummet (Pichard, 1987).

Cultural hegemony and educational attitudes

It has been argued (by such as Beveridge and Turnbull, 1989) that Scotland is an economic colony of England and that education (among other things) has been used as a means to have the Scots accept this lowly position. This has been refuted by McCrone (1996) who disputes that Scotland or the Scots have any real attributes of the colony or the colonized, except perhaps one: the cultural content of the independence movement is not strong. It is as if the Scots have accepted the inferiority of their own culture to such an extent as to almost discount it entirely. This ties in with Fanon's (1963) assertion that the colonized must accept the inferiority of his/her own culture. None the less it is indisputable that the economic power bases lie outwith Scotland; the economic conditions in the country are precarious and are dependent on outsiders often with little or no local interest. In the case of French Switzerland, there has been a generalized gravitation of major banks and other industries towards Zurich and the other major cities of North Central Switzerland, an area which acts like the south-east of England as a jobs magnet. Just as Scotland has on average a much higher rate of unemployment than has England then so, too, has French Switzerland than the German part. The Swiss French have never had to suffer the extremes of unemployment of the Scots but they have had their share, as Mitchison puts it with regard to Scotland, of 'having to suffer periodic checks to expansion ... without having experienced the expansion itself' (Mitchison, 1993, p. 411).

A major part of cultural hegemony is being ignored. Perhaps a more important part is in learning to ignore oneself. The Scots have been successfully ignored in 'British' writings for as long as Scotland has been part of the United Kingdom. They have ignored themselves for just as long. Gikandi (1996) tells us how Thomas Carlyle and John Stuart Mill, both Scots, argued over the impact of slavery on English culture and England and how each defended his stance as being consistent with his own Englishness! We have mentioned how at least one writer on intercultural education can ignore the Scots. Mason (1995) in his *Race and Ethnicity in Modern Britain* (whose Foreword describes it as 'a comprehensive and authoritative overview of major issues for students of all levels' (p. vii)) manages not to even mention the country of Scotland. The Irish qualify for inclusion as they now increasingly do on Equal Opportunities questionnaires for job applications. If we believe in ethnicity at all (and that is a concept open to dispute) then since the Irish and the Scots are genetically about as close as you can get, the inclusion of the one with the exclusion of the other does seem at best odd.

Until very recently, the Scots managed also to downgrade their own history. Scottish history was fine for primary school children and children in lower secondary school. After the options were chosen (in the third year of secondary school), then 'serious' history began. This was perhaps unsurprisingly the history of England. Grant (1982) claimed that the Scots were perhaps unique in teaching someone else's history in preference to their own. Alas he was wrong in this as Catherine Matheson's experience at school in the Canton of Valais demonstrates. Catherine learned Swiss history at primary school while in secondary school she was taught every detail of the history of France. Another experience we had in common concerned the teaching of geography. Local geography was for primary and lower secondary. 'Real' geography (in Catherine's case that of the rest of Europe, in David's that of England and then the rest of Europe and thence outwards) took over in the upper reaches of secondary school. In other words, the 'native' history and geography moved aside at those points in the curriculum which were most important. Against this backdrop, it is no surprise that 'native' literature fell by a similar wayside. However, an essential difference in our experiences is of course in the fact that Scotland was and is under the political dominance of England, French Switzerland is not under that of France.

Various parallels have been drawn between the *assimilados*, those native inhabitants of Portuguese colonies who adopted the cultural attributes of the colonizer and became assimilated to Portuguese culture (a notion which had its parallels in the British and French colonies), and the steps needed for educational and social success in Scotland (Grant, 1982; Kay, 1986) and similar can be argued for French Switzerland. Ignoring native history, or at least diminishing it, and doing likewise with 'native' literature are powerful mechanisms for maintaining cultural hegemony. In the Scottish case with its centralized government there is as little excuse as there is in the French Swiss case with its decentralized government. Both regions in their own way were and are responsible for schooling and what goes on in it. The Scots are proud of having resisted the imposition of a national curriculum *à l'Anglaise*. The French Swiss have never had to do this. In both cases, it is at the level of fairly local government that decisions as to curricular content have been taken, especially as regards lower secondary school and primary school, and yet 'native' material has, when it has appeared at all, been presented as quaint and not to be taken for 'the real thing.' It has, however, to be accepted that money has played an important role, especially where literature is concerned and also in textbook production. Economies of scale mean that textbooks produced for small populations (5 million in all in Scotland, 1.5 million in French Switzerland) will cost more than those produced for use in England (48 million) or France (57 million). Writers of literature have long been drawn to London and to Paris. They adapt their output to the majority culture and so their writings may in the end be Scottish or French Swiss only in so far as the place of the writer's birth.

Indigenous languages: a curse to be wiped away or a blessing?

The notion of the superiority of one language over another is intimately linked with aspects of cultural imperialism. French has established its superiority over Patois, English over Scots and Gaelic. In both cases, these claims to superiority were and are clearly political. What is a continuing source of wonderment to these writers is the sheer amount of effort which has been put into destroying languages. There seems no end to missionary zeal of the dedicated monoglot educationists. Of course, measures employed varied from place to place and from moment to moment, ranging as they did from persuading parents that their native tongue was a millstone round their children's necks, through simply ignoring the native tongue and confining all teaching to the target language, to punishing in various barbaric manners whether this be the Welsh *not* or the *màide-crochaidh*[4] of the Scottish Highland school. In this light, the Patois was ignored or beaten out of its pupils (depending on the area) or propagandized to death. The result is that it is a language in its death throes, gone in half a century from being the lingua franca of most of rural French Switzerland (especially in the mountains[5]) to being a echo, heard only in the occasional word slipped inadvertently into a conversation in French. Gaelic was attacked on all sides, even to the extent that Dr Johnson himself pleaded in its favour (Bell and Grant, 1977). Scots has simply been reduced to comedy and drunkenness, as well as the caricature of the Scots thug. Where style dominates substance, then Scots may be acceptable in public speech. However, all is not as bleak now as it was until recently.

Minority languages are now very much a point of discussion and activity. It is no longer accepted that there exists a 'bilingual deficit' whereby the mind can only take on a second language by losing competence in the first. Rather second languages are increasingly held to amplify and stimulate competence in first languages (Corson, 1998). As a teacher on the Isle of Skye put it with regard to monoglot Gaelic children entering what would *become* for them an English-medium school: 'We build on the Gaelic, teach them English as well, and in a couple of years they are completely fluent in both' (quoted in Grant, 1988, p. 158). Problems arise when the parents' competency in the majority language is incomplete and they effectively teach their children a deficient version of the majority language. The result is the so-called *Halbsprechern*, the half-speakers who speak neither the parents' language nor the majority language but a mixture of the two. Thus we have seen increasingly over recent years funding being allocated to supporting minority languages, to sustaining minority cultures, and this especially in the sphere of education. There is an enormous literature which argues for such initiatives and the beneficial effects, not just for the learners and their cultures but for wider society, which can accrue. As we have argued elsewhere (Matheson and Matheson, 1998), native language support is *perhaps* less critical in the case of major languages as even if, for example, Punjabi were never again to be heard on the streets of Glasgow, it would still be heard in the Punjab. Where such support is absolutely critical is the case of the small and very small indigenous languages of the areas we are considering. In this light, it is heartening to see Gaelic no longer stigmatized but offered not only as a 'foreign' language but also as a medium of instruction in an increasing number of primary schools in Scotland and several secondary schools. It features as one of the European Union's official 'lesser used languages' (http://www.eblul.org/minor-gb.htm) but, contrary to Jones's (1999) claim, Gaelic in Scotland has no official status. None the less it is funded in its revival by central government and by the European Union, hence a sudden increase in the amount of Gaelic on television in Scotland and not just in the Highlands and Islands, ranging from *Pàidrig Post* (Postman Pat, the children's animation programme) to *Eorpa* (a current affairs programme on European minority languages and cultures).

The Patois is in an even more precarious situation than Gaelic. It has yet to break through into the schools, There are no evening classes in Patois in the Migros Club Schools (http://www.migros.ch/index) – the largest provider of adult education in Switzerland – or even in the much smaller Université populaire. Instead we find at Vissoie, for example, in the Canton of Valais a *Musée des patoisants*, a museum of those who speak Patois! There are efforts afoot to revive the language, most notably in the University of Neuchâtel where work is in progress on a glossary of Patois (see http://www-dialecto.unine.ch for details).

Neither Gaelic nor Patois are in a position to survive *and* thrive without external help. They are now no longer attacked but rather in receipt of official support. Each is seen as an important part of the national heritage. Scots, on the other hand, is still stigmatized even to the extent of denying that many Scots speakers even speak the language (or dialect). It is curious indeed to note that the same European Bureau of Lesser Used Languages which admits *rural* Scots into its catalogue, denies any place to *urban* Scots which forms the varieties of the language most spoken in Scotland (http://www.eblul.org/minor-gb.htm). Scots is, however, making a breakthrough by other means, and is moving away from being simply a speech form which is acceptable only among the socio-economically deprived or in fora where style is more important than substance and comic (or other stereotypical) effect is sought.

Cultural renaissances: Scotland

We live in an age when we are often exhorted to think globally and act locally. In the UK we see the Westminster government having to bend to decisions taken in Brussels. In French Switzerland, we see the presence of a high proportion of foreigners and an increasing acknowledgement that the government in Berne and the principle of direct democracy are perhaps not best adapted to the transnational era (Germann, 1994). Indeed the European Economic Community (EEC – as was) gave the then regional councils in Scotland an occasion not to be missed: to bypass Westminster and set up offices at the heart of EEC power. It is arguable that this initiative encouraged many Scots to realize that they could do things on an international front without having to go through London, and while such moves may have encouraged the Conservatives, in 1996, to abolish the Regions (in the face of overwhelming support for the Regions in referenda held by the Regional Authorities under the auspices of the Electoral Reform Society), they may well also have contributed to the massive 'Yes' vote in the referendum on a Scottish Parliament with tax-varying powers which occurred in 1998. At the same time, let us not lose sight of the *Braveheart* effect. This film may have been historically somewhat wide of the mark (the thought of William Wallace in woad and with long hair! He had a beard, short hair, probably never wore a kilt or fought with a broadsword) but its impact on the Scots psyche was immense. It was, as Fanon (1963) suggests as a necessary precursor to seeking independence, reinterpreting ancient folk tales for modern effect. Indeed, we have seen over recent years a sudden explosion in literary and filmic output from Scotland. Old ways of defining oneself, such as Tartanry, Kailyard and Clydesidism[6] which are marked overall by a depressing sense of hopelessness, are yielding bit by bit to a sense of dynamism and even pride in oneself, rather than by opposition to some Other (usually the English).

Concomitant with this renaissance has been the development of the Scots Language Society (SLS) and the Scots Language Resource Centre (SLRC). This latter was the object of much mirth for its Canny Spell spellchecker program, an unfortunate pun since *canny* may mean wise but *cannae* (a homonym) means cannot. Rather predictably, many of the detractors appeared to think *ah widnae bother*.

Both the SLS and the SLRC depend much on the good offices of Perth and Kinross Council whose web site (http://www.pkc.gov.uk/slrc) contains their web pages. These societies are attempting to rebirth the Scots language in a manner more akin to the ways in which it is actually used. This contrasts with the attempts at synthetic Scots, *Lallans*, which more or less fell flat if for no other reason but that it represented an amalgam of rural Scots dialects and roundly ignored the urban varieties. The current result, mind you, is initially fairly incomprehensible to the average speaker of Scots who, while well able to understand a multitude of spoken dialects of the language, has problems making the leap into the written form. A little effort is, however, all that is required to get used to seeing the words in print and to learning various terms that may not figure in one's native dialect. It is not, incidentally, the mixture of Scots and English which Burns used but, rather, an attempt to distance Scots from English in much the same way as Norwegian was distanced from Danish with the construction of Nynorsk. Whether it will achieve the same result as Nynorsk is doubtful but one innovation, perhaps attributable to the SLS, is the inclusion of spoken Scots in the curricula for the new Higher Still upper secondary school programme in English and Communication (SQA, 1998). Candidates are no longer required to attempt to extirpate their native tongue from the oral parts of these examinations. Rather the emphasis is on communication. If the meaning is transmitted (and received) then that is all that is required of the idiom employed.

In the History programmes at secondary school, in keeping with the moves towards social history evident across many school systems, candidates to Standard Grade History (General Certificate of Secondary Education – GCSE – equivalent, eleventh year of school) can no longer avoid the history of Scotland and the Scottish people. In the Higher Still programme, the space given to Scottish history is now greater than ever before (SQA, 1997).

Cultural renaissances: French Switzerland

The French Swiss have largely given up on the Patois, except for the few native speakers left and the even fewer who try to learn it. It is now so peripheral to the lives of the majority of the inhabitants of the area that whether it survives or vanishes will have little or no impact on them. Much more important is the growth of French Swiss identity as a definable concept.

Switzerland is a country held together by its cracks. This seemingly odd observation is not the oxymoron it might at first seem. As has been noted by many observers (see, for example, Kerr, 1974; Martin, 1959; Matheson, 1992) historically the schisms in Swiss society cross-cut one another. The schisms were basically: urban–rural, mountain–plateau, Catholic–Protestant, French–German (the italophones were deemed sufficiently distinct as not to generally figure in these equations). The image is perhaps akin to the crystalline structure of steel: steel is full of micro-fissures and faults which cause it to try to fall apart in different directions. The apparently paradoxical result is that it stays together! Switzerland has been the same. The religious divide in itself militated against the formation of language blocks, communications difficulties militated against blocks which united town and country or mountain and plateau. Times have changed. Religion is no longer the force of division it once was; Switzerland's communication infrastructure is a phenomenon of modern engineering. As other forces of division decline, the language blocks have begun to assert themselves.

Evidence for this comes in a variety of forms. There is, for example, the concentration of economic bases of power in fewer and fewer areas (generally in the industrialized areas of German Switzerland) with the result that companies under economic pressure tend to retreat into these areas. Perhaps most critical is the pattern emerging in voting. There are referenda almost weekly throughout much of the year in most Swiss communes and Cantons. Federal votations are somewhat rarer and it is to these that we direct our attention. If a schism is developing between the French and German Swiss then there should be evidence for it here.

Schisms between the two main language blocks are not totally new: the First World War saw the Germanophile General Wille elected to head the Swiss Army[7] and, as Joye and Zendali (1999) put it, this almost tore the country apart with the German Swiss siding massively with the Central Powers, the French Swiss with the Entente Cordiale. This same general brought the army on to the streets to crush the 1918 General Strike which itself had brought the country to the brink of a left-wing revolution. However, national solidarity was fully restored in the Second World War with the election of the Vaudois (and therefore native francophone) General Guisan who used German most of the time to underscore that national unity was his first priority.

The current schism is seen in the manner in which the French Swiss vote, whenever the occasion arises, in favour of greater openness to the rest of Europe, for example, and the German Swiss vote against. The French Swiss have a greater tendency to vote in favour of social reform than their German Swiss compatriots (Schneider, 1999). As Dayer (1996) reminds us, for more than a century each main language block has been becoming more and more homogenous in its voting patterns. She further informs us that the French Swiss have a greater tendency to vote against any motion which removes power from the Cantons to give it to the Federal government. The French Swiss are also reported to be considerably more aware of the language schism than are the German Swiss.[8]

The growing schism between the French and German Swiss is a major cause for concern in Switzerland. As the title of one academic publication puts it, Is the cohesion of the nation threatened? (*La cohésion nationale menacée?* – Weibel, 1997). The Swiss are not known for dramatic headlines or titles but increasingly this is what we are witnessing. The weekly news magazine *L'Hebdo*, for example, headed a major article on 17 June 1999 'Requiem for a dying Switzerland' (*Requiem pour une Suisse mourante*). For many commentators, the writing seems to be on the wall. But what other signs are there of a growing French Swiss sense of self?

One which is critical appears in the field of education. The former heavy reliance on school books imported from France is declining in favour of home-produced material. The catalyst in this has been the appearance of a French Swiss section of the Council of Directors of Public Education which has encouraged and cajoled cantonal education authorities to co-operate in first agreeing a broad outline programme for compulsory school.[9] Similar events have taken place across the German Swiss sections of the council. In French Switzerland, there has been a dramatic increase in the number of school texts of all sorts which are being produced for use across French Switzerland. There is concern that the programme for the Federal Maturity examination (actually a cantonal qualification but moderated at Federal level and recognized nationally) be harmonized throughout the area (Fournier, 1998). In short, where previously Cantons would carefully go their own way, they are now openly collaborating. The notion of a common French Swiss school programme, while still a long way off, is getting closer all the time. In short, education is replicating what we already see on the political front.

A name which has been attached to French Switzerland is *Romandie*. A rose by any other name may smell as sweet but political entities and entities which have political potential can be very much influenced by the name attached. *Romandie* implies something more than a simple linguistic area: it implies cultural links at the very least. The use of this name has provoked reactions beyond expectations. In our research over the years, we have found those who will use the name and those who deny it any validity whatsoever. In 1978, Pichard could entitle a portrait of the French Swiss Cantons, *La Romandie n'existe pas*. His basic thesis was that there was such divergence on so many fronts between the francophone Cantons, it was almost ridiculous to consider them as forming anything other than an area in which a common language was spoken. This appears decreasingly true. In fact, whether it was even true in 1978 is debatable. In 1947, for example, the *Tour de Romandie* for cyclists began and has thrived ever since. Although the French Swiss accept being termed *Suisse romand* or simply *Romand* they may employ *Romandie* when they wish to distance themselves both from France and, above all, from the German Swiss (Perregaux, 1996). A flag for Romandie appeared from 1981, as a sort of amalgam between the French Tricolor, the Swiss flag and six stars (for the francophone Cantons). There are certainly nationalists (for want of a better term) among the French Swiss and, if the voting patterns are anything to go by, they may well increase in number. What such nationalists might want is of course another question, whether it be separation (as was attempted between Protestant and Catholic Cantons in the last Swiss civil war of 1847) or something short of this. However, it is indisputable that the rare voices in the wilderness, such as the Valaisan priest, Abbé Clovis Lugon (1983), are finding themselves with company.

Scotland and French Switzerland: emerging nations in a supranational age?

The nation is an odd concept. It is yet another term that we all think we can define until we actually try to do it. John White's (1996) article 'Education and nationality' demonstrates just how slippery a concept 'nation' and hence 'nationality' can be. White unfortunately, while attempting to tackle the notion of 'Britishness', does not quite manage to avoid tacitly equating Britishness with Englishness, discussing as he does the English/Welsh 'National' Curriculum as if it pertained to the whole of the United Kingdom. White is far from alone in the conflation of English and British, as Phillips *et al.* (1999) remind us has happened in the ideas of British and English identity which appear in that self-same English/Welsh 'National' Curriculum. White does, however, raise the important question of how to define nation and nationality and does not manage quite to answer it.

In the case of the two areas we are examining, Scotland has been described as a 'nation without a state' (Foster 1980), as a 'stateless nation' (McCrone, 1996). The nation-state of which it is part dates from the Union of the Parliaments of 1707. Or does it date from the Union of the Crowns in 1603? For the French Swiss, the situation is hardly less confused. The history of Switzerland, for most of its time span, does not concern most of what is now French Switzerland.

Switzerland has its official origins in a pact said to have been signed on 1 August 1291. This was 'discovered' as the National Day in 1870 (Furter, 1983) and the year 1291 became the founding year of the Confederation from 1891 when the Cantons of Uri, Schwyz and Unterwald celebrated 600 years of *their* confederacy (Anderson, 1983). This situation is, mind you, no more odd than that of the USA, it is just a little more extreme.

Revisionism in dating nations is quite common. And in this light we suggest that the nation is as old as we wish it to be. The nation-state, where the inhabitants (at least most of them) are expected to feel some sort of loyalty towards the state and its institutions, is of much more recent vintage. Furter (1983) places the birth of the nation-state at the time of the *Kulturkampf* of the 1870s. This time is also when he locates the discovery (or invention?) of William Tell as a Swiss national hero (see Bergier, 1988). The year 1870 is also of course the year in which for many diverse reasons, England (to be followed by Scotland two years later) introduced the State *as we know it* into education in the United Kingdom in the form of the first Education Act.

The Swiss have always occupied an odd role in the world of nations. One does not, for example, become a Swiss citizen. One is first accepted into a Commune. On the basis of this acceptance, one is accepted into a Canton and hence has the right to carry a Swiss passport and exercise all the functions which a citizen in Switzerland is entitled to exercise. The unusual part is the emphasis on the small locality which is the Commune. This goes beyond mere formality: all the documents relating to one's civic status are kept in the Commune of which one is a citizen (or *bourgeois*). In this way, the documents relating to our family reside in a tiny village, perched high on a cliff in the Canton of Valais. The Swiss do not imagine themselves a community. And this to an even lesser extent than do the British.

Wirt (in Furter, 1983, p. 231) argues that there has been a policy of assimilation in Great Britain with respect to the Scots. Were the British to actually form a community then assimilation would be irrelevant, not just unnecessary. That the Scots have not been more fully assimilated is witness to the failure of this policy. None the less, the manner in which Scots languages, history, heritage and culture for so long played second fiddle to the dominant discourse from England (and this may or may not have been wished by England) demonstrates the reality of Wirt's point. The French Swiss for their part would be hard put to demonstrate any real attempt at assimilation by their German Swiss compatriots. A point, however, which the French Swiss and the Scots have had in common is that each has seen that by going beyond the immediately dominant discourse (on the one hand that from Westminster, on the other hand that from Berne and the German Cantons – given the role of direct democracy) or at least in opening oneself up to the 'exterior', it is possible to reassert oneself as part of a greater whole in which even those under whose dominance one finds oneself are themselves in a hegemonical minority position. The Scots tried this in their Regions by appealing directly to Brussels. It is improbable that the Scottish Parliament will not do the same sooner or later. The French Swiss cannot *yet* go outwith the discourse of the Swiss Germans but they can, and have, recognized a certain measure of common interest, indeed common-ality, among themselves. However, they are clearly pulling very frequently in a direction opposite to that of the Swiss Germans and there is only so much pulling that a country can take before it starts to tear itself apart.

So where does this leave the nation? And notions of national identity?

We have perhaps become quite used to nations being fixed entities, especially in the UK where we easily forget that it was only in 1921 that the current borders of this United Kingdom were fixed, 'provisionally' as was said at the time. The borders of Switzerland were fixed in 1815.

We often hear about our global economy, we are reminded of global events and even of global weather patterns. In short, we are very much aware of living on and sharing a planet. It is arguable that the nation as we knew it was dependent for its existence on ignorance of the Other. We are still pretty ignorant but compared to our parents when they were our age, we have a phenomenal amount of information about the world available to us all the time. It may be biased, it may be distorted but we are increasingly aware that it *is* subject to such bias and distortion. We are aware, however badly, of the situations of others.

It is said in comparative education that by looking around us we slowly begin to see ourselves as others see us and to use tools of critical analysis, developed to examine 'elsewhere', to examine our own 'backyard'. In this light, in our globalized society, with our education (and political) systems having to take ever more account of 'elsewhere', we turn our regard Janus-like to look both inwards and outwards. We would suggest that the growth of regional awareness throughout Europe (albeit with sometimes calamitous effects) bears witness to this phenomenon. We see this not only in Scotland and French Switzerland and in certain parts of ex-Yugoslavia, but also in England and France where the smaller parts of the whole are wishing to be noticed and to have account taken of them. In this light, the nation-state as we know it is perhaps on its way out. In the supranational state, all previous majorities are likely to be in a minority. The danger is that the supranational state attempts to reconcile too many differences, that it attempts to homogenize, that it merely replaces one dominant discourse with another. The quandary is to respect and even encourage diversity whilst encouraging tolerance of diversity and yet maintain links between groups. Our previous views of nation-states as fairly homogenous groupings are increasingly false, if indeed they ever were true (see Grant, 1997). We notice and recognize the multiculturality on our doorstep, however much some of us might try to deny it. Our education systems are increasingly called upon to act in intercultural manners, to change education for diversity (Corson, 1998) for, it is argued, it is only in educating for diversity that we can increase equality of opportunity, not just in terms of permission but also power. The problem is how to achieve this without atomizing the nation-state as we know it. This is a constant backdrop to the growth of awareness of cultural identity and encouragement of such growth. We can accept or repudiate parts of our cultural identity without rejecting the whole and without losing an overall identification with our culture. But how many of us can do the same with a nation? How many of us can actually identify with a nation? With bits of it certainly. But in the absence of an external threat who can identify with the whole entity? *Gie few an ther aa deid.*

Notes

1. An interesting, if frequently forgotten, fact is that for the ancient Greeks *all* foreigners were barbarians, all non-Greek languages being held to sound like 'bar-bar', in other words they were gibberish (Grant, 1988). Given the relationship which existed between Egypt and Greece at the time, such an attitude could make one wonder whether in practice, rather than in theory, the term *barbaroi* was in fact pejorative.

2. In Nigel Grant's version of the centre of Europe game, the centre eventually lands on either Fort William or Aviemore, both being towns in the Highlands of Scotland. The irony in this lies in the fact that the Highlands of Scotland are described as peripheral not only in the European Union but even in the United Kingdom

3. Rangers has since its inception been associated with Protestantism and has a large following among Northern Irish Protestants, a number of whom travel across the Irish Sea to Scotland to see them play each week. Celtic for its part was founded by a Marist Brother and had similar associations with Catholicism. Rangers, until very few years ago, banned all Catholics from playing for it. Celtic had no similar prohibition of Protestants and its most successful manager was an active member of the Protestant Orange Lodge.

4. These were devices hung round a child's neck if s/he was caught speaking the banned language. The routine was generally that the victim wore the device until s/he caught another child making the same error and so it passed from child to child until the child found wearing it at the end of some prescribed period was physically punished. These devices (and Scotland and Wales are not isolated cases) not only

worked to eliminate the language under attack but got the very speakers of the language to do much of the work entailed.

5. See Bjerrome (1957) who reports how, even in in the mid-1950s, the Patois was alive and thriving in the Gruyère, the Vaudois Alps, the Jura and the Valais.

6. Kailyard, Tartanry and, to a lesser extent, Clydesidism are stereotypes, or rather the mythical structures, which form Scottish kitsch and many of the means by which Scotland and things Scottish are identified both within and outwith Scotland. Kailyard focuses on a quaint vision of Lowland rural Scotland marked by bucolic intrigues. Tartanry is similarly rural but focused on a romantic vision of Highland Scotland. Clydesidism harks back to an urban, industrial past where the honest workers are oppressed by tyrannical bosses but keep their self-esteem intact. An important point in each of these constructions is that they are essentially backward-looking (see Matheson and Matheson, 1998).

7. The Swiss Federal Assembly elects a general to head the army in times of national crisis, usually war. At other times, the most senior officer is a colonel.

8. The linguistic schism is examined in detail in Kriesi *et al.* (1992) who reported on it to the Federal Chancellery.

9. This appears under various titles depending on the Canton but the basic content is the same. The Cantons have agreed the *minimum* content. Each can add to it but not subtract from it.

References

Anderson, B. (1983) *Imagined Communities*. London: Verso.

Antonietta, T. (1991) 'Die Handlaner der Krieges und ihre noblen Unternehmer: Eine ethnographische Betrachtung des Walliser Solddienst in 18. und 19. Jahrhundert', in *Valais d'Emigration*. Sion: Musée cantonal d'histoire et d'ethnographie Valère.

Bell, R. and Grant, N. (1977) *Patterns of Education in the British Isles*. London: Unwin Education Books.

Bergier, J.-F. (1988) *Guillaume Tell*. Genève: Fayard.

Beveridge, C. and Turnbull, R. (1989) *The Eclipse of Scottish Culture*. Edinburgh: Polygon.

Bjerrome, G. (1957) *Le Patois de Bagnes (Valais)*. Stockholm: Almqvist.

Breitenbach, E., Brown, A. and Myers, F. (1998) 'Understanding women in Scotland'. *Feminist Review*, 58 (1), 44–65.

Brock, C. and Tulasiewicz, W. (1985) 'The concept of identity: editors' introduction', in C. Brock and W. Tulasiewicz (eds) *Cultural Identity and Educational Policy*. London and Sydney: Croom Helm.

Cassini, G. (1991) 'La guerre est-elle un art qui détruit tous les autres? Du service étranger comme source de production et d'inspiration artistique dans le Valais de l'Ancien Régime', in *Valais d'Emigration*. Sion: Musée cantonal d'histoire et d'ethnographie Valère.

Chérix, F. (1997) *La Suisse est morte? Vive la Suisse! lettre ouverte aux déçus de l'immobilisme*. Lausanne: Editions d'En bas.

Corbett, J. (1997) *Language and Scottish Literature*. Edinburgh: Edinburgh University Press.

Corson, D. (1998) *Changing Education for Diversity*. Buckingham: Open University Press.

Dayer, A. (1996) 'Le retour de la question romande'. *L'Hebdo*, 23 May.

Fanon, F. (1963) *The Wretched of the Earth*. Harmondsworth: Penguin.

Favre, A. (1981) *Moi, Adéline, accoucheuse*. Sierre: Editions Monographie.

Foster, C.R. (1980) *Nations without a State*. New York: Praeger.

Fournier, G.F. (1998) Délégué aux questions universitaires, Canton of Valais, personal communication.

Furter, P. (1983) *Les Espaces de la Formation*. Lausanne: Presses polytechniques romandes.

Germann, R.E. (1991) 'L'Europe et la double majorité' in B. Prongué, J. Rieder, C. Hauser and F. Python, (eds) *Passé pluriel: en hommage au professeur Roland Ruffieux*. Fribourg: Editions universitaires Fribourg Suisse.

Germann, R.E. (1994) 'La diplomatie référendaire de la Suisse dans l'Europe transnationale', in Y. Papadopoulos (ed.) *Présent et Avenir de la Démocratie directe*. Genève: Georg.

Gikandi, S. (1996) *Maps of Englishness*. New York: Columbia University Press.

Grant, N. (1982) *The Crisis of Scottish Education*. Edinburgh: The Saltire Society.

Grant, N. (1988) 'The education of minority and peripheral cultures'. *Comparative Education*, 24 (2), 155–64.

Grant, N. (1996) 'European and cultural identity at the European, national and regional levels: further comparisons', in T. Winther-Jensen (ed.) *Challenges to European Education*. Bern: Peter Lang.

Grant, N. (1997) 'Intercultural education in the United Kingdom', in D. Woodrow, G.K. Verma, M.B. Rocha-Trinidade, G. Campani and C. Bagley (eds) *Intercultural Education: Theories, Policies and Practice*. Aldershot: Ashgate.

Grant, N. (1999) Emeritus Professor of Education, University of Glasgow, personal communication.

Griffiths, M. (1995) *Feminisms and the Self*. London: Routledge.

Jones, C. (1999) 'Warfare, state identity and education in Europe'. *European Journal of Intercultural Education*, 10 (1), 5–16.

Joye, P.-A. and Zendali, M. (1999) 'Requiem pour une Suisse mourante'. *L'Hebdo*, 17 June.

Kay, B. (1986) *Scots: The Mither Tongue*. Edinburgh: Mainstream.

Kerr, H. (1974) *Switzerland: Social Cleavages and Partisan Conflict*. London: Sage.

Kriesi, H., Wernli, B., Sciarini, P. and Gianni, M. (1992) *Le clivage linguistique: problèmes de compréhension entre les communautés linguistiques en Suisse*. Berne: Chancellerie fédérale.

Lugon, C. (1983) *Quand la Suisse française s'éveillera*. Genève: Editions Perret-Gentil.

McCrone, D. (1996) *Understanding Scotland: The Sociology of a Stateless Nation*. London: Routledge.

Martin, W. (1959) *L'Histoire de la Suisse*. Lausanne: Payot.

Mason, D. (1995) *Race and Ethnicity in Modern Britain*. Oxford: Oxford University Press.

Matheson, C. and Matheson, D. (1998) 'Problématique régionale et questions linguistiques en Ecosse', in S. Perez, (ed.) *La Mosaïque linguistique: regards éducatifs sur les pays industrialisés*. Paris: L'Harmattan.

Matheson, D. (1989) 'Opportunities in post-compulsory education in the Highland Region in Scotland and the Canton of Valais in Switzerland'. Glasgow University: unpublished MEd thesis.

Matheson, D. (1992) 'Post-compulsory Education in Suisse romande'. Glasgow University: unpublished PhD thesis.

Matheson, D. (1999) 'Review of Woodrow, D., Verma, G.K., Rocha-Trinidade, M. B., Campani, G. and Bagley, C. (eds) *Intercultural Education: Theories, Policies and Practice* Aldershot: Ashgate'. *Compare*, 29 (1), 100–1.

Mitchison, R. (1993) *A History of Scotland*. London: Routledge.

Papadopoulos, Y. (ed.) (1994) *Présent et Avenir de la Démocratie directe*. Genève: Georg.

Papilloud, J.-H., Arlettaz, G. and S., Evéquoz-Dayen, M., Morand M. C., Clavien, A. and

Tschopp-Bessero, M.-P. (1992) *Le Valais et les étrangers*. Sion: Société et culture du Valais contemporain.

Perregaux, B. (1996) 'Ne dites plus jamais Romandie!' *L'Hebdo*, 23 May.

Phillips, R., Goalen, P., McCully, A. and Wood, S. (1999) 'Four histories, one nation? History teaching, nationhood and a British identity'. *Compare*, 29 (2), 153–69.

Pichard, A. (1978) *La Romandie n'existe pas*. Lausanne: Editions 24 Heures.

Pichard, A. (1987) *La Suisse dans tous ses Etats*. Lausanne: Editions 24 Heures.

Rébaud, H. (1964) *Géographie de la Suisse*. Lausanne: Payot.

Schneider, M. (1999) Swiss Federal Statistical Office, Berne, personal communication.

Scottish Qualifications Authority (SQA) (1997) *Arrangements for History* (Higher Still). Glasgow and Dalkeith: SQA.

Scottish Qualifications Authority (SQA) (1998) *Arrangements for English and Communications* (Higher Still). Glasgow and Dalkeith: SQA.

Steffen, H. (1991) 'Der Solddienst zur Zeit Stockalpers (17. Jahrhundert)', in *Valais d'Emigration*. Sion: Musée cantonal d'histoire et d'ethnographie Valère.

Valais d'Emigration (1991) Sion: Musée cantonal d'histoire et d'ethnographie Valère.

Verma, G. (1997) 'Inequality and intercultural education' in D. Woodrow, G. K. Verma, M. B. Rocha-Trinidade, G. Campani and C. Bagley (eds) *Intercultural Education: Theories, Policies and Practice*. Aldershot: Ashgate.

Weibel, E. (président) (1997) *La cohésion nationale menacée?* Neuchâtel: Institut de Sociologie et de Science politique, Université de Neuchâtel.

White, J. (1996) 'Education and nationality'. *Journal of Philosophy of Education*, 30 (3), 327–43.

3

Education and Religion

David Limond

Introduction

Whoever embarks on a piece of work about religion without some trepidation has probably misunderstood what s/he has been asked to do. For the believer religion is not simply a matter of life and death – it is a matter of afterlife and death. When they think themselves to be misrepresented, members of religious communities are apt to announce that they have been offended. And indeed certain groups may be right when they protest that they are often ungenerously depicted particularly in the mass (atheist dominated?) media (Said, 1997). This chapter does not seek to offend anyone but as there is nothing, however trivial, which might not offend someone, perceived offensiveness cannot be understood as a side constraint, a limit on action. An attempt at neutrality between religions is signalled by the choice of the formulation 'god(s)' when speaking of the object(s) of religious interest. This will offend monotheists who cannot countenance that there are gods and it will offend *all* theists in ignoring the convention of capitalization. But Martin Luther could 'do no other', 'And what can David say more . . .?' (II Samuel 7:10).

Meaning of religion

A specialist reference work cautions that 'Whatever it [religion] is . . . no single or simple definition will suffice' (Pyle, 1984, p. 270) and what follows is not a definition. Instead what is offered here are notes towards compiling an account of the use of the word 'religion'. *Religion* is a portmanteau term encompassing both *belief* and *practice*. The former is possible without the latter, belief may be private, and the latter is possible without the former, practice may be a sham. An *organized religion* exists where these two coincide in a group of people of some appreciable size (no fixed lower limit can be given here, 'appreciable' will have to do). Most members of an organized religion must believe most of its tenets most of the time. Typically religious beliefs are doctrines concerned with metaphysics and morals. The most common sort of religious metaphysical doctrine is one positing a 'metaphysics of creation'. Even when sophisticated religious believers accept scientific claims as to the nature of the universe they still claim that there must be a necessary place in any account of it for god(s). The appearance of life, matter, space, time, even probability may all admit of non-religious explanations but in any religious metaphysics of creation there is a place reserved for god(s) in bringing about *possibility* (Davies, 1993). Religious moralities vary in their details but they often overlap with metaphysical doctrines in that they posit states – to be attained, avoided or accepted – that are moral in nature such as nirvana or purgatory. Religious practices are often described as rituals. That is, they are repeated behaviours to which moral significance attaches. Such practices are typically performed in public and in communal contexts. Even the very non-ritualistic Society of Friends (Quakers) are a *society*, they have *meetings* (thus emphasizing the need for community). Although what they do is sit together and wait for one amongst them to be moved to 'testify', this is something they do *regularly* and which they deem *important* so that it *is* a ritual. Metaphysics, morality, ritual and community are highly characteristic features of organized religions (Smart, 1977, pp. 15–21).

Meaning of education

These are some tentative criteria for a description of the nature of organized religion. It might be possible at this point to labour over several pages of explanation on the nature of education. But this seems to be less pressing than was the need to give at least some account of the meaning of religion. In all that follows education can simply be stipulated as being synonymous with formal education and as a practical proposition the discussion can be limited to schools. That there is something we can call informal education cannot be denied. Further, it is certainly true that the study of informal education is neglected in the general run of educational writing. There is scope for discussing informal education and religion at one and the same time. This is so if only because organized religions have often been major providers of informal education (Ellis, 1990). The history of Europe's universities is intimately bound up with the history of the Christian church(es) in a relationship which remained close until quite recently (Anderson, 1992). But these are matters that will not be discussed here. Some stipulation such as 'religion can for present purposes be taken to mean organized churches and comparable groups', might also have saved effort but there is danger in any overly restrictive and unexplained demarcation of what constitutes (true) religion. No one has ever gone to war over the nature of education but it may well be that human beings have fought over nothing so much as they have over religion. Interfaith dialogue has tended to be extraordinarily difficult (any conversation in which each party is liable to imagine the other to be in thrall to diabolical power can be vexed) and religious war has shown itself to be a depressingly easy alternative. Some have even despaired at the seeming incompatibility of organized religion and civil life (Gellner, 1996, pp. 44–60). Any war between religious groups necessarily involves each denying that the other is in fact a religious group. Thus any time spent on offering an inclusive account of the nature of religion(s) is never time wasted.

A brief history of education and religion

Histories of any aspect of education in the UK, the USA or elsewhere in the 'western world', even when they are fantastically brief surveys such as this will be, often begin with some remarks as to the situation in classical Athens or biblical Israel. But here it is possible to break with convention by seeking a specifically British start to a generally British survey. Formal education and organized religion may have been yoked together for as long as there has been priestly knowledge to transmit from generation to generation. This knowledge may originally have been of a highly practical type. The first priests were perhaps the first fire-makers (Goudsblom, 1992). But over time such knowledge may progressively have come to involve more conspicuously religious elements; that is, more metaphysics and more morality, with these perhaps both engendered by the encounter with fire, a 'substance' or an 'entity' (actually it is a fast chemical reaction in the vapour phase) which seems to be utterly 'other' in nature but which bestows benefits on those who 'serve' it.

The first organized religion in Britain of which there is anything even approaching reliable knowledge is that of the Druids. Unfortunately even relatively scholarly works concerned with the Druids are often little more than exercises in wish fulfilment (Berresford Ellis, 1995). 'They were early feminists; they had a highly developed 'green' consciousness; they were advocates constructively communist rather than destructively competitive . . . modern moral sensibilities revel in retrospective vindication. But it *is* known that the druids had schools (Berresford Ellis, 1995, pp. 157–61). Or, to make a precise distinction, they engaged in *schooling*. Their schools had no necessary physical existence so that 'school' here means a group of learners gathered around a teacher. The origin of schools as places lies in the regularization of arrangements for schooling as an activity. These schools (or this schooling) served what might be called an internally rather than an externally directed purpose. Their concern was to prepare successive generations of Druids.

When the Romans settled in Britain (which they did not do to any great extent until after 43 CE[1]) they brought with them the idea of schools that were recognizably externally directed. These they planted in some degree at least in that part of Britain now known as England from perhaps 78 CE (Lawson and Silver 1973). But these were externally directed schools. They existed to fulfil many functions (not least converting the sons of local nobility to Roman ways and, literally, 'civilizing' them – making them citizens of Rome) but they did *not* function to perpetuate priestly knowledge as had those of the Druids. This distinction is crucial. Roman culture was civic (worldly) before it was religious. Early Christian culture was religious before civic. In the pivotal fourth century CE

Rome was converted to Christianity and Christianity was Romanized. Like Druidic schools the operation of early Christian education was internally directed. Only through the collision of Christian religion and Rome civics did this change, a point perhaps best illustrated by example.

The effective penetration of Christianity into Britain can be dated to around 400 CE with Ninian's mission to the Picts (Lynch, 1994). It did not enjoy a very secure footing until the next century. 'About 500 [CE] a school for *missionaries* (my emphasis) was taught by the semi-legendary St Illtud, abbot of a Celtic community at Llantwit Major' (Lawson and Silver, 1973, p. 8). This was schooling which served to prepare successive generations of priestly interpreters and communicators of specifically religious knowledge. Christian schools grew up subsequently around monasteries and cathedrals. At first these still existed to provide priestly training but by the latter half of the twelfth century CE they had expanded their role. This came about because imparting at least rudimentary literacy was essential in the bookish Christian religion (Bible, Gk *biblion* = book). In time, literacy became a generally socially useful skill in a way that the secret knowledge of Druids (whatever that consisted in) never did (Goody and Watt, 1992). There was now secular teaching, albeit limited, in these schools. The Christian church in Britain thus increased the range of its educational activities from the internally directed preparation of priests to include the externally directed teaching of some lay pupils. The next significant development in the history of formal education in Britain was the advent of lay schools. But these were still (indirectly) subject to clerical authority. This regulatory function was managed in various ways. When cathedrals first established schools each needed a teacher. Such a teacher was originally the *scholasticus* but as the rights and responsibilities attached to that office increased over time the *scholasticus* became the grander chancellor (Lawson and Silver, 1973). Chancellors came to be involved with teaching, their predecessors' original function, only vicariously. Thus they appointed those who did the work of teaching in cathedral schools and granted (or withheld) licences for teachers in lay schools. In time this role would pass to others (Lawson and Silver, 1973; Scotland, 1969) but a regulatory role was established in this way in order that even when the Church did not have exclusive power over education it might still have much influence. This role consisted in assessing the suitability of teachers and ensuring that they were not impious people who would teach anything which would go against the interests of the Church, which were assumed to be the interests of society as a whole.

The Church was now involved in formal education in at least three ways. It was a provider of education for its own purpose, that of preparing clergy and members of religious orders. It was a provider of education to some members of the lay population and it was a regulator of the character of even the lay education it did not provide. In many respects this is how the position remains even now though the overt regulatory role has been replaced by one which seeks to influence the tone and content of lay schooling in certain ways.

At this point the historical canter becomes a gallop. Increased literacy was certainly both a cause and an effect of the Reformation of religion in Europe in the sixteenth century (Ozment, 1993). In immediate post-Reformation Scotland these were heady times. It seemed possible (and necessary) to make education serve the purpose of protecting the revolutionary theocratic state then emerging but also to involve it in the salvation of individual souls as never before. This was attempted in the combined Church and State constitution proposed in the *First Book of Discipline* (1560). This, despite its fearsome name (only coined later and apt to be misunderstood, discipline in this context simply means 'organization') included a surprisingly liberal proposal for a network of schools to be paid for from property taxes. The Reformed churches denied that any priest could mediate grace. Universal literacy was necessary if all were to read the good news of scripture, each for him/herself. On this occasion, however, victory went to those who preferred to serve Mammon and these proposals were significantly amended in the *Second Book of Discipline* so that the powerful landowners of the day were not obliged to finance anything as reckless as a mass education system (Lynch, 1994). But the Church of Scotland continued to see the provision of education as a sacred duty. For some 300 years it would struggle along as best it could in the provision of a national system of schools.

Meanwhile, in England and Wales, there was marginally less fervent commitment to the provision of schools by the Church of England and by the various dissenting churches whose rights of worship were recognized from the late seventeenth century. But there was commitment. This found expression in a variety of ways. Some efforts were broadly ecumenical, representing all the Protestant denominations, such as those of the Society for Promoting Christian Knowledge founded in the early 1700s (Lawson and Silver, 1973). Other groups served specific denominations such as the Anglican National Society for Promoting the Education of the Poor in the Principles of the Established Church (a name mercifully most often abbreviated to 'the National Society') established in 1811. In parallel with the National Society stood the British and Foreign Schools Society, funded by members of the dissenting churches.

As best they could until they enjoyed full legal rights from the mid to late nineteenth century, minority religious communities such as the Jews and the Catholics satisfied their own needs under a variety of arrangements too diverse to describe in detail. In Ireland in all this time there were several calculated attempts at the mass conversion of Catholics by means of education, for example, through the network of Charter Schools established in the 1700s but these were never successful (Dowling, 1971). The effective primacy of Catholicism in all but the north-east quarter of the island (Ulster) was recognized by successive British governments from the early to mid-nineteenth century onwards and, with State sanction and even funding, responsibility for Ireland's schools was largely ceded to the Catholic Church (Bowen, 1980).

By the 1870s the provision of at least elementary education became a shared community responsibility throughout Britain. In the early twentieth century, signifying definitively the normalization of Catholic life in Britain, Catholic schools were incorporated under this umbrella. The establishment of this form of provision, financed by local and central taxes and under joint local and central political direction, was, however, significantly delayed by wrangles amongst various religious groups. In particular, in England and Wales the dissenters feared politicians would give the Anglican Church an excessive degree of influence in the schooling of all pupils, be they Anglican or not. There was also considerable lobbying in the late nineteenth century for overtly and avowedly secular schools, though this idea was overridden (Lawson and Silver, 1973). Contemporary arrangements represent the accumulation of generations of compromise. For the most part organized religions have won out over their secular/atheistic rivals and the current systems in operation throughout the UK clearly favour the interests of historically dominant religious groups.

Education and religion today: religious schools

The current state of affairs can be summarized quite swiftly but understanding the *implications* of the continued involvement of organized religious groups in formal schooling is far from easy. In England and Wales those schools run in accord with specific religious principles are more correctly known as voluntary schools. The parents/guardians of the pupils who attend them have chosen to expose their children to a particular religious ethos. Voluntary schools differ in certain technical arrangements. Voluntary-*aided* schools receive less direct funding from the public purse than do voluntary-*controlled* schools but much as the respective names suggest voluntary-controlled schools have less autonomy as a result. In a few other cases schools operate under so-called special agreements by which they receive less finance than even voluntary-aided schools but have correspondingly more freedom. These are to be found only at secondary level (Mackinnon, Stratham and Hales, 1998). The ratio of voluntary to other schools is something in the order of 1:2 amongst primaries but no more than a fifth of secondary schools are voluntary (*ibid.*). The majority of English and Welsh voluntary schools are run under the aegis of the Church of England or the Catholic Church, though some others are represented in this sector including the Jewish and Muslim communities.

Specifically religious schools are provided in Scotland by local authorities, which makes them quite unlike voluntary schools which English/Welsh local authorities only *help* to provide (Clark, 1997). But, *de facto*, a separate religious sector does exist in Scotland as in England/Wales. To all intents and purposes the Church of Scotland withdrew from the provision of schools in 1872 and has not returned since. (Strictly speaking, as it continued to maintain a private boarding-school for the daughters of ministers after 1870 and as its school for expatriate Christians in Israel continues to thrive, so it has never altogether withdrawn from the provision of schools.) Thus the major group involved with explicitly religious schools in Scotland today is the Catholic Church. From the 1870s to 1918 Scottish Catholics funded and ran their own schools. They were not confident that satisfactory arrangements could, and would, be made for Catholic educational needs (the teaching/learning of *particular* doctrines and teaching/learning *generally* in accord with Catholic principles) in the publicly funded schools established after 1872 (Fitzpatrick, 1999). The pressure of financing these schools finally obliged them to rethink the position in 1918. But by then (non-Catholic) Scottish national sentiment had swung behind the proposition that the current situation was unreasonable and the deal made for the transfer of Catholic schools included the long-sought assurances of absolute protection for religious conscience which had hitherto been denied. Other faith communities in Scotland do now have schools under similar arrangements but these are very few.

In Northern Ireland, where of course the fault lines of religious conflict are tragically stark, a distinction is drawn between voluntary (maintained) and voluntary (non-maintained) schools (Mackinnon, Stratham and Hales, 1998). As in England and Wales the differences between these are not necessarily immediately obvious but they concern the sharing of the burden of finance between church groups and the public purse. There are voluntary schools serving the Catholic community and others serving Protestants. All other schools not privately owned and operated are controlled schools. The innovative system of public provision of schooling which began in the early 1830s and forms the basis of the mass schooling traditions of both the 'north' and the 'south' was only intended to ensure that there would be a chance of schooling for all. It held some brief to integrate that schooling but more recently there have been experiments to this end through the establishment of controlled integrated schools aimed at promoting interfaith/community links (*ibid.*).

The position on explicitly religious schools can then be summarized as follows: Catholic children can, and generally do, receive a specifically Catholic schooling in all parts of the United Kingdom. Even in Scotland where 'Catholic schools' are not run directly by the Catholic Church there is surety of the Catholicity of what is taught through the exercise of a priestly veto on appointments of teachers. This, however, applies only in limited circumstances, with emphasis on official approval, not only for those teachers working in the fields of Religious Education (which is hardly surprising) but also teachers of Biology – where sex rears its head generally as does the issue of abortion more specifically (Fitzpatrick, 1999). Anglican children can likewise attend Anglican schools in England though not all do. Parents/guardians who want more specific guarantees as to the religious tone and content of their children's schooling must make other arrangements. Private religious schools exist, the Catholic boarding-school Blairs in Scotland is an example as is Ampleforth in England (Rae, 1999). Parents are free in law to send their children to such schools. (This is subject to general requirements as to the educational and other needs of the children concerned. Fire-worshippers might have a difficult time persuading local authority building inspectors that their in-school shrine was safe.)

Education and religion today: religion in other schools

Even if the UK's is a secular society (which can be taken to mean that it is a society in which relatively few engage in organized religious practices though this is not necessarily a measure as to their religious *beliefs*) its people are not subjects of a secular *state*. There are two established (that is, officially sanctioned and protected) churches, the Church of England and the Church of Scotland. In many respects they differ as much as any two Christian churches might. Where the Church of Scotland is presbyterian in organization (more or less democratic with authority shared amongst clergy and laity) the Church of England is episcopalian (organized around the top-down rule of bishops). The Church of Scotland is reformed in its doctrines and practices but the Church of England claims the fine technical position of being a part of the Catholic Church though one not recognizing Papal authority. But for all these differences (and wars have been fought over whether Anglican practices and organization would be acceptable in Scotland[2]) these two are yoked together. In a country which has a history of established religion in this way it would seem all but impossible that the State should refrain from being generally supportive of there being a religious element in the teaching/learning of all its schools. (This is a fact often lost on many educational commentators who fail to appreciate the gulf between their own atheistic or secular positions and that of the State.) Since the advent of the 1988 Education Reform Act (ERA) it has been incumbent on schools in England and Wales to provide a daily act of collective worship (ERA, section 6). Phrasing of a sort beloved of those who draft legislation stipulates that this worship be 'wholly or mainly of a broadly Christian character' but without following the forms of service of any Christian group in particular (section 7). Ironically, contrary to the intentions of the ERA's sponsors, this wording, rich as it is in ambiguity, has probably allowed some teachers to experiment with the syncretistic New Age spirituality to which many are known to be attracted (Heelas, 1997). As this often involves irrational mysticism and can be devoid of any morality beyond self-satisfaction and a more or less misanthropic 'green' ethic, it can be hard to imagine where its value might lie.) There must also be provision for religious education and this is required to reflect the nature of Christian history/heritage while giving account to other traditions (section 8). These requirements can be waived in certain circumstances but sections 6 to 8 set the norm from which anything else must therefore be a deviation.

By contrast to England and Wales, Scotland was not beset by sweeping – and controversial – educational change in the late 1980s. There are legal requirements of the same sort as those described above in force – the Education (Scotland) Act, 1980. But these were not as stridently insisted on as essential by their partisans or as bitterly contested by their opponents when they were introduced and, impressionistically, one has the sense that they are more honoured in the breach in Scotland than in England. Needless to say only a government with little political wisdom would hasten to impose universal duties of worship and the like in Northern Ireland, and successive governments, of all hues, have concentrated their efforts on the promotion of integrated schools (Mackinnon, Stratham and Hales, 1998).

The life of religious schools: general

It has already been suggested that there are three principal ways in which organized religion(s) can operate in and through formal education. Religious groups have characteristically made their own educational arrangements for the preparation of successive generations of monks/nuns, priests and ministers. This continues to be the case but need not detain us further because this provision is now confined to post-school education in seminaries and the like. It is no longer considered appropriate to prepare children for a specifically religious life. One slight amendment to this might come in observing that Blairs has historically been strongly associated with the preparation of teenage boys who think they may have a vocation and hope to be *considered* for training as Catholic priests. But this is a far cry from oblation, the raising and educating of foundling boys from infancy in medieval monasteries with the express intention that they would become monks. Thus, it is possible to concentrate on religious groups as providers of education for other, externally directed, purposes (that is, as educators of lay people) and as agents acting either to regulate or at least influence the conduct of formal education more generally.

The life of religious schools: Catholic

It is surprisingly easy (amongst non-Catholics) to gain continued acceptance for the belief that the life of Catholic schools is dominated by the promotion of unswerving and uncritical loyalty to Catholic doctrine. But this assumption may reflect a lack of appreciation of recent change in Catholic culture on the part of certain philosophers of education.[3] (See Barrow and Woods, compare pp. 78–9 in the edition of 1975 with pp. 80–1 in the substantially unaltered edition of 1998.) A more realistic portrait of life and learning in Catholic schools is called for.

Certainly Catholicism has been at war with modernity and change since the Reformation if not for longer. The intensity of this conflict only increased with the advent of the French Revolution, and reached its highest pitch in the nineteenth century during and after the European revolutions of 1848. It increased again with the advent of the Russian Revolution and has waxed and waned since. That is to say, the Catholic Church has opposed the emergence of meaningful human individuality. It has opposed both scientific method in general and certain scientific discoveries and technological developments in particular. Most obviously these have included its opposition to abortion (Vidler, 1990). It has opposed the overturning of established political orders not simply because these have often been bloody in practice but because it has denied any need for change in principle.

All this is typified by the events of 1848. Despite a brief flirtation with Italian liberalism and nationalism, Pius IX definitively set the church he led against the liberal nationalist modernity represented by the revolutionaries of that period (Vidler, 1990). The world on which he turned his back, and ordered Catholics to turn theirs as well, was one that came quickly to be ever more characterized by science, industry, mass political ideology and changed social roles. Even more so than it had been before, Catholic schooling after the middle of the nineteenth century became a marked force for conservatism in many parts of the world. After 1848 the spirit that had imbued Jesuit attempts to counter first the Reformation and later the French Revolution through education, expressed in the rigid orthodoxy of the curriculum known as the *Ratio Studiorum*, became widespread (Bowen,

1980). Catholic schools became dominated by an all-embracing Ultramontanism. Literally, a tendency to look 'over the mountains' in all things. The mountains in question are the Alps and the original Ultramontane Catholics were French so that the image is of looking always to Italy, more precisely to Rome, for guidance. It is usually with this Ultramontanist period of Catholic history in mind, rather than necessarily in reflection of any contemporary reality, that Catholic education is depicted as doctrinaire in the extreme. This is not to say that contemporary Catholic schooling cannot still be inflexibly doctrinaire and that Ultramontanism is not alive and aggressively well. The incumbent Pope has after all charged the Jesuits with re-evangelizing the erstwhile socialist commonwealth of central and eastern Europe and the secretive *Opus Dei* group gives many concern (Urquhart, 1995). But a more charitable picture of contemporary Catholic schools – though one also somewhat more realistic – might cast them as varied almost to the same extent as modern Catholicism itself, that is, stretched from the liberal to the conservative. The possibilities for serious doctrinal debate within Catholic ranks were significantly increased in the 1960s as a result of the Second Vatican Council, and debates initiated then have not cooled since. The diversity of present-day Catholic thought is reflected in the operation of Catholic schools. In liberal Catholic journals such as *Concilium* it is possible to hear the voices of Catholic feminists and others whose very existence belies any claim as to Catholicism's monolithic nature. Catholic teachers are certainly as influenced by the discourses of modernity as are those of other, or no, religious tradition and this has obvious implications for their teaching and the example(s) they set to pupils.

The life of religious schools: Anglican

The modern day Anglican Church is often satirized, but fondly so, for its seemingly excessive mildness. But its past is no less bloody than that of any other powerful religious group and the assumptions behind this apparent mildness have a curious history. Anglican beliefs and practices have been forced with greater or lesser degrees of success on recusant Catholics and intransigent Presbyterians alike. The discourses of Anglicanism emphasize its rationality and thus the irrationality of those who oppose it. Wilful refusal to accept that 'rationality' has resulted in persecution for many. Only from the eighteenth century was Anglicanism's temporal power curbed as the drift to the cities prompted by industrialization denuded its rural parishes. Loosened from the strictures of orthodoxy many of the new urban population moved away from religious practice and the only option available was to *persuade* them to return (Hempton, 1994). This was attempted in part through the National Society. Under its auspices, Anglicans were involved in the provision of elementary education at the time of the 1870 Act. The Act itself allowed that where such voluntary provision could be shown to be working successfully it would be retained.

Over time the State steadily advanced in its provision of schooling but by both quantitative and qualitative measures Anglican provision has remained high. There are still many Church of England primary schools and though the number of its secondary schools is fewer it is far from being an insignificant provider at this level. But more than this, the standing of Anglican voluntary schools is generally high in public perception (Judd, 1999). Indeed so high is it that Anglican schools are consistently oversubscribed and can sometimes be obliged to turn away the parents of prospective pupils. At the time of writing this is set to become the subject of an inquiry as the Anglican hierarchy looks for ways of consolidating its success and extending its provision (Judd, 1999). Admission to Anglican schools is contingent on religious observance and, while this might not seem unreasonable in itself, there may be a measure of 'rice bowl Christianity' as a result. Like Catholicism, contemporary Anglicanism is hardly monolithic and its schools reflect the diversity of its component groups with both Evangelicals and Anglo-Catholics in evidence amongst parents, heads, teachers, governors, bishops and clergy, all of whom contribute to setting the tone in any given Church of England school.

The life of religious schools: others

As yet there are still only trivially few religious schools not in the hands of the traditionally significant providers. But there are times when a study of trends can be more useful than looking at absolute numbers. Thus, while the provision of specifically Jewish education, in both publicly funded and private schools, has remained essentially stable for generations, as has that of such communities as the Methodists, demand for and provision of Muslim schooling, both publicly and privately funded, has grown considerably in recent years. The various Islamic communities (and there are as many of these as there are Christian groups) have lobbied hard to see a precedent set for the extension of the voluntary arrangements in England and Wales beyond their original exclusively Christian remit. They continue also to press for the inclusion of questions touching on religious affiliation in future censuses. This, they hope, will give solid statistical evidence to support their contention that the growth in Muslim belief and practice warrants the development of a distinct sector of Islamic schools comparable in kind, if not scale, to the Anglican and Catholic sectors. (This growth is a product of demographic change through immigration in large part, though the small but steady flow of converts to Islam cannot be ignored.)

Serious Muslim scholars no doubt grow tired explaining that many practices associated with Islam in the collective 'Western mind' are products of specific cultures and have no sanction in the Koran or elsewhere in Islamic scripture (Ahmed, 1992). The excesses sometimes visited on Muslim women (such as the horror of clitoral excision) find their 'justification' in traditional beliefs specific to certain parts of the world. The fact that such things are done by Muslims does not make them Islamic any more than persecution of Jews is Christian. In each case the relationship is contingent rather than necessary. But there remain liberal concerns as to aspects of life for Muslims that undoubtedly *do* have scriptural warrant. An obvious case here is posed by the modesty requirements which operate for males and females alike but more obviously for the latter ('women ... [must] guard their unseen parts', Koran ch. 4). This is not to say that such a requirement is universally observed amongst Muslim women but even the most liberal of Islamic theologians do not consider it optional. Such is the closed nature of Muslim theology, which will not admit of any interpretation of scripture which denies that it is divinely inspired and must be obeyed whole and entire, that they *cannot* (Ahmed, 1992). Where modest dress (and *full* body covering is another product only of traditional practice) is truly chosen liberalism does not allow an objection but whether schools can legitimately be permitted to 'construct' choice from an early age remains an open question. (In passing, it is worth noting that a compromise solution to the problem(s) caused for some by the relative paucity of specifically Muslim schools has emerged through the tendency of some Islamic parents to favour sending their daughters to Catholic schools where – all the more so if these are single sex – they consider the moral tone and general circumstances to be more to their liking than in the state school mainstream. This they have been able in law to do since the early 1980s.)

Religious life in other schools

The formal requirements incumbent on those involved in the operation of schools which do not have a specific(ally) religious ethos have been discussed above. These requirements are a product of the consistent success of at least the major Christian churches in contributing to educational policy. The Church of England was successful in ensuring that the 1870 Act suited its purposes. The Catholic Church in Scotland held out until it got what it wanted in 1918. The Catholic bishops did not win all that they wanted from the 1944 Education Act in England and Wales (Barber, 1994) but the Church of England was a significant participant in the formation of policy in the war years. The Church of England played a major part in influencing sections of the ERA. And it is in this way that various churches continue the regulatory function first developed when the pre-Reformation church was obliged to loosen its absolute monopoly on the provision of formal schooling. That is to say, the major Christian churches act as what might be called the conscience of the State in matters educational. (This is also true in other aspects of social policy though these lie beyond our present remit.) This influence can best be understood by exploring briefly two examples.

During the Second World War a tone arose in public debate which emphasized the need to develop post-war social structures which would make meaningful the claim that war was being waged in defence of democracy. One way it seemed possible to do this was the designing of a school system that would exclude no one from the benefits of progressing beyond the elementary schooling which had been the lot of most children hitherto. This aspiration was powerfully described in an influential work by the then Archbishop of Canterbury, William Temple. Significant features of the post-war education settlement were presaged in his 1942 book *Christianity and Social Order* (Temple, 1994). If this represents an example of advice taken generally willingly it is important to remember that the voice of conscience is not always so welcome though it may eventually be heeded. Thus throughout the 1980s the Church and Nation Committee of the Church of Scotland spoke loudly on the need to preserve aspects of Scottish life from the encroachment of ideas which had been the source of bitter social and political controversy in England and Wales (Rosie, 1992). Church and Nation continued this advocacy of Scottish solutions to Scottish problems in education and elsewhere after the advent of the ERA and into the 1990s. In particular, from 1991 it put its considerable influence behind lobbying for a Scottish parliament – an ambition now achieved – which would have control over Scottish education.

Contemporary issues in education and religion

This chapter is not concerned exclusively with the ERA. But in so far as it represents the most apparently explicit attempt to re-evangelize life and learning in the 'north-western' world in the post-war period it is a useful case study. Much of the initial response to the ERA from amongst teachers and educationalists was hostile but it was sometimes thoughtful and insightful. The ambiguities of the ERA's language, its intentions and its likely effects were all given critical consideration. It was pointed out that the ERA had been framed as a response to lapsed religious provisions of post-war school legislation but that it had been created without any great thought as to *why* those requirements had been so patchily satisfied. It was pointed out that the ERA gave no hint of its own justification. What *was* so good and so important about religious worship and religious knowledge? Was the intention to produce believers, or to produce people sensitized to life's spiritual possibilities, was it aimed at some civic moral purpose or at something else altogether? It was pointed out that the emphasis on the non-doctrinal nature of daily worship seemed to be some sort of attempt to settle disputes which had long since settled themselves, doctrinal ecumenism having been the order of the day amongst the major churches for some considerable time. No longer do (most?) Baptists, say, fear the pernicious effects of Anglican services on their children, with both happy to worship together under many circumstances. Though in passing we may note that one objection to the ERA does fail. The complaint that 'in the USA worship in non-Church schools is not only lacking, it is expressly forbidden' (Cox, 1989, p. 37) with the implied question 'why can it not be so here?' is wide of the mark. The schools of the USA *do* in fact have a daily act of collective worship. If the oath of allegiance does not constitute an act of worship it is hard to imagine what it is. The fact that it can be difficult to know exactly *what* is being worshipped – it may as well be the reified or even deified 'nation' as anything else – is another matter.

The religious component of the ERA does, however, certainly verge on being incoherent in several respects. The most obvious and important of these is its basic confusion of religious *education* and religious *instruction*. It is quite simply unclear whether the ERA intends to develop knowledge and understanding of religion in pupils as an academic exercise (religious education) or to bring them to the acceptance of certain doctrines (religious instruction).

Over there and over here: the UK and the USA

As a yearning for the (supposed) 'American way' (state-sanctioned secularism) was an aspect of the ERA debate it may be useful and convenient to note some comparative points before concluding this work. For all its faults, the ERA was certainly not as crude a device for re-evangelizing society through education as the inclusion of teaching on 'special creation' and the exclusion of evolutionary biology in school curricula recently mandated in Kansas (Vulliamy, 1999). (Kentucky and Oklahoma have since taken similar steps.) A 'headline event' like this can draw more short-term attention than its long-term significance may warrant, and may reveal more than anything quite how much leverage relatively few people can have in a representative democracy if they are determined and lucky. (The Kansas decision required a majority of two on a committee of ten – not exactly a grassroots revolt (Appell, 1999, p. 15).) But this is still a useful starting point. It reminds us that the contradictions in and around the matter of religion in the political discourse of the USA are legion. It is the secular state (Bill of Rights, article I, 'Congress shall make no law respecting an establishment of religion . . .') which is 'indivisible under God'. Its origins as a polity lie in the deism of the eighteenth century. That is, depersonalized religion which, in the words of the Declaration of Independence, looks to 'Divine Providence' as a cosmological force rather than, say, the highly individual (and more than a little sarcastic) Jehovah who spoke from the whirlwind (Job, 38–41).

It is here that the loophole lies. Deism locates god(s) in all things. Deism is metaphysics as religion. The largely deistic Founding Fathers could not imagine a world without god(s), because deism takes god(s), to be a manifest presence in creation but they could – and did – imagine a polity without churches because deism has much less need of organized practice than is common amongst religions. Their commitment to the idea that reason would ultimately prevail ensured that they did not regulate *against* organized religion(s) but their own religiosity ensured that they did not mandate the secular state to pursue a project of secularization. It is in this vacuum that those concerned with the advocacy of organized religious belief *and* practice have been able to manoeuvre, promoting a direct linking of education and religious purposes of a sort not seen in the UK for several centuries.

Conclusion

Whoever embarks on concluding any piece of writing on religion without having some degree of trepidation has certainly misunderstood what s/he has been asked to do. Religion concerns itself with what are said to be eternal verities, debates on such matters are not easily summed up. In keeping with a well-established theme, what follow are no more than notes towards some conclusion. The atavistic urges which motivated the religious component of the ERA and which motivate the imposition of the bad science and bad theology of creationism in some US school curricula are devoid of any subtlety. They are also illiberal. The general moral lesson to be extracted from such attempts at re-evangelizing largely secular societies is simply this: compelling religious practice through religious instruction is relatively easy. The history of religion in education has generally been characterized in this way. Promoting religious knowledge in schools may possibly contribute to fostering religious belief (as knowledge of the humanities can tend to humanize and as knowledge of science can produce respect for scientific method). But as there is no necessary relation between religious belief and religious practice so there is no necessary relation between religious knowledge (knowledge *about* religion(s)) and either religious belief *or* religious practice. The failure implicit in promoting compulsory religious instruction is a failure of faith. The truly faithful will always have the courage to accept that it is practically wiser and in principle more moral to hope for the development of belief and practice through the fostering of religious knowledge.

Notes

1. The distinction between dates which are C(ommon) E(ra) and B(efore the) CE equates to that between AD and BC but is often preferred as being less culturally loaded.
2. First Bishops' War 1639; Second Bishops' War 1640. Though (re)unification of the Church of Scotland and the Scottish Episcopalian Church may soon occur if recent reports are to be believed (O'Sullivan, 2000.)
3. A more pertinent example of religious indoctrination might be the Sunni Muslim schools of Pakistan from which young men issue forth to fight in Afghanistan's insatiable wars.

References

Ahmed, A.S. (1992) *Postmodernism and Islam: Predicament and Promise*. London: Routledge.

Anderson, R.D. (1992) *Universities and Elites in Britain Since 1800*. London: Economic History Society.

Appell, D. (1999) 'Speaking up for science'. *Scientific American*, November, 15–18.

Barber, M. (1994) *The Making of the 1944 Education Act*. London: Cassell.

Barrow, R. St C. and Woods, R. G. (1975, 1998) *An Introduction to Philosophy of Education*. London: Methuen.

Berresford Ellis, P. (1995) *The Druids*. London: Constable.

Bowen, J. (1980) *A History of Western Education*, vol. 3. London: Methuen.

Clark, M. (1997) 'Education in Scotland: setting the scene', in M. Clark and P. Munn (eds) *Education in Scotland: Policy and Practice from Pre-school to Secondary*. London: Routledge.

Cox, E. (1989) 'Collective worship in schools: Education Reform Act 1988, sections 6, 7 and 12', in E. Cox and J. Cairns (eds) *Reforming Religious Education: The Religious Clauses of the 1988 Education Reform Act*. London: Kogan Page.

Davies, P. (1993) *The Mind of God: Science and the Search for Ultimate Meaning*. Harmondsworth: Penguin.

Dowling, P. (1971) *A History of Irish Education: A Study in Conflicting Loyalties*. Cork: Mercier Press.

Ellis, J.W. (1990) 'Informal education: a Christian perspective', in T. Jeffs and M. Smith (eds) *Using Informal Education*. Buckingham: Open University Press.

Fitzpatrick, T. (1999) 'Catholic education in Scotland', in T. Bryce and W. Humes (eds) *Scottish Education*. Edinburgh: Edinburgh University Press.

Gellner, E. (1996) *Conditions of Liberty: Civil Society and Its Rivals*. Harmondsworth: Penguin.

Goody, J. and Watt, I. (1990) 'The consequences of literacy', in P. Giglioli (ed.) *Language and Social Context*. Harmondsworth: Penguin.

Goudsblom, J. (1992) *Fire and Civilisation*. Harmondsworth: Penguin.

Heelas, P. (1997) *The New Age Movement: The Celebration of Self and the Sacralization of Modernity*. Oxford: Basil Blackwell.

Hempton, D. (1994) 'Religious life in industrial Britain 1830–1914', in S. Gilley and W. Sheils (eds) *A History of Religion in Britain: Practice and Belief from Pre-Roman Times to the Present*. Oxford: Basil Blackwell.

Judd, J. (1999) 'Archbishop sets up church school inquiry', *The Independent*, 14 October, p. 10

Lawson, J. and Silver, H. (1973) *A Social History of Education in England*. London: Methuen.

Lynch, M. (1994) *Scotland: A New History*. London: Pimlico.

Mackinnon, D., Stratham, J. and Hales, M. (1998) *Education in the UK: Facts and Figures*. London: Hodder and Stoughton.

O'Sullivan, J. (2000) 'Scotland's main Protestant Churches to end schism and unite', *The Independent*, 13 April, p. 13.

Ozment, S. (1993) *Protestants: The Birth of a Revolution*. London: HarperCollins.

Pyle, E. H. (1984) 'Religion', in J. Hinells (ed.) *The Penguin Dictionary of Religions*. Harmondsworth: Penguin.

Rae, J. (1999) *Letters to Parents: How to Get the Best Available Education for Your Child*. London: HarperCollins.

Rosie, G. (1992) 'Religion', in M. Linklater and R. Denniston (eds) *Anatomy of Scotland: How Scotland Works*. Edinburgh: Chambers.

Said, E. (1997) *Covering Islam*. London: Vintage.

Scotland, J. (1969) *The History of Scottish Education*, vol. 1. London: University of London Press.

Smart, N. (1977) *The Religious Experience of Mankind*. Glasgow: Collins.

Temple, W. (1994) Extract from *Christianity and Social Order*, in J. Atherton (ed.) *Social Christianity: A Reader*. London: SPCK.

Urquhart, G. (1995) *The Pope's Armada*. London: Bantam Books.

Vidler, A.R. (1990) *The Church in an Age of Revolution: 1789 to the Present Day*. Harmondsworth: Penguin.

Vulliamy, E. (1999) 'Anti-Darwinism makes a monkey out of Kansas'. *The Observer*, 3 October, p. 25.

4

Education and Citizenship[1]

Jon Davison and James Arthur

Introduction

A child born in France is a *citizen*: a child born in the England is a *subject*. The term 'citizenship' appears to have little meaning for residents of this country (Kerr, 1999). As a consequence, perhaps, there has never been very strong support for a separate subject of Citizenship to be placed upon school timetables. Nevertheless, Rowe (1997) has identified eight models of citizenship education in England that comprise, *inter alia*, aspects of the following: values development, inculcation of good habits, knowledge and understanding of legal rights and responsibilities, and of the parliamentary system. Pupils' development in these areas is believed to be supported by direct teaching located within the Personal and Social Development curricular area in schools and by exposure to adult role models and positive school ethos. This somewhat marginal nature of citizenship education was, perhaps, reinforced by the production of *Curriculum Guidance 8: Citizenship Education* (National Curriculum Council, 1990a) when the English/Welsh National Curriculum was introduced. This document and others in the series had only little impact on the work of schools as they struggled to meet the timetabling demands of the National Curriculum with its specified percentages for core and foundation subjects. Increasingly, however, the personal, social, spiritual, moral and cultural development of the pupil has been seen to be significant, so much so that it forms part of the inspection framework for the Office for Standards in Education (OFSTED).

In November 1997 the Advisory Group on Citizenship Education, chaired by Professor Bernard Crick, was established to provide advice on effective education for citizenship in schools. The so-called Crick Report was published by the Department for Education and Employment (DfEE) in 1998 and contained recommendations relating to the development of the knowledge, skills, under-standing and values necessary for 'active citizenship' (DfEE, 1998, p. 10). The report highlights three 'mutually dependent' aspects believed to underpin an effective education for citizenship: 'social and moral responsibility, community involvement and political literacy' (pp. 11–13). In other words, the development of what has been called elsewhere, 'social literacy' (Arthur and Davison, 2000).

In this chapter the term 'social literacy' is used to describe the knowledge, skills, understandings and values which comprise the complex process of children's social maturation. While the school plays a role in this development, it can, in the words of the Crick Report, 'only do so much' (DfEE, 1998, p. 9). Such development is also the product of the complex interactions between children and their homes, and between children and the wider community in which they grow. The use of the term 'social literacy' also reflects the model of citizenship education proposed later in this chapter: one which empowers, not just enables; one which is critical, not just functional. Further, in order to fully acknowledge the centrality of 'discourse' to 'active citizenship' (DfEE, 1998, p. 14), the chapter extends the definition of social literacy by drawing upon the work of socio-linguists in relation to discourse theory. This chapter also argues that, if pupils are to become truly active citizens as adults, any programme of citizenship education must be underpinned by the development in all school subjects of a pedagogy that makes transparent the discourses which underpin: the education system; teaching and learning; National Curriculum subjects; and citizenship education itself.

Social development

The acquisition of social literacy is historically and culturally conditioned and context specific. Babies engage in social activity before they are 'taught' it: babies are disposed to be *social* before they learn what are the components or processes of *sociability*. There are two distinct views of social development. The first is *normative and communal*: children learn from their culture customs that provide them with a guide to act in ways that minimize conflict with others. Children are persuaded of the moral force of acting socially through their voluntary associations within their immediate circle, such as with members of the family, and within the wider community, for example, through interaction with members of a church or club. In this normative view the child will not only know the correct behaviour but will perform the role without the need for regular, conscious reference to the rules governing it. The second view is *pragmatic and individualistic*: the social order of children is maintained by explicit and implicit agreements entered into by self-seeking individuals to avert the worst consequences of their 'self-ish' instincts. Formal agreements and sanctions underpin social order. Individuals obey rules because they confer personal advantage.

While it might be agreed that schools play a significant role in the social maturation of pupils, the question of whether schools should be assessing know-ledge and understanding of a social behaviour, or the ability to perform the behaviour, is an area of contention. Therefore, an exploration of the nature of 'social literacy' is required.

Social education and social literacy

Social Education, Personal and Social Education, Personal, Social and Health Education are all phrases commonly used in schools to describe the social dimension of the school curriculum (DfEE, 1998, p. 23). The aims of such social education usually cite the development of factual knowledge and understanding, a commitment to desirable values and attitudes, a range of social and life skills, and desirable qualities of character (Scrimshaw, 1989, p. 28).

The term 'social literacy' has not been used to describe such education in the UK. It originated in Australia in the 1980s in relation to multicultural education (Kalantzis and Cope, 1983). The Education Faculty, University of Waikato, New Zealand also used the term to include children learning from the study and teaching of social studies in schools. New Zealand's national curriculum describes children as acquiring social literacy through an engagement with social studies premised upon the social *processes* of enquiry, values exploration and social decision-making. These earlier versions of social literacy incorporate the acquisition of knowledge and understanding linked to the development of social skills that promote responsible behaviour. Goleman (1996) gives an account of the development of education located in the areas of Social Literacy and Emotional Intelligence in the USA.

England and Wales

In England and Wales a quarter of a century ago, the Schools Council Humanities Project and Schools Council Social Education Project proposed that there should be a clear connection between learning *from* the social sciences curriculum and the acquisition of social skills necessary to function effectively within a community or society. The Social Education Project report (see Rennie, Lunzer and Williams, 1974, p. 119) declared the fundamental principle 'that everyone needs to develop the skills to examine, challenge and control his immediate situation in school and community'. While both projects linked the teaching of the humanities and social education explicitly with children's social development, neither used the term 'social literacy' in project reports. In the same decade, Elliot and Pring (1975, p. 8) described four aims for social education: to learn about the local society; to understand how society works; to learn to be responsible and to have the right social attitudes. These social aims are clearly reflected in the Crick Report (DfEE, 1998, pp. 13–21).

However, the 1988 Education Reform Act effectively ended the development of social studies in schools in England and Wales by prescribing a curriculum comprising a range of 'traditional' subjects defined in abstract academic terms. Social aspects of the curriculum were progressively marginalized as 'traditional' academic subjects sought status and respectability in the hierarchy of academic credibility created by the structures of the new National Curriculum: the primary concerns of *core* and *foundation* subjects were not the social and practical aspects of daily life. Increasingly, however, there grew the realization that in order for the National Curriculum to reflect the 1998 Education Reform Act's curricular aim of preparing pupils for life and the world of work, there would need to be an element of cross-curricular integration of the teaching of the social component of the school curriculum. Subsequently, the National Curriculum Council (1990a–d) produced a range of cross-curricular documentation that included Citizenship, Health Education, Economic and Industrial Understanding. As a result, social education was not totally removed from the school curriculum. National Curriculum Council *Curriculum Guidance 3: The Whole Curriculum* (NCC, 1990b) stated that it was schools' responsibility to prepare young people for their roles in adult life and that individuals should be enabled to think and act for themselves 'with an acceptable set of personal qualities which also meet the wider social demands of adult life'.

Arguably, the curriculum reflects the political and social context within which it is constructed (Kerr, 1999, pp. 3–6). In its *Statement of Values* (QCA, 1999b), the revised National Curriculum for the year 2000 includes the following: the development of children's social responsibility; community involvement; the development of effective relationships; knowledge and understanding of society; participation in the affairs of society; respect for others and children's contribution to the building up of the common good, including their development of independence and self-esteem. Additionally, the government intends that citizenship education will become a statutory part of the school curriculum by 2002 in secondary schools and that primary schools will be expected to deliver citizenship education through personal and social education, which is to be made more coherent within a new, non-statutory, framework. The government requires schools to provide a curriculum that will contribute to meeting specific learning outcomes which involve inculcating pupils with social and moral dispositions as an essential precondition to civic and political education, thus promoting social cohesion and inclusion within society. Schools will be expected to motivate pupils and encourage their participation in the political processes of democratic society. The draft frameworks (QCA, 1999a & b) makes it clear that schools are expected to help 'equip them with the values and knowledge to deal with the difficult moral and social questions they face'. The questions of with *which*, or *whose*, values pupils might be equipped are ignored. Indeed, until now the values that underpin the National Curriculum have rarely been addressed in official documentation, beyond an evocation of 'standards'. The central metaphor of the National Curriculum is *delivery*. Many question whether this is an appropriate description of teaching and learning of core and foundation subjects. Perhaps more questionable is the notion of teachers *delivering* values defined in National Curriculum documentation. While all 'stakeholders' in the education system might agree that 'standards' and 'values' are 'Good Things', there is little evidence of rigorous engagement with the problematic nature of their definition.

The draft framework for personal, social, health education and citizenship at key stages 1–4 (QCA, 1999b) expects young people to learn specific social skills. In this framework social literacy is perceived to be an *achievement* on the part of the child, for it is defined as the ability to understand and operate successfully within a complex and interdependent social world. It involves the acquisition of the skills of active and confident social participation, including the skills, knowledge and attitudes that enable an individual to make reasoned judgements in a community. At key stage 1, children will be expected to learn how to share, take turns, play and resolve simple arguments. At key stage 2, children are expected to take increasing responsibility for their social behaviour in and out of the classroom and understand the effect of their choices on the community. At key stage 3, children will build on these social skills by developing higher order skills which help them to confidently take part in aspects of the community's social life. Finally, at key stage 4, young people will be expected to have acquired a greater knowledge and understanding of social issues and be able to articulate and discuss these issues with each other and with other members of the wider community. It would appear that this framework proposes a simple linear development of social literacy linked to age and key stage in the same way that knowledge and understanding of the content of core and foundation subjects is believed to be developed by delivery. Despite acknowledging that pupils will have to operate successfully in a complex social world, such a model of development ignores the complexity of the processes through which social literacy is developed. Unlike scientific or mathematical knowledge which, in the main, may be developed in the school context, children's values, beliefs and attitudes are also developed within the home and in the wider community. Indeed, some children's 'home' values may be in direct opposition to those espoused by the school, or, indeed, at variance with those of other children.

Social literacy is concerned with the empowerment of the social and ethical self, which includes the ability to understand and explain differences within individual experiences. Robinson and Shallcross have reviewed the many attempts to explain or rationalize social behaviour and have highlighted how complex the process is. They summarize their research:

> Social action occurs at two levels simultaneously. It occurs at the level of large institutions that shape the nature of the social, political, economic and cultural landscapes within which individuals develop their identities and it also takes place at the grass roots level, the level of action at which we, as individuals, have the free will to make choices but largely not in circumstances of our own making. (Robinson and Shallcross, 1998, p. 69)

Combs and Slaby (1977, p. 162) define social skill as 'the ability to interact with others in a given social context in specific ways that are societally acceptable or valued and at the same time personally beneficial, mutually beneficial, or beneficial primarily to others'. A key pillar of the National Curriculum is the assessment of achievement in key stages. Any model of assessment of social development needs to acknowledge the complexities discussed here. Obviously, children daily manifest a whole range of positive social competencies, but to reduce a study of children's social roles to the measurement of 'competencies' or behaviours that involve positive and negative consequences would be both narrow and restricting. Simply providing children with a 'social first-aid kit' runs the danger of being totally instrumental in approach; rather, there needs to be a recognition of the intrinsic values within all human interaction that are difficult to ignore. Consequently, the determination of what social attributes or behaviours a child might exhibit in order to be judged socially literate is only a small part of the process and, ultimately, reductive. However, before proceeding further in the discussion of social literacy, there is a need for some clarity over the form of citizenship which schooling might seek to inculcate.

Citizenship and citizenship education

The social dimension of education is interrelated with, but also distinct from, the political dimension, but it is when they combine that citizenship education begins to take shape. A stated aim of the Crick Report is 'a change in the political culture of this country both nationally and locally: for people to think of themselves as active citizens' (DfEE, 1998, p. 7). It is possible, therefore, to locate versions of citizenship on a continuum having the poles *passive* and *active. Passive*, or functional, citizenship may be the product of an education which seeks only to develop knowledge, understandings and behaviours – competence – in order to *enable* an individual to participate in society. Citizenship education for passive, functional citizenship would, in the main, comprise a content-based curriculum, aimed at developing in pupils knowledge of legal rights and responsibilities, the Law, the electoral system, the workings of national, regional and local government, the processes of the welfare state and so on. Its purpose would be to create citizens who could function in society by performing the roles expected of them as adult members of that society. Conversely, *active*, or powerful, citizenship may result from citizenship education that not only enables individuals to develop the knowledge, understandings and behaviours necessary for them to function in society as described above, but which, through the development of levels of *criticality*, also *empowers* individuals so that they might question, critique and debate the workings and processes of society. Such, indeed, appears to be the intention of the recommendations of the Crick Report. Further, this approach to citizenship education might produce citizens who would take a leadership role in proposing alternative models of the structures and processes of democracy.

The draft framework for personal, social, health education and citizenship at key stages 1–4 (QCA, 1999b) not only avoids the values issues highlighted earlier, it also presents citizenship as if it is a simple, homogenous, value-free state of being. Figure 4.1 provides a means to explore types of citizenship by drawing a distinction between the *normative* and *individualistic* views of social development discussed at the beginning of this chapter and between *active* and *passive* versions of citizenship. It thus highlights the beliefs and values that might be seen as characterizing versions of citizenship. The horizontal line represents the continuum from passive to active citizenship whilst the vertical line moves up from the individualistic to the normative views of how children acquire social literacy. The quadrants in

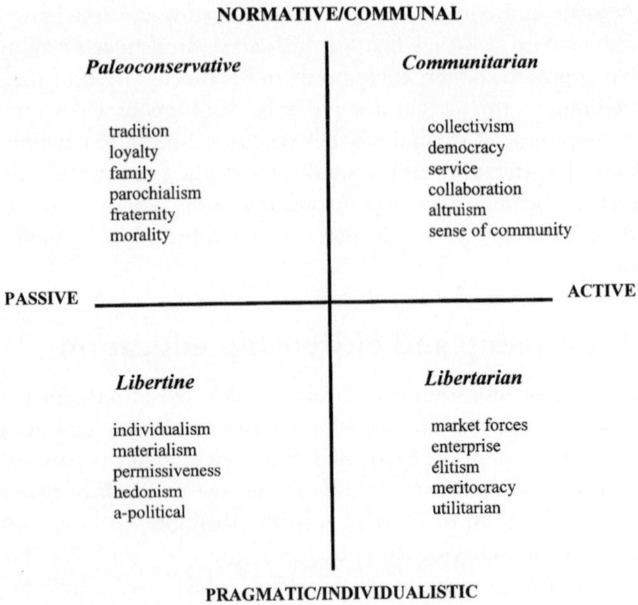

NORMATIVE/COMMUNAL

Paleoconservative

tradition
loyalty
family
parochialism
fraternity
morality

Communitarian

collectivism
democracy
service
collaboration
altruism
sense of community

PASSIVE ⎯⎯⎯⎯⎯⎯⎯⎯⎯⎯⎯⎯⎯⎯⎯⎯⎯⎯⎯⎯ ACTIVE

Libertine

individualism
materialism
permissiveness
hedonism
a-political

Libertarian

market forces
enterprise
élitism
meritocracy
utilitarian

PRAGMATIC/INDIVIDUALISTIC

Figure 4.1 Types of Citizenship.

Figure 4.1 are: *communitarian* citizens (the upper right), *paleoconservative* citizens (the upper left), *libertine* citizens (the lower left) and *libertarian* citizens (the lower right). In a chapter of this length any characterization of beliefs and values of the various types of citizen is not exhaustive and runs the risk of appearing reductive. Without question there are many other values, beliefs and attitudes that might be attributed to the quadrants. The choice of values and beliefs has not been made with any agenda other than aiming to show that it is too simplistic to refer to citizenship as if it were not a debatable term. Similarly, the beliefs and values listed in each quadrant are not necessarily only confined to the particular quadrant in which they appear. For example, the idea of *service* would naturally exist in both upper quadrants, but the versions of service would be markedly different, for example, acceptance of imposed rules in the upper left quadrant, opposed to collective engagement in the construction of rules in the upper right. Further, we offer this figure as a means to explore the concept of citizenship and the values which underpin its varying forms, as it illustrates some of the features which might be seen as characterizing types of citizens.

The following paragraphs are brief descriptions of the types of citizens that may characterize the quadrants in Figure 4.1. They are not exhaustive analyses, but illustrative thumbnail sketches. While *libertarian* citizens might be seen as valuing involvement in politics, their aim is to reduce government at every level and to increase the nature and scope of the market in the form of property rights and the sanctity of contracts. They are typically not hostile to community, but not much interested either. Libertarian citizenship education would at best be about developing the child's competence to operate successfully within the capitalist system, to understand the rules and develop the dispositions of utilitarian creativity and entrepreneurial drive. At worst, it could encourage the practice of deceit, fraud and hypocrisy which are destructive of community and lethal to democracy. The widening social and economic divisions apparent in society in the 1980s and the infamous collapse of Barings Bank, perhaps, serve as an illustration of the more negative aspects of the promotion of libertarian citizenship. The Crick Report is rightly concerned about libertarian citizenship which is manifested by 'apathy, ignorance and cynicism about public life' (DfEE, 1998, p. 8).

Libertine citizens may become marginally involved in political activities but tend to be antisocial. Such citizens are generally hostile to social institutions and their philosophy might be described as eat, drink and copulate, for tomorrow we die. Libertine citizenship education would be radically critical of concepts such as virtue, community and tradition, and its aim would not be to extend the common good. Instead, this type of citizenship education would engage in an ongoing struggle to ensure the maximum freedom for each individual with everything up for questioning and argument. At worst, this libertine approach could cause division, fragmentation and strife within a community.

The term *paleoconservative* has been coined for the upper left quadrant, to describe the form of conservatism which manifested itself prior to so-called 'Thatcherism': a libertarian form of citizenship. This distinction has been made in order to avoid confusion with the now more common use of the term 'conservatism', which tends to be used to describe post-Thatcher 'conservatism'. It is also important to make this distinction, because the oppositional location of the two quadrants clearly illustrates the debates between the Thatcherite and so-called 'Wet' versions of conservatism that clashed in the last two decades of the twentieth century. Paleoconservative citizens are socially conservative, traditional and generally tend to be optimistic about the ability of society to manage itself free from government interference. However, they typically favour state laws to enforce traditional concepts of morality. Citizenship education for the paleoconservative would mainly be about complying with various kinds of authority. At best this type of citizenship education would encourage dispositions like respect, responsibility and self-discipline, at worst, submission, conformity and docility.

Communitarian citizens can be progressive or conservative, for they place great emphasis on putting aside personal interests for the sake of community. They seek to balance the social good of the community against the good of the individual. Communitarian citizenship education would emphasize the role, depending on the ideological perspective, of 'mediating' social institutions in addition to schools, in the belief that society as a whole is educative. At best, this would not restrict itself to the transmission of a set of social procedures, but would aim to strengthen the democratic and participative spirit within each individual. At worst, it could become majoritarian in approach; insisting on the acceptance of the moral position of the majority in society. From an examination of the 'Terms of reference of the Advisory Group on Citizenship' (DfEE, 1998, p. 4), it is apparent that it is to the best ideal of the communitarian citizen that New Labour aspires, in its revision of the National Curriculum. In this sense New Labour has an agenda which is to produce a majority of citizens who will express communitarian sentiments, in the same way that Thatcherism attempted to encourage citizens to feel at home in expressing libertarian sentiments (see Arthur, 1998, 1999). That communitarianism may be progressive or conservative (or, perhaps, both) is highlighted in the debates over the New Labour government's policies on education since the general election of 1997.

Clearly, this brief exploration illustrates that it is, perhaps, too simplistic to begin to develop citizenship education without discussing the nature of citizenship itself. Further, the term 'social literacy' is not unproblematic for the means by which children acquire social literacy can privilege some over others. By using the 'right' behaviour and language in the 'right way', that is, by entering the dominant discourse, socially literate citizens have avenues opened for them to the social goods and powers of society. The New Labour government seeks to use teaching and the school curriculum as a means to redress deficiencies in the prior social acquisition of children in the name of social inclusion. The socially empowered person is 'characterised by the possession of a sound and detailed understanding of himself and others, and also by his [*sic*] ability to behave in an intelligent way in relation to others', Scrimshaw (1975, p. 73). Despite being articulated a quarter of a century ago, these aims for social education are almost identical to the aims enunciated by the National Forum for Values and the Community (QCA, 1999c). The Forum's ideals of valuing self, families and relationships with others are incorporated into the revised National Curriculum. The final report of the advisory group in citizenship (DfEE, 1998, p. 14) maintained, 'discourse is obviously fundamental to active citizenship'. The rest of this chapter now examines the central role of language in the development social literacy and active citizenship.

Discourse

Adult illiteracy is perceived to result from a lack of the skills needed by people in order to survive, or function, at a minimally determined, adequate level within society. Discussions of the level of adult illiteracy often cite causal factors related to economic or educational inequality, or an individual's or a group's lack of social power. In reality, of course, such factors are enmeshed. The work of socio-linguists James Paul Gee, Colin Lankshear and Neil Mercer enables us further to develop the concept of social literacy. Gee (1987) proposes that individuals belong to a community and increase their social power within that community by learning and controlling discourses. Gee draws a distinction between 'discourse' which he defines as 'connected stretches of language that make sense' found within 'Discourses' (Gee, 1990, p. 143), and 'Discourse' which he defines as 'a socially accepted association among ways of using language, of thinking, and of acting that can be used to identify oneself as a member of a socially meaningful group or "social network" ' (*ibid.*). Gee's definition of Discourse is important because, significantly, it is always greater than language ('discourse') as it encompasses beliefs, values, ways of thinking, of behaving and of using language.

Gee further proposes that an individual's *primary* Discourse is in most instances acquired through socialization into the family. The acquisition of thoughts, values, attitudes and ways of using language creates an individual's world-view. In terms of social development, it may be located within the normative view described earlier in this chapter as social engagement here is most likely to be one to one, face to face. Human beings develop through a process of reflection upon action: a conscious objectification of their own and others' actions through investigation, contemplation and comment (Freire, 1972). Through engagement in such a process, individuals become active historical and cultural agents. Such 'becoming' is achieved through a process of 'dialogue' (Freire, 1985, pp. 49–59). Another context for 'dialogue' is in the meeting of *primary* and *secondary* Discourses.

Individuals encounter *secondary* Discourses through engagement in diverse social institutions: schools, churches, societies, clubs and through participation in aspects of popular culture, for example. Such secondary Discourses also involve uses of language, ways of thinking, believing, valuing and behaving, which may offer human beings new and different ways of seeing the world. Each quadrant identified in Figure 4.1 has its own secondary Discourse, as shown by the examples of beliefs, values and attitudes identified. Pursuing Gee's analysis, Lankshear (1997, p. 17) proposes that 'Education, socialisation, training, apprenticeship and enculturation are among the terms we use to refer to processes by which individuals are initiated into the Discourses of their identity formations.' Schools are complex discourse communities. The language, values, ways of being and membership of various facets of the school, whether by staff or pupils, define and are defined by individuals' engagement with Discourses. However, although schools invariably draw up statements, or policies, concerning ethos and values in general terms, the very values, beliefs and ways of thinking which specifically underpin the Discourses of the subjects in the curriculum are rarely, if ever, made explicit. Rather, the content of subjects is 'delivered'. Similarly, the values underpinning a National Curriculum of core and foundation subjects and their relative worth are rarely examined.

Gee (1992, pp. 25–26) defines 'powerful literacy' as 'control of a secondary use of language in a secondary Discourse'. However, powerful literacy is not a particular literacy, *per se*, but a particular *use* of literacy. Gee believes that such control over language not only enables the individual to participate in that Discourse, but that it also serves as a meta-discourse to critique an individual's primary Discourse. Further, it also enables an individual to critique other secondary Discourses as the debate in recent years between the communitarians and libertarians illustrates.

Pupils are empowered though *learning* the meta-level linguistic cognitive and linguistic skills, as opposed to *acquiring* the language of the secondary Discourse. An illustration of this difference might be slavishly following a teacher-provided model structure to write up an experiment in a science lesson (*acquisition*) as opposed to understanding the values that underpin scientific enquiry which impose certain methodological demands upon those conducting experiments (*learning*). Lankshear sums up the importance of this meta-level knowledge as:

knowledge about what is involved in participating in some Discourse(s). It is more than merely knowing how (i.e. being able) to engage successfully in a particular discursive practice. Rather, meta-level knowledge is knowing about the nature of that practice, its constitutive values and beliefs, its meaning and significance, how it relates to other practices, what it is about successful performance that makes it successful, and so on. (Lankshear, 1997, p. 72)

Lankshear argues that such knowledge empowers the individual in at least three ways. First, the individual's level of social performance within the Discourse is enhanced which increases the chances of access to social 'goods'. This mode of empowerment is easily related to success in the education system. Second, control over secondary language uses provides the means by which a Discourse may be analysed to see how skills and knowledge may be used in new ways and directions *within* that Discourse. Finally, the meta-level knowledge of a number of secondary Discourses makes it possible to critique and transform a secondary Discourse. Furthermore, critical awareness of alternative Discourses allows the possibility of *choice* among them. Critical choice among Discourses, opposed to simple acquisition, or rejection of Discourses without such learning and understanding, is empowerment; and it is the essence of social literacy and active citizenship. Consequently, the development of social literacy is an essential precondition for the successful preparation of children to participate fully in the life of their communities and within the wider society after they leave school.

The school curriculum

Fundamentally, the school is an agency of socialization which exerts pressures on those involved to accept its social values as their own. Successful engagement with learning through an induction into 'educated discourse' (Mercer, 1995, p. 84) will determine pupils' future acquisition of social 'goods': for example, particular employment paths, further and higher education, and, ultimately, status and wealth. In *The Challenge for the Comprehensive School* Hargreaves (1982, pp. 34–5) details his belief that schools lost their corporate vocabulary, because phrases such as 'team spirit', '*esprit de corps*' and 'loyalty to the school' had declined in favour of a culture of individualism. He believes that the comprehensive school should make more of a contribution to the social solidarity of society. He also argues that citizenship education must include experiential learning of the kind offered by community service. Hargreaves proposes three educational goals for comprehensive schools: to increase greater democratic participation, to stimulate greater social solidarity and to help resolve conflict between different communities. All three goals would sit extremely well within a model of communitarian citizenship education proposed by the New Labour government. Similarly, such an approach would have importance for the development of social literacy, as it would give pupils the opportunity to encounter a range of secondary Discourses.

Hargreaves proposes a community-centred curriculum of which community studies, including practical community service, are an integral part. Such a curriculum would be compulsory for all and consist of a core of 'traditional' subjects organized around community studies. The influence of external examinations would be reduced in favour of increased teacher assessment in schools. Traditional school subjects would be more integrated and team-taught. The general objectives of Hargreaves's model curriculum would be translated into a flexible timetable and core subjects would be reshaped into new forms and contexts. Schools prepare children for membership of several communities and, therefore, Hargreaves (1982) believes, the purpose of the school curriculum is to provide children with the knowledge, understanding and skills required for them to participate effectively in all communities because 'it is when we belong to many groups and communities, and play an active role within them, that we are most likely to learn about them, and resolve, the tension between solidarity and conflict' (*ibid.*, p. 144). Hargreaves presents a bold vision and a daunting challenge, but believes nevertheless that schools need to increase community participation and asks: 'what other major agency apart from the school has any hope of success?' (*idem*) Educational legislation in the intervening seventeen years has constructed a model of the curriculum that is, in many ways, the antithesis of Hargreaves's model. It is interesting to note, however, that, with the return of a Labour government for the first time in as many years, such ideas have resurfaced and much of what Hargreaves proposes can be found in the Crick Report. (Professor Hargreaves is acknowledged in the Crick Report as having contributed to the work of the Advisory Group on Citizenship (DfEE, 1998, p. 83).)

This observation appears confirmed by a widely publicized DEMOS[2] text, *Learning Beyond the Classroom* (Bentley, 1998), which develops many of Hargreaves's ideas into the late 1990s. Although DEMOS is an independent think-tank, at the time he wrote the book, Bentley was not only an adviser to David Blunkett, MP, Secretary of State for Education and Employment, he was also a member of the Advisory Group on Citizenship (DfEE, 1998, p. 5). Bentley proposes 'active, community-based learning' (Bentley, 1998, p. 30) aimed at developing a capacity in individuals to be responsible, independent learners. Many of the opportunities for young people to engage in voluntary activities that he details are geared towards preparation for employability. Young people, Bentley argues, should be given real responsibility through devolving a range of decision-making to them so that positive learning can take place in genuine communities.

If adopted, the radical, and perhaps idealistic, proposals of Hargreaves and Bentley would require major changes not only to the curriculum, but also to the organization of schools – changes which are highly unlikely to be made. How then is it proposed that the National Curriculum in schools advance the child's social literacy? The new National Curriculum will provide non-statutory guidance, particularly in English, geography and history, highlighting links between citizenship and these subjects in an attempt to reinforce citizenship education. The traditional subjects of the school curriculum focus almost entirely on cognitive aspects of teaching and learning. However, the knowledge and learning processes that they impart can have a value in directing activity towards desired social ends.

History serves as a useful example to explore this assertion. History is, above all else, about people and has an important and unique contribution to make to social education. In the primary school history develops certain skills which can be said to be key aspects of social literacy: the ability to reflect on evidence and draw conclusions; the ability to consider various interpretations of the same event, developing a respect for evidence. History also develops attitudes that a social being needs: a critical approach to evidence; respect for the value of reasoned argument; tolerance of various viewpoints. The study of the past is increasingly set in a cultural and moral context, looking at law-making, abuse of power, introducing persecution and religious conflict, as well as ideas such as cultural interdependence, diversity of beliefs and philanthropy. Children would increasingly be asked to consider political and social actions in a contemporary moral context.

Other subjects within the National Curriculum can offer similar contributions to the development of social literacy; for example, the examination of the ethical dimensions of aspects scientific advancement, the consideration of an individual's empathy with characters in English literature, the moral dimensions of world trade in geography. As yet, however, there has been little systematic articulation of what contributions might be made by subjects.

Furthermore, the work of socio-linguists such as Gee, Lankshear, Mercer and others offers teachers the possibility of developing pupils' social literacy through participation, collaboration and negotiation; by making Discourses visible through exploring the underpinning values and beliefs. Whatever the subject, the role of classroom talk and, in particular, 'exploratory talk' in the classroom cannot be underestimated: 'It typifies language which embodies certain principles – of accountability, of clarity, of constructive criticism and receptiveness to well-argued proposals – which are highly valued in many societies' (Mercer, 1995, p. 106). In key social institutions such as the law, government, administration, research in the sciences and arts, and business, language is used in sophisticated ways, for example, to interrogate the quality of the claims, hypotheses and proposals, to articulate understandings, to reach consensual agreement and to make joint decisions. Mercer reminds us that it is in such language that 'reasoning is made visible' and 'knowledge is made accountable', not in any absolute terms, but in 'accord with the "ground rules" of the relevant discourse community' (*ibid.*).

Social literacy is fundamental to pupils' development as active citizens. If teachers are to develop pupils' social literacy, they need to make the ground rules of exploratory talk in the classroom visible. These ground rules are: sharing relevant information; providing reasons for any assertions or opinions; asking for reasons where appropriate; reaching agreement; accepting that the group, rather than any individual, was responsible for decisions and actions and, ultimately, for any ensuing success or failure (Mercer, 1995, p. 108). By enabling pupils to *learn* these ground rules, rather than leaving them implicit and expecting pupils to *acquire* them, teachers will develop pupils' social literacy and promote their development as active citizens.

Conclusion

At the beginning of the twenty-first century the English National Curriculum remains dominated by cognate subject areas without any real attempt to articulate the values and beliefs which they help form in young people. By itself, curriculum content will be insufficient to produce active citizens who will participate fully in the life of their communities and in the wider society. It is not enough only to inform pupils *about* aspects of citizenship – how Parliament works, legal rights and so on. Such an approach to citizenship education is at the passive end of the continuum. Simply engaging pupils in voluntary work within the community (cited by the Crick Report) will not of itself empower them. The values and beliefs embedded in communities, in facets of society, in the very aspects of citizenship about which pupils are being informed, need to be made visible and debated. Similarly, the values and beliefs that underpin the educational discourse of the school need to be made visible to pupils, for the school is the social setting wherein they learn this educational discourse. Ultimately, the Discourse of citizenship education itself needs to be made visible to pupils so that they can critique its underpinning social values and beliefs in order that they may become active, transformed citizens. Such ideas are indeed challenging for curriculum developers and for teachers in school, for they would entail developing articulate, well-informed pupils who would be able to critique any curriculum offer. Social literacy is both a prerequisite for and an essential requirement of citizenship education. It involves learning a series of social and linguistic skills and developing a social knowledge base from which to understand and interpret the range of social issues which citizens must address in their lives.

Notes

1. A version of this chapter was presented as a paper to the Citizenship Conference, Institute of Education, University of London, July 1999.
2. 'DEMOS is an independent think-tank and research institute based in London. Launched in 1993, its role is to help reinvigorate public policy and political thinking and to develop radical solutions to long-term problems' (see http://www.demos.co.uk/index.htm). It receives core and project funding from a wide range of companies and charitable organizations. Some of its project funding also comes from national and local governments.

References

Arthur, J. (1998) 'Communitarianism: what are the implications for education'. *Educational Studies*, 24 (3), 353–68.

Arthur, J. (1999) *Schools and Community: The Communitarian Agenda in Education*. London: Falmer Press.

Arthur, J. and Davison, J. (2000) *Social Literacy and the School Curriculum*. London: Falmer Press.

Bentley, T. (1998) *Learning Beyond the Classroom: Education for a Changing World*. London: DEMOS/Routledge.

Combs, M. and Slaby, D. (1977) 'Social skills training with children', in B. Lahey, B. Crick and A. Porter (eds) *Political Education and Political Literacy*. London: Longman.

Department for Education and Employment (DfEE) (1998) (The Crick Report) *Education for Citizenship and the Teaching of Democracy in Schools: Final Report of the Advisory Group in Citizenship*. London: QCA.

Elliott, J. and Pring, R. (eds) (1975) *Social Education and Social Understanding*. London: University of London Press.

Freire, P. (1972) *Pedagogy of the Oppressed*. Harmondsworth: Penguin.

Freire, P. (1985) *The Politics of Education: Culture, Power and Liberation*. London: Macmillan.

Gee, J. (1987) *The Social Mind: Language, Ideology and Social Praxis*. Bergin and New York: Garvey.

Gee, J. P. (1990) *Social Linguistics and Litercies: Ideology in Discourses*. London: Falmer.

Gee, J. (1992) 'What is literacy?' in P. Shannon (ed.) *Becoming Political*. Portsmouth, NH: Heinemann.

Goleman, D. (1996) *Emotional Intelligence*. London: Bloomsbury.

Hargreaves, D. (1982) *The Challenge for the Comprehensive School: Culture, Curriculum and Community*. London: Routledge and Kegan Paul.

Kalantzis, M. and Cope, B. (1997) *An Overview: The Teaching of Social Literacy*. Sydney: Common Ground.

Kerr, D. (1999) *Re-examining Citizenship: The Case of England*. Slough: NFER.

Lankshear, C. (1997) *Changing Literacies*. Buckingham: Open University Press.

Mercer, N. (1995) *The Guided Construction of Knowledge*. Clevedon: Multilingual Matters.

National Curriculum Council (NCC) (1990a) *Curriculum Guidance 8: Citizenship Education*. York: NCC.

National Curriculum Council (NCC) (1990b) *Curriculum Guidance 3: The Whole Curriculum*, York: NCC.

National Curriculum Council (NCC) (1990c) *Curriculum Guidance 4: Education for Economic and Industrial Understanding*. York: NCC.

National Curriculum Council (NCC) (1990d) *Curriculum Guidance 5: Health Education*. York: NCC.

QCA (1996–7) National Forum on Values and Community. London: QCA.

QCA (1999a) *Draft Programmes of Study and Attainment Target for a Proposed New Foundation Subject for Citizenship at Key Stages 3–4*, May. London: The Stationery Office.

QCA (1999b) *National Curriculum Review Consultation, Part 2: A Framework for Personal, Social and Health Education (PSHE) and Citizenship at Key Stages 1–4*. London: The Stationery Office.

QCA (1999c) *National Curriculum for England: Statement of Values by the National Forum for Values in Education and the Community*. London: HMSO.

Rennie, J., Lunzer, E. and Williams, W. (1974) 'Social education: an experiment in four secondary schools', *Schools Council Working Paper 51*. London: Evans and Methuen.

Robinson, T. and Shallcross, T. (1998) 'Social change and education for sustainable living'. *Curriculum Studies*, 6 (1), 69–84.

Rowe, D. (1997) 'Value pluralism, democracy and education for citizenship', in M. Leicester, C. Modgil and F. Modgil (eds) *Values, Culture and Education: Political and Citizenship Education*. London: Cassell.

Scrimshaw, P. (1975) 'The language of social education', in J. Elliott and R. Pring (eds) *Social Education and Social Understanding*, London: University of London Press.

Scrimshaw, P. (1989) 'Pro-social education', in J. Thacker, R. Pring and D. Evans (eds) *Personal and Social and Moral Education in a Changing World*. London: NFER/Nelson.

5

Education and Professionalism

Catherine Matheson

Introduction

After some discussion of the concepts of profession, professional and profession-alism and professionalization, this chapter will examine historically the evolving idea of the teacher as a professional by looking at various concepts and meanings of what it is to be a professional in terms of the role and the status of teachers, primary and secondary education, the kind of knowledge that is valued in teachers and notions of accountability and autonomy. The chapter will focus mainly on England but examples will be drawn from other European countries.

Definitions and concepts

Profession, professionalization, professional

The concept of 'profession' is an abstract model in which the core elements are most fully exhibited by the so-called true professions. These core elements are more easily listed by example than defined according to their characteristics or distinctive qualities. In the UK 'profession' is restricted to particular kinds of occupations and has connotations of a higher level, exclusivity, a body of specialized knowledge, intensive academic preparation, lengthy training and a code of ethics (Jarvis, 1983). The main image in a profession is that of a community of specialist knowledge, both professional and tacit, where there are particular shared and learned values. The members of this community are seen as autonomous and responsible. They are individual practitioners applying expert knowledge, free from administrative control and dealing with the particular problems presented *voluntarily* to them by *clients*. The notion of tacit knowledge in addition to professional knowledge is important since it is this that, literally, gives the practitioner a professional *feel* to the manner in which s/he carries out the job. The professional is more than an executor of decisions taken elsewhere but rather one who can call upon an ever-increasing learned set of 'intuitions' based on experience otherwise known as 'reflection-in-action' and/or 'knowledge-in-use' (Schön, 1983) which in reality are a reflection of an accumulated body of *savoir-faire*.

To acquire such professional and tacit knowledge necessitates long training, marked in the popular imagination (and probably in reality also) by arduous preparation for stringent examinations. These factors combine to give an aura of mystery about the profession. To add to the mystique, a profession may well cloak itself in ritual, and a highly technical language. It will act to aggrandize its own position by projecting itself as a domain belonging to an élite. The overall effect is to impress the public with the feelings of awe and inferiority that secure a mandate for the wide exercise of professional autonomy (Tight, 1996). In this way, everybody would accept medicine, law and accountancy as professions. The rituals and self-imposed mystery that surround much of medical practice need no elaboration. Suffice to say that when we encounter a non-patronizing medical practitioner, to many of us it will come as a surprise. A medical practitioner who demystifies our ailment and its treatment may well be just as unusual. Lawyers and accountants tend to be similar (and are directly paid for their services unlike most medical practitioners encountered within a national health service such as in the UK, and also most teachers) although it is unlikely that we should have as much acquaintance with either of these groups as with medical practitioners. It is a rare one of us who has not been sick but we could easily go from one end of our lives to the other without ever having recourse to a lawyer or accountant. None the less, with each of these practitioners, we meet them under very special circumstances and, other than exceptionally, spend little time in their company. This is an important point whose significance will become clearer as we go on.

Occupations become professions through the process of *professionalization*, a deliberate action on the part of occupational members. The status of a profession is based largely on a claim to specialized knowledge acquired through advanced training and education, although the status of the profession in a society may depend on the value attributed to it by users and by society at large. Profession-alization is a 'complex process in which an occupation comes to exhibit a number of attributes which are essentially professional and are said to be the core elements of professionalism' (Johnson, 1993, p. 22).

An assumption regarding professionals is that they are experts in the specific branch of learning upon which their occupation is based and that they continually seek to maintain the mastery of that learning in order to offer a service to the client (Jarvis, 1983). Seeking and maintaining mastery is done by way of continued professional development which has been institutionalized by most professions. As shall see 'the foundation of every occupation claiming professional status is wledge and its application' (Jarvis, 1983, p. 29).

Professionalism, professional autonomy and professional accountability

From an ideological perspective professionalism is the 'commitment to professional ideals and career ... expressed in attitudes, ideas and beliefs' (Freidson, 1970, p. 151). Three main types of professionalism can be distinguished: generic, occupational and personal. Professionalism is both a concept and a form of behaviour which is influenced by historical context and national culture.

The central features of professionalism are a specialist knowledge base, autonomy and service. These have been affected by socio-cultural changes over the last two and a half decades. Specialist knowledge has expanded but at the same time it has begun to be challenged and criticized. Questions are being raised as to whose interests are served by the way in which specialist knowledge is created, represented and used. 'Specialist knowledge confers status and provides the centrepiece of its claim to autonomy, the argument being that only fellow members of the profession are sufficiently knowledgeable to judge the work of their colleagues' (Eraut, 1994, p. 223).

The ideal of autonomy applies at the level of the whole profession and at the individual level. Only the profession can define and assess the competence and good conduct of its members. At the individual level, autonomy is about the control of one's work, even if it means rejecting the recommendations of the professional body. (Eraut, 1994).

Logically it would seem reasonable to think that the greater the autonomy, the greater the responsibility and accountability. For sociological and historical reasons, however, this equation has not tended to be the case in the UK, where accountability has tended to be perceived by professionals as 'an external control mechanism rather than as a strengthening of their moral and professional obligations and hence a threat to autonomy rather than the consequence of it' (Eraut, 1996, p. 225).

Advocates of professionalization and of professionalism argue that it is a movement which helps protect the public from the hazards of the marketplace in which their ignorance might put them in jeopardy. Critics by contrast are of the opinion that professionalization helps corporate power increase an occupation's leverage against the public through reducing competition or public accountability (Bullock, Stallybrass and Trombley, 1988). There is a contradiction between the service ideal and the needs of the clients and the needs of the professional and/or society. Because of their specialist knowledge the belief was that only professionals could determine the needs of their clients. This conception has been widely challenged by notions of clients' rights and clients' choice and especially notions of children's rights.

It is interesting to note that economists have consistently – even more so since some of the practices of the market have been adapted to the delivery of services such as education and health – questioned the benefits of professionalism, pointing instead to the harmful monopolistic practices of professional associations. While professionalism had until the 1980s guaranteed more professional freedom against bureaucratic tyranny, most professionals are now salaried employees. The ideology of professionalism, however, seems to assume that professionals are self-employed or partners in small practices. The level of power and autonomy is more a dream than a reality as most professionals are employed in the public sector and industry (*Eraut, 1994*).

Not all occupations meet the criteria of a profession. According to Dreeben (1970, p. 15) 'professional occupations are associated with high income, high prestige, respect and power-judgments that follow in part from the fact that professional persons are highly educated, perform demanding skills and provide valued services.' As Gosden (1972, p. 1) underlines, in order to qualify as a profession it is necessary for an occupation to also have some recognition by society of 'the profession's right to influence the way in which the service it offers is administered'. Traditionally professionalism in the UK has meant more rather than less autonomy and less rather than more accountability, but ever since the introduction of market principles in the delivery of the health and education services, professionalism has increasingly meant more rather than less accountability and less rather than more autonomy.

From autonomy to accountability

Tawney [1922] quoted in Brooks (1991), a historian who sat on two of the Hadow committees, believed, unlike Callaghan, Thatcher and Blair, that the influence of industry on education was both restrictive and narrowing, and he favoured liberal education, that is, a specifically non-vocational education. Tawney thought that central government's hold on the curriculum should be removed for fear it would not serve the interests of pupils or the teachers but those of industry or political ideology. He thought that teachers were to be trusted to know best, whereas Callaghan in the 1976 Ruskin Speech believed (as did Thatcher and Blair) that teachers have the expertise and the professional approach but must satisfy parents and industry that what they are doing meets their requirements and the needs of our children. If the public is not convinced, then the profession will be laying up trouble for itself in the future (Barber, 1996).

The 1988 Education Reform Act (England) and the National Curriculum which it introduced can be traced back to the Ruskin Speech and to the Great Debate (Brooks, 1991). Labour Prime Minister, James Callaghan, made a key speech on education on 18 October 1976 at Ruskin College, Oxford. It launched the Great Debate on education and set the political agenda on education for the next fifteen years. Declining standards, unevenness between schools as well as neglect of attainment targets in mathematics and modern languages were cited to implicitly criticize progressive methods and support a national curriculum, national assessment and national standards. The curriculum should be no longer a 'secret garden' but a matter of public concern, and central government should increase its control in education. Schools must satisfy parents and industry and emphasize vocational skills and not just academic knowledge. The local education authorities (LEAs), parents, teachers and industry should work together in a closer relationship where resources should be more carefully monitored in the national interest, that is, with greater intervention by central government and the inspectorate of schools. All teachers should receive in-service education during their careers and initial teacher training should be more academically and professionally rigorous, and the entry requirements raised (Brooks, 1991).

Margaret Thatcher took the principles of the Ruskin Speech a stage further and declared that education had failed because professionals and LEAs sought to appropriate control of a service from its proper source, the parents, and that the teachers should therefore be directly accountable to parents, to the boards of governors and to the headteachers. The provision of the 1988 ERA introduced more than 300 new powers for the Secretary of State for Education as well as a market-derived terminology (accountability, efficiency, effectiveness, value for money, cost control, customer satisfaction, service delivery, planning unit, quality assurance). The ERA 'directly challenges and seeks to displace the received assumptions' that had been embedded in English education since its last major piece of educational legislation in 1944 (Kogan, 1989, p. 41).

The ERA transferred power from local to central state but gave more autonomy in the sense of accountability to schools. It dramatically reduced the power of the LEAs, giving individual schools control over their own budgets and allowing them to apply to opt out of LEA control and receive grant maintained status. The mere threat of schools opting out of council control was enough to change the climate, forcing local authorities to delegate more money and to give headteachers more independence, power and control over staff (Bridges and McLaughlin, 1994). The shifting balance of accountability meant that headteachers felt they were account-able to parents and no longer to the LEAs. As the headteacher of one primary school explained:

My account is to governors firstly then parents. The legislation has shifted the point of accountability away from the LEAs to the schools. I don't feel accountable to the LEAs. [They are] accountable to me for providing value for money for [their] services. (Radnor, Ball and Vincent, 1997, p. 217)

The ERA limited the professional autonomy of teachers and curbed the power of the trade unions regarding policy-making and salary negotiating. 'By deregulating major aspects of education, the state wants to ensure social justice, but in increasing a limited number of state powers it has actually strengthened its capacity to foster particular interests while appearing to stand outside the frame' (Whitty, 1997, p. 302). Teaching was no longer seen as 'a professional mandate to act on behalf of the state in the best interests of its citizens' but as needing to be 'subjected to the rigours of the market and/or greater control and surveillance on the part of the re-formed state' (Whitty, 1997, p. 303).

According to Sinclair, Ironside and Seifert (1993) quoted in Whitty (1997):

Headteachers are no longer partners in the process of educating pupils, but they become allocators of resources within the school, managers who are driven to ensure that the activities of employees are appropriate to the needs of the business, and givers of rewards to those whose contribution to the business is most highly regarded (*ibid.*, p. 305).

A study conducted by Campbell and Neill (1994) highlighted that teachers felt the burden of having to be more accountable to headteachers. They thought they had more responsibility and less power as the blame was shifted to them. The increase in policy control and in accountability meant that the professional autonomy they had enjoyed and the greater autonomy that they expected was largely eroded. As headteachers became key actors with new powers the concepts of 'professional' changed from autonomous in charge of a non-compulsory curriculum to accountable and responsible for implementing a compulsory National Curriculum, and from loyalty to a larger corporate identity seen as the provider of a public service to loyalty to an institution providing a marketable commodity. Many teachers also experienced tiredness, discouragement and depression. Teachers felt increasingly left out of the decision-making process as they faced increased workloads, budgetary restrictions and increased accountability (Campbell and Neill, 1994; Sinclair, Ironside and Seifert, 1993).

According to McMurtry (1991) there are fundamental contradictions between the market and education models in terms of goals, motivations, methods, standards of excellence, as long-term development of education and civilization requires the autonomy of education from market influences. Similarly for Wringe (1994), Grace (1989, 1994) and Winch (1996), it is an error to treat education as a marketable commodity because it is a public good. The market model is detrimental to public interest or subversive of essential social institutions. Market transactions are unsuitable for the distribution of necessities which individuals are unable to meet through no fault of their own or which are beyond the means of ordinary individuals, or when individuals are unqualified to judge their own needs or the quality of the services provided. The State should provide education without direct charge and enforce the criteria of adequacy. The parents should be seen as co-educators and not customers, which implies certain parental responsibilities rather than consumer rights (Winch, 1996).

Much of the new managerial school accountability in the form of outputs of standards and quality (examinations results, tests results and league tables or the new performance indicators such as truancy rates, percentage of pupils staying on beyond the compulsory age or first destination of leavers) is alien to the older means of accountability – the process of inspection which focused on the quality of inputs and of recommending desirable processes or practices (Lawton and Gordon, 1996).

Accountability in the sense of applying managerial or business efficiency to education has nevertheless become part of the educational discourse. Discussion about the role and status of teachers in the UK has to be put in the framework of both its educational historical context and the current market discourse which has shaped educational provision for the past twenty years. Before the arrival of that discourse, teachers used to believe that professional status would be achieved by having an all-graduate profession, compulsory initial teacher training, a self-regulated professional body and hence more say over their terms of employment. The age of market-oriented accountability found teachers ill equipped to meet the new challenge whereby professionalism meant accountability and no longer autonomy. For the various above-mentioned historical reasons professional accountability in the UK has been viewed as a threat rather than as the consequence of autonomy. The 1950s and 1960s are considered to represent the height of teacher professionalism and freedom, but this autonomy was always relative. At the level of the secondary curriculum 'assessment systems of university-based boards of examination exerted a significant check upon the freedom of action of many teachers' (Helsby, 1995, p. 339).

The ERA had a major impact on teachers' sense of professionalism in the sense of being a professional and behaving professionally. These two key aspects of professionalism were investigated by Helsby (1995) who found that teachers thought they measured up quite well to the high standards they imposed on themselves but that they were confused as to whether behaving professionally meant being in control and planning or following instructions, however misguided. Teachers saw themselves as meeting most of the identified requirements of being professionals but lacking autonomy and public recognition of their professional status. Helsby (1996) emphasized local contexts and especially departmental cultures as being influential in shaping teachers' sense of professionalism. These ranged from a sense of isolation and non-involvement because instructions had to be followed, to having collaborative cultures in which colleagues discussed their work and shared their experiences and were thus given an opportunity to influence the way things were done.

The notion of accountability has existed as long as teachers have existed. Socrates as a citizen rather than as a teacher had to answer for what he did. He was accountable to the city-state and when found lacking, not doing what was expected of a teacher, was famously tried and sentenced to death in 399 BC by being made to drink hemlock for 'corrupting the youth and religious innovation'. Eraut (1981) distinguishes three kinds of accountability in education: moral, legal and professional accountability Professionalism and professional accountability are complex and controversial issues. Within the market discourse teachers' accountability and appraisal often take the form of an encouragement to reflective practice to help them meet their attainment targets, or at least understand what prevents them from meeting their attainment targets. Reflective practice, however, necessarily implies both self-critique and institutional critique. One cannot have one without the other (Elliott, 1990, p. 23). The latter is usually not welcome or taken into account during teachers' appraisal. Ideas of interactive and collaborative professionalism or collegiality are sometimes found to be encouraged within certain local contexts and departmental cultures (Helsby, 1996). Collaborative cultures according to Quicke (1999) should maximize the scope for making moral choices and also for developing insights into how power operates in an institutional context since the awareness of internalized constraints is integral to critical reflection and to a collaborative culture. Apple (1999) suggests that rather than continuing down the path of tighter control and surveillance through more detailed assessment of technical skills, it would be more realistic to examine teachers according to certain underlying principles such as a commitment to social justice, closer working relationships between schools and pupils/communities, more collegial control and autonomy.

In England the government's newest idea to both increase accountability and raise the status of the profession is performance related pay (PRP). The Green Paper (DfEE, 1998), *Teachers – Meeting the Challenge for Change*, proposed 'a new vision of the profession which offers better rewards and support in return for higher standards' and 'improve[s] the image, morale and status of the profession' by means of the following key features:

- Appraisal should influence teachers' pay as well as supporting their professional development.
- Teachers whose performance was judged satisfactory could expect to receive annual increments up to the threshold. Those who fall below expectations might not gain an increment each year, while excellent performers might be awarded two.
- Assessment arrangements would combine internal and external assessment against new national standards with strong classroom performance at their core.
- Teachers above the threshold would have higher pay ranges and new professional expectations. A teacher's individual pay range at this level would depend on performance and responsibility, with any further pay steps based on a review of their performance (DfEE, 1998).

The National Union of Teachers (NUT) in England is against individual payment by results, believing it will cause staffroom division. The General Secretary of the NUT announced that in their own survey of September 1998 it was found that 30 per cent of teachers were very relaxed about performance related pay, which was taken to mean that 70 per cent who are against. He said that it was his role to move the 30 per cent away from their support of performance related pay (Rafferty 1999). Of course, without further evidence, it may well be that the 30 per cent who are 'very relaxed' are in reality to be compared with the 70 per cent who are simply less than 'very relaxed' about the issue of PRP. The extrapolation made by the General Secretary of the NUT whereby not being 'very relaxed' is taken as a sign of animosity towards the concept of PRP is, on the face of it, a symptom of faulty logic. In this we have a problem: if a senior representative of teachers in England is unable (or unwilling) to be more rigorous in his use of language then how can the general public, many of whom may well have spotted this extrapolation, be expected to take the union, and hence the members who comprise it, seriously and as professionals? None the less, it remains to be seen if PRP will raise the status of the teaching profession.

How can the status of teachers be raised?

In the 1960s and 1970s discussions about whether teaching was a profession argued that teaching was a semi-profession because it did not have the attributes of the 'true' professions of law or medicine and because it was highly feminized (Etzioni, 1969; Legatt, 1970; Simpson and Simpson, 1969). Many professions 'maintain a code of ethics, over and above the law of the land, which governs relationships between members of the profession and their clients' (Aldrich, 1996, p. 69). Teaching on the other hand is under government control and teachers have very little freedom for developing their own ideas and making their own informed judgements. 'Teachers . . . have had considerable difficulty in approximating to the professional model' (*ibid.*). In Scotland there is no National Curriculum though in practice most schools follow the recommendations of the 5–14 Development Programme (Bryce and Humes, 1999).

The control over the entry to the profession is another factor deemed to have affected the professional status of teaching which is accessible to more individuals since the entry requirement are lower than those needed to enter medicine, the law or accountancy. Since 1965 Scotland, unlike England, has had a General Teaching Council (GTC) containing a majority of teacher representatives which controls entry to the profession, accredits initial teacher training courses and has responsibility for the assessment of probationary teachers. The very existence of the GTC is testimony to the relative status of teaching as a profession in Scotland. In practice this means that the situation of teachers in England without a degree or a teaching qualification cannot exist in Scotland even to teach in private school since most private schools would want GTC registration before employing someone as a teacher.

A further factor which has affected the professional status of teachers is that their clients have low status as they are children who go to school because they have to and not adults who choose a particular service. A teacher is not someone who is often admired in society, unlike doctors, lawyers and accountants. People tend to think that what a teacher does is easy compared with other professions. Teachers tend to lack prestige because 'no aura of mystery surrounds the work they do' (Kelsall and Kelsall, 1969, p. 146). This is reinforced because we have all been in a classroom situation with a teacher and we think we know exactly what their job involves. Teaching, however, is 'a most complex and challenging occupation, not least because it takes place with reference to children (for whom the teacher stands *in loco parentis*) rather than adults' (Aldrich, 1996, p. 73).

It is worth noting that teachers have been one of the least successful groups in bringing public opinion on to their side. This is in part due to the fact that all teachers at primary and secondary level are seen by the public as the same thing and in part to their inability to form one body and prevent creating in the public's mind an image of squabbling unions (Bottery, 1996). The latter is not so true of Scotland, though the former is. In the past, teachers' unions like the NUT have been criticized for their use of strike action over issues such as pay, working conditions and duties expected of them. They have been called unprofessional because they took a stance against their lack of acknowledgement of a professional status. If teaching had been widely recognized as a profession there would have been no need for teachers to take such strike action.

Whereas demands made upon teachers have increased since the late 1980s (implementation of the National Curriculum with increased bureaucracy and national assessments at 7, 11 and 14, literacy and numeracy hours, teaching citizenship as from 2002 [see Chapter 4] and pastoral responsibilities), account-ability has increased and initial teacher training in England has been arguably 'de-professionalized' by encouraging a restricted notion of professionalism as opposed to a broader one and emphasizing particular competence or standards on an 'apprenticeship basis' in schools.

Eraut (1994) distinguishes between continued professional education (CPE) which takes place through courses, conferences or formal educational events and continued professional development (CPD) which also includes various kinds of experiential and work-based learning that contributes to professional growth. The relationship between the two is often unclear, although recent government policy on both initial and in-service education has increasingly emphasized the latter at the expense of the former (Helsby, 1996).

At all levels the emphasis has been on the improvement of skills at the expense of knowledge, e.g. problem oriented and workshop based rather than advanced work which is discipline based and theoretical in the form of MAs, MScs and EdDs, and PhDs reflecting trends in educational research with an emphasis on action research and applied projects (Gilroy, 1991).

While some have suggested that there seems to be a brand of anti-intellectualism that is encouraged in school teaching, there are still many teachers who place sufficient value on the kind of professional development or education that award-bearing in-service courses can provide. They are prepared to give both their time and money to ensure access to such experiences. However, as teachers' time and money have other demands placed upon them, it is not impossible that in the near future the number of teachers able to afford to take part in even part-time award-bearing courses will decrease, especially if course fees increase substantially. 'If and when that happens in-service educators will have finally lost the last vestiges of their professional autonomy' (Gilroy, 1991, p. 15).

Professional education and development are the acquisition and improvement of knowledge and *skills* or competencies required for effective professional practice to benefit the client. The improvement of *skills* is not likely to enhance professional status because it does not follow a model of professionalization which is based on medicine and law and emphasizes *knowledge* and not skills. If you improve skills and competencies you are unlikely to raise the status because skills are narrow and associated with training while knowledge is broad and associated with education. At all levels teachers are increasingly urged to reflect on their own practices or competencies in the context of the classroom. Paradoxically, these particular trends in teacher professionalization or professionalism with practitioners determining the nature of their own development might detract from the standing of teaching as a profession (Hoyle, 1985).

Historical perspectives on teachers and professionalism

Primary school teachers

In nineteenth-century England, and especially after 1870 when elementary school teachers were desperately needed, anyone who was willing to teach could do so. Many 'combined teaching with a second occupation, cobbling or tailoring, taking in washing or mending' (Aldrich, 1996, p. 69). Autonomy was non-existent and accountability was such that it partly determined the pay of teachers. In 1862 the *Revised Code* regulated very closely what happened in the elementary school classroom. This payment-by-results system was introduced to make maximum use of resources whereby teachers were directly accountable to their employers (Brooks, 1991).

Both the status and the pay of teachers were extremely low. As Lord Macauley said of teachers in 1847 in a speech to the House of Commons:

> [They are] the refuse of all other callings, discarded footmen, ruined pedlars, men who cannot work a sum in the rule of three, men who do not know whether earth is a sphere or a cube, men who do not know if Jerusalem is in Asia or in America. And to such men, men to whom none of us would entrust the key of his cellar, we have entrusted the mind of the rising generation. (Quoted in Watts, 1974, p. 24)

The Report of the Commissioners of Inquiry into the state of education in Wales the same year underlined that:

> No person, really qualified for the office of schoolmaster by moral character, mental energy, amiability of temper and proficiency in all the elementary branches of education, together with aptitude in imparting knowledge, will doom himself to the worst paid labour and almost the least appreciated office to be met with in the country. (Quoted in Maclure, 1973, p. 59)

Teaching was often used as a stepping-stone for individuals 'on their way to more lucrative employment in Church or state' (Aldrich, 1996, p. 69). Even the teachers of the boys' public schools (i.e. prestigious *private* schools) did not have a very high professional status. The only teachers who were considered professionals were headteachers of boys' public schools. They were considered to be of high professional status in line with, for example, other professionals such as the masters of Oxford and Cambridge (Aldrich, 1996, p. 69).

Earlier in the nineteenth century things had fared better for teachers in Scotland. There were the schoolmasters in burgh schools and academies, the dominies and the local parish schoolmasters. They were all appointed for their moral as well as educational qualifications. With the formation of the Educational Institute for Scotland (EIS) in 1847, Scottish teachers acquired the formal means of expressing their wish to have a true professional voice. Teaching, however, was changing irreversibly and the EIS was unsuccessful in winning professional authority because the new city schools had no connection with the parish schools of a former age and urbanization saw the destruction of their former, albeit modest, authority. Legislation enacted in London was applied to Scotland as well as England and Wales and introduced new systems of control which diminished their autonomy (Gatherer, 1999).

The appalling status of elementary school teachers in England in the nineteenth century contrasts vividly with that of Prussian teachers. As early as 1763 Frederick the Great of Prussia's ordinances enshrined in the *Prussian School Code* provided for compulsory attendance of children, the maintenance of a complete school term each year (i.e. no more *ad hoc* absences such as to bring in the corn), the curricular requirements, methods of instruction, and the education and compensation of teachers. Most radically of all, Frederick made available payments to families to compensate for the loss of children's earnings as they attended school between the ages of 5 and 14 (Boyd, 1972; Pollard, 1974). By 1794, the Prussians had introduced further reforms with the creation of the Prussian Board of Education to take control of schooling. In 1794 the Prussian *General Civil Code* stipulated a high degree of central control, fines for parents who failed to send their children to school, teacher qualifications, designated texts and annual inspections. The Prussian government realized early that the success of its elementary and secondary schools depended more on the quality of the teachers than on any other single factor (Binder, 1970). By 1800 there were about a dozen teacher-training seminaries. Prussia led the way among all other European states in providing competent and thoroughly trained elementary school teachers. The qualifications were determined by examinations and no teacher could be given a post without the qualifications and without having his/her nomination receive royal ratification (Pollard, 1974). After the defeat of Prussia by Napoleon at Jena in 1806 a series of reforms were inaugurated to bring back Prussia to new life and vigour. 'Blameless patriotism was believed to be the most sacred duty of all schoolmasters and mistresses' (Wilds and Lottish, 1970). Forty years before the English 1870 Elementary Schools Act, Prussia had made school compulsory for both boys and girls from ages 7 to 14 within a fully developed state controlled school system that included a ministry of education. The compulsion on attendance was rigorously enforced so that only those in the most isolated areas or in itinerant occupations could have their children escape the schoolmaster (Pollard, 1974).

Even France, which waited until 1882 to pass a law making primary education free, compulsory and without any religious teaching, gave a higher status and better pay to its teachers because Jules Ferry, the education minister who was responsible for the law of 1882, turned his 'army of black-coated elementary school-teachers into missionaries of a central state devoted to converting heathen provinces' (Wilds and Lottish, 1970). Even before the law of 1882 most elementary school teachers undertook a four year training course in the departmental *Ecole Normale*. Unlike in England, but as in Prussia, France gave to elementary or primary school teaching more professional status and more respectability.

In the years 1926–31 elementary teachers in England were given a large measure of autonomy over what was taught, and their power was increased with the adoption of child-centred teaching methods or learning by doing whereby teachers began to shape the curriculum according to their pupils' needs (or their own interests). In 1926 The Hadow Report set much of the agenda for later years (BECC, 1926) and in 1931 the Hadow Report on the primary school stated that 'The curriculum of the primary school is to be taught in terms of activity rather than knowledge to be acquired and facts to be stored'. Examinations should only play a subordinate role in the assessment of pupils. Teachers were encouraged to take the curiosity of children as the starting point of the school curriculum (BECC, 1931).

By 1945 primary school teachers possessed sufficient autonomy and power to be able to determine the nature of the curriculum. These changes in power relations came as a result of the rising level of qualifications that the teachers were expected to have, advances in the control of entry to the profession, greater involvement in the shaping of policy and the development of progressivism which helped legitimate all the above (Brooks, 1991). In the 1960s, with the generalization of comprehensive schools and the increasing abandonment of the 11 + examinations, teachers' assessment of pupils became of paramount importance. The Plowden Report in 1967 gave official recognition to progressive pedagogy encouraged since Hadow (BECC, 1926, 1931). Recommendations that subjects could disappear into co-operative projects and individual activities of children were officially supported (DES, 1967). Progressive pedagogy had few curriculum requirements, no mandatory or even systemic informal testing of children. More prevalent were individual or small-group activity within the framework of a topic or subject and some common objectives. Whole-class teaching occupied a small part of the day. Teacher curriculum design and child-centred teaching were demanding, however, especially when combined with expectations that the teacher was a substitute parent responsible for the moral, social and emotional development of each child. Distrust of parents meant that teachers did not enlist their help nor even expect that pupils would do very much schoolwork at home (Brooks, 1991). Although the Ruskin Speech in 1976 implicitly criticized progressivist teaching methods and the 1988 Education Reform Act (England) de-legitimized the discourse of progressivism by introducing the National Curriculum and a greater level of state control, child-centredness is still a dominant feature of English education and this may have implications for the professional status of primary school teachers.

A comparative study of the experiences of teachers working in areas of disadvantage in France and in England illustrates two conflicting dilemmas of teaching, each reflecting the priorities and expectations of what the role of the teacher is in these two countries. The French research team warned that in adapting too much to individual pupils there is a danger that with the best of intentions teachers will multiply references to daily life, emphasize affective relationships, claim against all the evidence that what they teach is 'useful', present knowledge in as pre-digested and contextualized a form as possible. 'There is a way of adapting to pupil needs which locks them in a relationship with knowledge "rapport au savoir" almost guaranteed to produce failure' (Charlot, Bautier and Rochex, 1992, p. 23, quoted in Osborn *et al.*, 1997, pp. 390–1). On the other hand, the English team thought more along the lines that in the pressure to ensure entitlement to a full curriculum, there is a risk of losing the ability to build bridges, to make links and to establish the relationships that are important in establishing an effective link to learning (Salzberger-Wittenberg, Henry and Osborne, 1983, quoted in Osborn *et al.*, 1997, p. 391). The balance is between challenging pupils and providing them with a safe haven. To provide one at the expense of the other is detrimental in different ways, with French and English teachers having a culturally embedded preference for the former and the latter respectively, that is offering a teacher-centred versus a pupil-centred experience.

Another comparative study perfectly illustrates the different conceptions of the role of the teacher and thus the importance of particular knowledge and skills associated with this role. Teachers in England were 'more likely to use questions in a way that built upon children's responses until the desired result was achieved' whereas French teachers 'would typically reject a child's response if it was not exactly what they wanted' (Broadfoot *et al.*, 1993, p. 70, quoted in Sharpe, 1997, p. 341). This has continued to be a prominent feature in the most recent comparative study. 'The French primary teachers employed more negative sanctions than their English counterparts and were less likely to use encouragement to motivate pupils' (Broadfoot *et al.*, 1995, p. 9, quoted in Sharpe, 1997, p. 341). Notions such as emergent and developmental learning so central to more pupil-centred English pedagogy are largely alien to French teachers (Sharpe, 1997). Learning by discovery and pupil activity are emphasized in England while in France the authoritative role of the teacher is the key feature even though a primary teacher until fairly recently did not need to have a degree-level qualification to teach. Not trying is the greatest fault a pupil can exhibit in England. The greatest fault in France is being wrong in the sense of failing to have the right answer. One system emphasizes individual development and the other the acquisition of skills to standardized national levels. If a pupil fails to reach the minimum standard he or she has to repeat the year. Thus we have a more diffuse role for English teachers and a more clearly defined role for French teachers, and these latter have a higher status. Do French teachers have a higher status because they have a more clearly defined and more authoritative role or because they are civil servants? Or is it that they can have such a high status because they are servants of the State charged with implementing a highly prescriptive national curriculum which is almost a quasi-constitution? Whatever the answer to these questions the State, the public and the parents acknowledge their authoritative role and their professional status. Different understandings surround not only what is the role and status of teachers but also notions of autonomy, accountability, inspection and assessment. In France teachers and not schools are inspected, and those teachers who come up with the best assessments are granted privileges such as extra money, less teaching or choosing what year and where they would like to teach.

In order to better control them elementary (and primary) school teachers in England were (and still are) told by the State and by society that teaching was a mission or a vocation and they were given a sense of responsibility and imbued with notions of professionalism but were never officially accorded the status of professionals. Elementary school teaching had low income and prestige, unregulated entry and tended to be highly feminized (Sullivan, 1998). Gender connotations are closely associated with notions of profession or professional, particularly in primary school teaching. 'No country should pride itself on its educational system if the teaching profession has become predominantly a world of women' (Langeveld, 1963, p. 404, quoted in Acker, 1994, p. 77) 'There can be little doubt that in the past much of the sense of a second-rate profession attached to teaching has been the fact that it was predominantly female in membership' (Moorish, 1978, p. 234, quoted in Acker, 1994, p. 75). Simpson and Simpson (1969) highlight the harm women do to the professional hopes of teaching and other semi-professions. Leggatt (1970) echoes the same thoughts as Simpson and Simpson (1969) and dwells on the negative consequences for the professionalization of teaching of the high proportion of women in teaching. Lortie (1975, p. 5) highlighted that the small number of male primary teachers in his sample had low commitment and low interest in their work. They nevertheless all hoped to be headteachers within five years. Choosing a career in teaching because it is more compatible with marriage and motherhood can be seen as a constraint as well as a choice, and may explain the high proportion of women (Lortie, 1975, p. 75). As Apple points out:

> Any occupation that is dominated by women is subject to less autonomy and greater outside control, lower pay and respect, and is apt to be blamed for social dislocations, tensions and inequalities over which it actually has little control. Calls for tighter control over teachers, teaching, and curriculum are a continuation of a much longer history in which schools and teachers are attacked during times of economic and social crisis. An understanding of this cannot be complete unless we see the history of gender relations that partly underpin it. (Apple, 1999, p. 44)

In the UK by the end of the nineteenth century elementary school teaching had become a predominantly female occupation. This feminization of teaching is one of the most important factors of its development. It was the consequence of a high demand for teachers. Women were nevertheless treated as cheaper and subordinate teachers. Interestingly, in France the proportion of women was smaller than in the UK which may also help to explain the higher status of elementary school teaching in France.

Secondary school teachers

Key characteristics of professionalism are culturally determined. Whereas professional groups in the UK tend to assume the role of semi-independent experts, in France their contribution is incorporated within the functions of the State. In the British context teachers may have been given the attributes of being professional but were never accorded the status or acknowledgement of the learned professions of divinity, medicine and law or university teaching (Sullivan, 1998). Only headteachers are considered professionals according to the Registrar-General's

Classification of Occupations 1911–98 classification but not other teachers. However, according to the latest *Office for National Statistics Classification of Occupations 2001 Onwards* (Hill, 1999, p. 86), teaching as well as nursing and social work are now classed as professions.

In France the status of secondary school teachers and those teaching in a *lycée* has always been far higher than that of primary teachers. In France teachers are called either *instituteur* or *institutrice* or *maître d'école* or *maîtresse d'école* if they work in the primary sector. They are called *professeur* if they work in the secondary sector. In the UK the term 'teacher' refers to primary, secondary and grammar school teachers, and can represent many different styles of teaching. It is difficult to see teaching as a profession since it comes in so many different forms. This has arguably raised the status of primary at the expense of secondary school teachers. Teaching in the UK covers a 'broad range of different areas and there is no clearly defined area of specialist of (esoteric) knowledge' (Aldrich, 1996, p. 69). In France teaching at the upper secondary level is to a great extent shrouded in esoteric knowledge, the direct consequence of historical developments in the nineteenth century.

In the eighteenth-century UK the prevailing political and commercial traditions were adverse to state action of any kind, least of all state interference with the private education of the upper and middle classes since any intervention along these lines was thought to be harmful. Some other countries thought the opposite. Peter the Great of Russia made education compulsory for the sons of the nobility in 1714, which caused much resentment but no outright rebellion. Except for his neglect of elementary education Napoleon took on all the ideas of the Revolution regarding education, that it was a civil affair aiming at developing both a national consciousness and the proficiency to serve the State in civil offices. In 1806 the State assumed central administrative control of education when all educational institutions were brought under the control of a state commission termed the *Université Impériale* (Ulich, 1967). Napoleon's chief interest was the establishment of a national system of education buttressed by a whole scaffolding of controls ending in the Ministry of Education. At both the secondary and tertiary level bursaries and incomes were provided for eminent scholars, especially scientists. Elementary or popular education never occupied his attention and he gave the Church general control over elementary education which was controlled locally and was to be supplemented by private effort (Wilds and Lottish, 1970).

Rational-encyclopaedic (*knowing that*) concepts of educational attainment and state prescription of national occupational needs have given unity to French upper secondary education. The coherence was established by the creation of the baccalaureate by Napoleon in 1808 as a state certificate by means of which the State could attest to the worth of the studies undertaken. Since the early nineteenth century the French *baccalauréat* obtained in a *lycée* has had a mystical significance with its symbolic functions as a true state mark of achievements (McLean, 1995). It is not only a mark of public status but also a true mark of citizenship that gives automatic rights of entry into higher education (McLean, 1995; Ulich, 1967). In 1808 Napoleon also created the *Ecole Normale Supérieure* (ENS), a rigid system for the selection of candidates to teaching positions in the higher classes of the *lycées* and at the undergraduate level of higher education. The *agrégation* created in 1821 under the Restoration (1815–30) is a highly competitive subject-based national examination given once a year and closely supervised by the Ministry of Education (Ulich, 1967). The successful passing of the examination which the candidate prepares for while attending the ENS or on his/her own gives the right to be appointed to the post of *professeur de lycée*. If there is no immediate opening available the salary is nevertheless paid. Only about one-third of the candidates are successful. Teachers in *lycées* are a powerful intellectual caste and have included many of France's leading intellectuals (McLean, 1995) such as Simone de Beauvoir, Jean-Paul Sartre and Pierre Bourdieu among many others.

In France education is highly centralized with a rigid hierarchy of administration and supervision. Schools are located according to central plans. Teachers are employed by central government which places them where they are needed. A highly prescriptive national curriculum is in place and examinations lead to certificates which have the imprint of the State. Programmes are framed as quasi-constitutions which begin with grand general aims before the details for implementation are elaborated. Teachers are state officials with as strong an obligation to serve the administration as the officials in ministries. Universities are part of the unified system just as well as schools (Binder, 1970; Wilds and Lottish, 1970).

All teachers in France are classified as high-grade civil servants. To qualify they must succeed in a competitive examination which passes only the number of teachers the country needs each year. Teachers have high status because they have overcome a tough entry hurdle. They enjoy comfortable working hours and job security. Teachers can boost their salaries and reduce their hours by passing additional competitive examinations. Those who have passed these have the highest status, enjoy even more comfortable working hours and have the highest salaries. All teachers have a clear professional role unencumbered by pastoral duties (Baker, 1999).

Conclusion

On the face of it, we might come to believe that the status of French teachers as civil servants is the key to their high social and professional standing. A similar conclusion might be reached by examining school teachers in Germany where they have the status, not of national civil servants, but of civil servants belonging to the *Land* in which they are employed. A glance at Japan would lend weight to this argument since in that country all teachers, although engaged by their local prefecture, are state civil servants employed by the Ministry of Education. However, one counter-example suffices to show the weakness in this argument. In Switzerland the teachers are neither civil servants nor have tough competitive hurdles to overcome, but have excellent pay, a highly valued public role and a high degree of autonomy, such as absolute authority within the classroom, which brings a high status. German, French and Swiss secondary school teachers regard themselves as specialists in their academic subject. They see themselves, and are encouraged to see themselves, as intellectuals. The acquisition of knowledge rather than skills is highly valued and rewarded by improved status, conditions and salary. This means that, like their German and French counterparts, the Swiss teachers have a clear notion of themselves and of what is expected of them. Their roles are well defined and are state supported.

In contrast, in England (and elsewhere in the UK) the prevalent child-centred as opposed to subject-centred approach can mean teachers taking responsibility for many of the failings of society and family, and then taking the blame for them. Teaching will gain higher status when it offers a clearer professional role, higher pay for those who are good at it, greater autonomy and tougher entry (Baker, 1999). Teachers in the UK have taken on a multiplicity of roles that arguably distract from their primary function of passing on skills, knowledge and attitudes, and have become in many respects a sort of frontline branch of social work. Unlike in France and Switzerland where there is a specialist to deal with pastoral care, teachers in the UK see this as one of their essential functions. They act *in loco parentis* but perhaps more as substitute parents. This leads to boundless duties and responsibilities. A clearer professional role would mean, at least, defining the limits of the teacher's responsibilities. Thus, we might also define the limits of those things that teachers can be blamed for.

References

Acker, S. (1994) *Gendered Education*. Buckingham: Open University Press.

Aldrich, R. (1996) *Education for the Nation*. London: Cassell.

Apple, M. W. (1999) 'If teacher assessment is the answer, what is the question?' *Education and Social Justice*, 1 (2), 43–7.

Baker, M. (1999) 'Pay alone is not the key, Mr Blunkett'. *Times Educational Supplement*, 29 January.

Barber, M. (1996) 'New Labour, 20 years on'. *Times Educational Supplement*, 11 October.

Binder, F. M. (1970) *Education in the History of Western Civilisation: Selected Readings*. London: Macmillan.

Board of Education Consultative Committee (BECC) (1926) *Report of the Consultative Committee on the Education of the Adolescent* (The Hadow 1926 Report). London: HMSO.

Board of Education Consultative Committee (BECC) (1931) *Report of the Consultative Committee on the Primary School* (The Hadow 1931 Report). London: HMSO.

Bottery, M. (1996) 'The challenge to professionals from the new public management: implications for the teaching profession'. *Oxford Review of Education*, 22 (2), 179–97.

Boyd, W. (1972) *The History of Western Education*. London: Adam and Charles.

Bridges, D. and McLaughlin, T. (1994) 'Education and the market place: an introduction', in D. Bridges and T. McLaughlin (eds) *Education and the Market Place*. London: Falmer.

Broadfoot, P., Osborn, M., Gilly, M. and Paillet, A. (1993) *Perceptions of Teaching: Primary School Teachers in England and France*. London: Cassell.

Broadfoot, P., Osborn, M., Planel, C. and Pollard, A. (1995) 'Systems, teachers and policy change: a comparison of English and French teachers at a turbulent time', presented to the European Conference on Educational Research, University of Bath.

Brooks, R. (1991) *Contemporary Debates in Education*. Harlow: Longman.

Bryce, T. and Humes, W. (1999) 'The distinctiveness of Scottish education', in T. Bryce and W. Humes (eds) *Scottish Education*. Edinburgh: Edinburgh University Press.

Bullock, A., Stallybrass, O. and Trombley, S. (1988) *The Fontana Dictionary of Modern Thought*. London: Fontana.

Campbell, J. and Neill, S. (1994) *Curriculum at Key Stage 1: Teacher Commitment and Policy Failure*. Harlow: Longman.

Charlot, B., Bautier, E. and Rochex, J. (1992) *Ecole et savoir dans les banlieues et ailleurs*. Paris: Armand Colin.

Department for Education and Employment (DfEE) (1998) *Teachers – Meeting the Challenge of Change*. London: The Stationery Office.

Department of Education and Science (DES) (1967) *Children and Their Primary Schools* (The Plowden Report). London: HMSO.

Dreeben, R. (1970) *The Nature of Teaching*. London: Scott, Foresman and Co.

Elliott, J. (1990) 'Teachers as researchers: implications for supervision and teacher education'. *Teaching and Teacher Education*, 6 (1), 1–26.

Eraut, M. (1981) 'Accountability and evaluation', in B. Simon and W. Taylor (eds) *Education in the 1980s*. London: Batsford.

Eraut, M. (1994) *Developing Professional Knowledge and Competence*. London: Falmer Press.

Etzioni, A. (ed.) (1969) *The Semi-Professions and Their Organization*. New York: Free Press.

Freidson, E. (1970) *Professional Dominance*. New York: Aherton Press.

Gatherer, B. (1999) 'Scottish teachers', in T. Bryce and W. Humes (eds) *Scottish Education*. Edinburgh: Edinburgh University Press.

Gilroy, D.P. (1991) 'The loss of professional autonomy: the relevance of Olga Matyash's paper to the brave new world of British education'. *Journal of Education for Teaching*, 17 (1), 11–15.

Gosden, P. (1972) *The Evolution of a Profession*. Oxford: Blackwell.

Grace, G. (1989) 'Education: commodity or public good?' *British Journal of Educational Studies*, 37 (3), 207–21.

Grace, G. (1994) 'Education is a public good: on the need to resist the domination of economic science', in D. Bridges and T. H. McLaughlin (eds) *Education in the Market Place*. London: Falmer.

Helsby, G. (1995) 'Teachers' construction of professionalism in England in the 1990s'. *Journal of Education for Teaching*, 21 (3), 317–32.

Helsby, G. (1996) 'Defining and developing professionalism in English secondary schools'. *Journal of Education for Teaching*, 22 (2), 135–48.

Hill, D. (1999) 'Social class and education', in D. Matheson and I. Grosvenor, (eds) *An Introduction to the Study of Education*. London: David Fulton.

Hoyle, E. (1985) 'The professionalization of teachers: a paradox', in P. Gordon (ed.) *Is Teaching a Profession?* Bedford Way Papers 15. London: Institute of Education, University of London.

Jarvis, P. (1983) *Professional Education*. London: Croom Helm.

Johnson, T. J. (1993) *Professions and Power*. Basingstoke: Macmillan.

Kelsall, R. K. and Kelsall, H. M. (1969) *The School Teacher in England and in the United States*. Oxford: Pergamon.

Kogan, M. (1989) 'Accountability and teacher professionalism', in W. Carr (ed.) *Quality in Teaching: Arguments for a Reflective Profession*. London: Falmer Press.

Langeveld, M.J. (1963) 'The psychology of teachers and the teaching profession', in G. D. Z. Bereday and J. A. Lauwerys (eds) *The Yearbook of Education 1963: The Education and Training of Teachers*. London: Evans Brothers.

Lawton, D. and Gordon, P. (1996) *Dictionary of Education*. London: Hodder and Stoughton.

Leggatt, T. (1970) 'Teaching as a profession', in J. A. Jackson (ed.) *Professions and Professionalisation*. Cambridge: Cambridge University Press.

Lortie D. C. (1975) *Schoolteacher: A Sociological Study*. Chicago: University of Chicago Press.

Maclure, J. S. (1973) *Educational Documents England and Wales 1816 to the Present Day*. London: Methuen.

McLean, M. (1995) *Educational Traditions Compared*. London: David Fulton.

McMurtry, J. (1991) 'Education and the market model'. *Journal of the Philosophy of Education*, 25 (2), 209–17.

Moorish, I. (1978) *The Sociology of Education*. London: Allen and Unwin.

Osborn, M., Broadfoot, P., Planel, C. and Pollard, A. (1997) 'Social class, educational opportunity and equal entitlement: dilemmas of schooling in England and France'. *Comparative Education*, 33 (3), 375–93.

Pollard, H. M. (1974) *Pioneers of Popular Education 1760–1850*. London: John Murray.

Quicke, J. (1999) *A Curriculum for Life: Schools for a Democratic Learning Society*. Buckingham: Open University Press.

Radnor, H., Ball, S. J. and Vincent, C. (1997) 'Whither democratic accountability in education? An investigation into headteachers' perspectives on accountability in the 1990s with reference to their relationships with their LEAs and governors'. *Research Papers in Education*, 12 (2), 205–22.

Rafferty, F. (1999) 'NUT says no to pay by results'. *Times Education Supplement*, 29 January.

Salzberger-Wittenberg, I., Henry, G. and Osborne, E. (1983) *The Emotional Experience of Teaching and Learning*. London: Routledge and Kegan Paul.

Schön, D. (1983) *The Reflective Practitioner*. New York: Temple Smith.

Sharpe, K. (1997) 'The Protestant ethic and the spirit of Catholicism: ideological and institutional constraints on system change in English and French primary schooling'. *Comparative Education*, 33 (3), 329–48.

Simpson, R. L. and Simpson, I. H. (1969) 'Women and bureaucracy in the semi-professions', in A. Etzioni (ed.) *The Semi-Professions and Their Organization*. New York: Free Press.

Sinclair, J., Ironside, M. and Seifert, R. (1993) 'Classroom struggle? Market oriented education reforms and their impact on teachers' professional autonomy, labour intensification and resistance', presented to the International Labour Process Conference, 1 April.

Sullivan, K. (1998) 'The great New Zealand education experiment and the issue of teachers as professionals', in K. Sullivan (ed.) *Education and Change in the Pacific Rim*. Wallingford: Triangle Books.

Tawney, R. H. (1922) (1989) *Secondary Education for All*. London: Hambledon.

Tight, M. (1996) *Key Concepts in Adult Education and Training*. London: Routledge.

Ulich, R. (1967) *The Education of Nations*. Cambridge, MA: Harvard University Press.

Watts, J. (1974) *The Professions: Teaching*. Newton Abbot: David and Charles.

Whitty, G. (1997) 'Marketization, the state, and the re-formation of the teaching profession' in A. H. Halsey, H. Lauder, P. Brown and A. Stuart Wells (eds) *Education, Culture, Economy, Society*. Oxford: Oxford University Press.

Wilds, E. H. and Lottish, K. V. (1970) *The Foundations of Modern Education*. New York: Holt, Rinehart and Winston.

Winch, C. (1996) *Quality and Education*. Oxford: Blackwell.

Wringe, C. (1994) 'Markets, values and education', in D. Bridges and T. H. McLaughlin (eds) *Education in the Market Place*. London: Falmer Press.

6

Education and Governance

Tim Peskett

Introduction

A recent tale of a headteacher's perception of the school governor's role ran as follows. A newly appointed governor with barely one meeting under her belt had chosen to attend a school speech day. At the end of the proceedings, and quite out of the blue, the headteacher asked her to walk on to the stage and offer words of thanks to the pupils and staff for their hard work. While she responded positively she had no inkling that such an activity would be required of her in her role as governor. It was explained later that as she was the only governor present there was no other option!

This true story at one level does not seem surprising; someone was required to carry out a function that had always been done by a person called a school governor. Yet at other levels it raises specific questions of roles and responsibilities, power and tensions, expectations and presumptions. This chapter will seek to examine the notion of school governance, briefly examine the principal tensions that can exist between some of the main players, extend the debate on decentralization within the parameters of current ideas on devolution of power and, finally, consider some of the implications of governors acting strategically.

Governors, governance and the governed

Sallis (1993) maintains that schools in the UK have always had governors of some kind. It is clear that the 1988 Education Reform Act in England and Wales reached new heights of intention by extending governors' responsibilities over a wide range of key functions (Sallis, 1993, p. 4). Yet there is still confusion over what governors *actually do*. Official guidance possesses some interesting contrasts in style. The

Department for Education and Employment (DfEE) identifies nine cogent powers and duties of the governing body. These are:

- deciding (with the head and the LEA if appropriate) the aims and policies of the school, and how the standards of education can be improved;
- deciding the conduct of the school – that is, how in general terms it should be run;
- helping to draw up (with the head and staff) the school development plan;
- deciding how to spend the school's budget;
- making sure that the National Curriculum and religious education are taught and reporting on National Curriculum assessments and examination results;
- selecting the head and deputy head;
- appointing, promoting, supporting and disciplining other staff in consultation with the head;
- acting as a link between the local community and the school; and
- drawing up an action plan after an inspection and monitoring how the plan is put into practice (DfEE, 1997b, p. 15).

The tone as well as the substance of this list is both challenging and daunting. The latter can be particularly ascribed to newly appointed governors when seeing such powers and duties for the first time. Note also the range of actions openly and principally reflected in the first word of each bullet point. These help to build an early picture of the likely functions emerging from such an officially stated range of duties. It is further evident within several of the statements that collective responsibility and some forms of partnership are expected.

A somewhat more summarized offering is presented by the Department of Education, Northern Ireland (DENI, 1997, p. 2) in a helpful yet brief flyer which attempts to encourage people to become school governors. Similar flyers have, from time to time, been made available by the DfEE in England and Wales but the DENI version makes for a more accessible appreciation of the 'wide ranging managerial responsibilities . . . working in partnership with the Principal' (DENI, 1997, p. 2):

- setting school aims and policies in relation to the curriculum, pupil admissions, charging for school activities, discipline, special educational needs and pastoral care;
- making sure that the statutory curriculum is taught and that pupils are assessed;
- making decisions on the school budget;
- selecting staff;
- promoting good relations between the school and the community;
- preparing information for parents, including an annual report on each child's performance;
- producing an Annual Report (so that parents can raise any matters about the way the board of governors, principal or education and library boards have carried out their responsibilities).

Clearly there is much common ground between the two lists. A great deal is covered under the DfEE's second bullet point of 'conduct of the school' which may subsume points one and six from the DENI booklet. Yet both stress the stark nature of power, duties and responsibilities held by volunteers. *No one* is compelled to be a school governor.

The then Scottish Office's (now Scottish Executive) legal guidance offers contrasts in both its format and, to a lesser extent, its focus upon the role of and relations with parents (Scottish Office, 1989, p. 1; 1996). The 'number of basic powers, duties and rights' are set out in the legislation under specific sections, schedules and regulations covering similar areas to those of both the DfEE and DENI. However, the overall focus is more specifically directed in Scotland to the parent body, where it is seen by government as 'perhaps one of the most important functions a Board will ever perform ... a mechanism for the two-way flow of information between parents, schools and education authorities' (Scottish Office, 1989, p. 1).

It is evident that one of the cornerstones of school governance in the UK is the notion of local representation. In one very real sense, governors have been regarded as one representation of the way in which a school relates to the world beyond and around it (Glatter, 1989). The representation of such groups as parents, local politicians and community or co-opted governors illustrates this point. There is, then, a coming together of a relatively diverse set of interests and experience with ostensibly the same aim, namely, the effective functioning of the school in keeping with its agreed aims. *School Governors – A Guide to the Law* (DfEE, 1997a, p. 15) cites one duty of governors as being responsible for deciding the conduct of the school, how, *in general terms*, it should be run.

As unhelpful as such an open term may be, 'general terms' also reflects a further key parameter of governance at its best. Governors do not have, nor were ever intended to have, responsibility for the day-to-day management of the school. Theirs in a step-away overview role, reinforced by their collective powers and responsibilities. Sallis has aptly stated it thus: 'that governors have responsibility at policy-making level, not in the day-by-day running of the school, and that power belongs to the governing body as a whole: the *individual* governor has no power to make decisions or take action' (Sallis, 1993, p. 5). Kogan *et al.* (1984) have suggested that governing bodies operate within four principal models, namely, accountable, advisory, supporting and mediating, and that the lay person as governor was seen as 'an outsider, a guest, on the territory of the professional' (*ibid.*, p. 47). Such ideal types are helpful in enabling a delineation of the range of roles and functions of school governors when assessed against the backgrounds of both official stipulation and actual performance.

Performance in the context of school governance is, in spite of Kogan *et al.*'s research, a recent perceptual phenomenon. A development of the four-model typology above has endeavoured to identify the different roles of every governing body by identifying these as central elements in the pursuit of improving the quality of education and standards of achievement (OFSTED/Audit Commission 1995, p. 4). These are:

- Steering role, e.g. agreeing policies, setting budgets, etc.
- Monitoring role, e.g. monitoring plans, budgets, standards, etc.
- Executive role, e.g. recruitment, discipline, etc.
- Accounting to parents, e.g. Annual report, publication of minutes, etc.
- Supporting role, e.g. supporting and advising the headteacher, etc. (*ibid.*).

These five roles encapsulate the view of their framers that each governing body needs to examine itself, in a kind of healthy governance check-up campaign, against each. Indeed, where governing bodies can find adequate quality time to carry out this exercise together, there is at least anecdotal evidence to suggest that it may assist in making sense of their roles within their current practice. Identification of governors' activities in this way can reinforce the concept of such roles while also encouraging some measured reflection on actual practice.

To what extent can the development of the partnership between governors and the other involved and interested parties in school life be gauged as effective? Schools are now faced, through the efforts of their own self-review processes and the external visits by inspectors, with having to assess the quality of the functioning of their governing bodies. Creese (1995) seeks to establish a proven link between effective schools and effective governance. He identifies six proposals which may contribute towards such a connection, namely:

- work in partnership with the staff;
- help towards the establishment of a climate for school improvement;
- work with staff to prepare a school development plan;
- appoint staff, especially senior staff, who are committed to school improvement;
- work with the staff to monitor and evaluate progress; and
- set an example by seeking to improve the performance of the governing body.

Creese (1995, p. 60) is insistent that: 'Where governors and staff can work in . . . partnership . . . the contribution of both groups is likely to be most effective.' This is not a new idealism. What has been lacking has been some tangible evidence of practice.

However, there is now some evidence to suggest (House of Commons, 1999) that such a link has research credibility at both a national political and higher education level. The general conclusions of *Improving the Effectiveness of School Governing Bodies* (Scanlon, Earley and Evans, 1999) found a 'clear association between effective schools and effective governing bodies'. Key factors found were:

- a positive attitude towards the governing body by the headteacher;
- chairs of governors were usually the most experienced or more senior;
- efficient working arrangements resulted in operating successfully;
- effective teamwork was evident within the governing body;
- high levels of governor commitment to the school;

- positive relationship with staff;
- governors were carefully selected;
- stable governing body and ease/difficulty of recruitment;
- benefits of training for individual governors and whole body; and
- governor characteristics, i.e. educational background, etc.

How do such conclusions assist us in identifying the links between prescribed practice, suggested roles and the measurable standards of effective governance? That they *do* create a blueprint for assessing the margins of positive practice we may be able to accept in part. What is debatable and of concern to governors and their supporters and trainers alike is the extent to which the identification of 'best practice' may inadvertently shield some of the negative influences that continue to create instability and indecision *within* some governing bodies.

Tensions and traumata

Differing perceptions and perspectives on the respective roles of governors and professional teachers often lie at the heart of the debate on roles and responsibilities (Deem, 1993; Thody, 1992). Confusions over actual and intended roles may even result from training, where perceptions of trainee governors later impact upon their governor colleagues and the professionals teaching and managing in their schools, so that all may feel the effect of reconsidered functions (Deem, Brehony and Heath, 1995). Research in Papua New Guinea (Maha, 1997) identified the usefulness of governing boards according to their levels of participation. Chief amongst these was the influence the school principal (cf. headteacher) appeared to exercise in allowing meaningful discussion and decision-making coupled with a willingness to implement any decisions taken. This in part concurs with the latest research in England and Wales (Scanlon, Earley and Evans, 1999) where partnership was identified as being aided by a positive attitude from the headteacher towards the governors and their work.

Understandable professional resentment may occur when reflective debate and discussion over respective roles has not been clarified and agreed in an open and democratic fashion. There is, however, a measure of necessary bravery attached to such an activity. The seeds of professional disquiet and territorial insularity generally result from indistinct boundaries acquired by word of mouth rather than by co-operative reflection. Sallis (1999) has identified these feelings astutely, citing them as 'very natural in the circumstances, since teachers have so long enjoyed a degree of protection of their territory against public intervention unknown in most other professions' (p. 41). Her attempt to reassure that fluctuating boundaries are unlikely to disappear in the short-term political arena is tinged with practical self-doubt.

Yet the attempts to promulgate demarcation lines have been singularly rare. One such effort (DfEE, 1996) produced suggestions in a variety of key areas, such as finance and the curriculum, though the acknowledged background influence to this was the impact of persuasive pressure groups and teacher trade unions which

Table 6.1 An example of the division of responsibilities between the governing body and the headteacher

The headteacher	The governing body
Draws up the school curriculum plan with the overall statutory framework and the policy framework set by the governing body	Determines a policy for delivering a broad and balanced curriculum within the statutory framework and in consultation with the headteacher, including a policy on sex education.

Source: DfEE (1996).

made up the broad representation on the consultative group that produced this otherwise excellent publication. One such area that can be particularly challenging for both parties is reproduced, in part, in Table 6.1.

How then are we to view any irreconcilable lay and professional views on their own respective roles in managing schools and learning? Any recent, emergent clarity has to be set against any prevailing national political debate and policy initiative that refers to this particular tension. Where governments made conscious decisions to raise the profile of school governors, there is likely to be an accompanying raising of the expectations, generally in a legal form, where additional or confirmatory responsibilities are reinforced.

A classic example of this is the position governors in England and Wales have been placed in with regard to the setting of school targets (DfEE, 1997c, p. 4). It has been made clear that governors have *the* responsibility when agreeing the setting of targets for school improvement. There is no suggestion that this is done in splendid isolation, far from professional advice and know-how, yet non-teachers are being asked to scrutinize professional judgements and then come to a reconciled decision about pupils' attainment on such a basis. Indeed, this document marks a subtle shift both in the role of governors *and* in the forms of governor scrutiny, from a position of relatively little guidance to one of structured involvement and questioning.

While there is an attempt in this clearly written document to emphasize some aspects of professional–lay partnership – though the word is not actually used – governors are offered described and defined roles supported by, literally, 'Questions governors might ask'. Hence four roles are outlined, namely:

- to ensure that the school meets its legal duties;
- to encourage open and honest discussion about the school's performance and how it can be further improved;
- to be strategic, i.e. determining values and goals and linking the process of target-setting with school development planning; and
- to support the head and staff in working through a cycle of school improvement which concentrates on pupil performance (*ibid.*).

These are significant expectations. A complementary publication (DfEE, 1997c) for professional staff sets out in more detail the proposed routes to the successful implementation of the target-setting process. Yet the legal basis of governors' responsibilities here is made paramount, a factor that initially caused some anxiety for even the most experienced and conscientious governors. In a real and very vital sense government has spelt out unambiguously the *importance* of the governor's role in this critical activity, forcing that role with measured intent. The three other stipulations push the pace of change to a remarkable extent. Once, then, governors have assumed that *theirs* is the responsibility in this area, an attempt is made to define the context of success by offering the challenge of 'open and honest discussion' (*ibid.*). To presuppose that this can be established readily and purposefully is naïve at best. Where this has emerged over some years of careful and fruitful development within an atmosphere of mutual trust and genuine partnership, ground rules will have been laid for such debate to be effectively broached. Where this has not occurred – likely in the majority of schools – a vital developmental process is being left to chance.

Clearly there is a role here for the governor support services of LEAs but even where training and support have been planned, governors take their experiences back to a context unknown in detail to such providers. What may emerge is more rather than less uncertainty, largely as a result of the prevailing school-based context of governor operation not having been debated openly and thought through to a workable level.

In setting a 'Five Stage Cycle for School Improvement' (DfEE, 1997d, p. 5) this particular target-setting exercise leaves markedly unresolved the problem of clarifying the lines of demarcation. Government may justifiably leave it to schools and their LEAs to resolve this, against the backcloth of their erstwhile suggestions. However, their further insistence, at least in writing, of reinforcing the endeavour with proposed questions at *every* stage is interesting. That the suggestions comply with the respected notion that the most effective questions from governors are often the most straightforward, even simple, cannot be disputed. A brief example from each of the five stages will serve to illustrate this point:

- How is our school currently performing?
- How should our school be doing?
- Do we need to revise any existing targets?
- Will our action plans ensure we meet our targets?
- Are we achieving our identified targets? (*ibid.*)

The issue here is of extreme significance for governors and their schools. Presumptions about partnerships will not solve the ongoing and enlivened debates about demarcations between professional and lay roles and responsibilities. The tensions raised by such a view both at national and local government levels serve only to obscure the debate over some of the principal realities of decentralization of power, duties and responsibilities.

Decentralization as devolution of power

Gamage (1993) maintains that community participation in school-based govern-ance can be seen as a formal alteration of the structures of governance, and that this entails 'making decisions in the domains of school's mission, goals, priorities, policies relating to financial, material and human resources' (p. 134). This largely covers the key elements in any attempt to ensure that governance has a local focus and influence. In an exhaustively comprehensive paper, Lauglo (1995) has attemp-ted to identify the main values invoked for decentralization, namely:

- a politically legitimate dispersal of authority;
- the quality of services rendered; and
- the efficient use of resources (p. 9).

These tangible entities all resound within the intention of developed countries and their current preoccupations inside the mini-world of school governance.

If we accept the premise that most systems of governance allow a wide spectrum of the community to participate in educational decision-making at the local community level (Maha, 1997), then there is a case for warming to Jones's argument that, in England and Wales at least, governance continues to be a brave experiment in local democracy (Jones, 1998, p. 330). Trying to define the outworkings of this view is, however, more challenging.

Sallis (1999) has persuasively stated that lack of clarification between delegated and representative roles, combined with an occasionally dismissive attitude on the part of some headteachers and fellow governors, may result in confusion and ineffectiveness. While no one on a governing body is a delegate, 'representative status confers ... a duty to listen to constituents, to convey their views to the governing body and to report back to their constituents on any matters not classified as confidential' (*ibid.*, p. 113). This communicating role, Sallis asserts, is not to be denied. She further insists that where this function is properly recognized and acknowledged it can add to governing body effectiveness and the acceptability of its decisions, '*if it acts with maximum awareness of the views of the groups represented*' (*ibid.*, my italics).

Here lies one of the key factors in facilitating local democracy through school governance. *How* the different views, interests and opinions are assimilated, compromised or rejected will inevitably set perceptions both within and outside the governing body. Hence the current stress in England and Wales on supporting the enhanced roles of governors by encouraging them to be more effective through, for example, their own process of self-review (Northamptonshire County Council, 1999). In countries such as Australia, England, Wales and Scotland, there is a growing devolutionary link between effective schooling and the aspirant roles and responsibilities of school governors (Gamage, 1993). While Blackledge (1995) concludes that empowerment for some is no empowerment at all, the pursuit of parental involvement through school governance is, in these countries in particular, being increased. Yet the political machinations are subtle. Sallis (1988) has maintained that devolution of power to schools 'may well in the short run benefit professionals more than parents' (p. 98). Increasingly the role of parents within the different forms of school governance can reflect a distinct shift in political intention.

The Scottish Boards model with parent members as a majority (Scottish Office, 1989) is similarly reflected in New South Wales, Australia. Here the roles of parent organizations and the school councils (cf. boards) are seen as complementary, but it is stated clearly that 'Parent organizations have an advisory function but school councils are a decision-making body' (New South Wales Department of Education and Training, 1998, part 3, p. 1). While parent representatives are but one of five groups intended to reflect 'all groups of the school community' (*ibid.*), they can combine their influence with the school's parents' organization in seeking to address their collective concerns and aspirations.

Set limitations of the power of such bodies are also delineated. Policies of the New South Wales government cannot be ignored by a school council. Also, the principal (cf. headteacher) remains accountable for the management of school finances, in contrast to the English and Welsh model, where governors share the responsibility with the headteacher, as governor (DfEE, 1997b). Increasingly the debate over finances has tended to focus on 'value for money' issues, in England and Wales largely in response to the Office for Standards in Education inspections, but here too there is a real element of local appraisal of 'taxpayers' money' being appropriately deployed for young persons' learning. Yet the connections here are tenuous. School governors in England and Wales receive devolved budgets over which they have control *at the moment of receipt*. Only those members of governing bodies who are elected local authority councillors may have been party to voting any current year's figures over a defined geographical area as an entity. Therefore to regard the devolution of finance as wholly democratic may be less than reasonable. 'Localness' with regard to the uses of school finances *can* be regarded as an attempt at democratic participation, though the boast that this has filtered down from national to local government and then to governing bodies via a single process of democratization of intent remains questionable.

Corson (1998) has highlighted the differences in developments between contrasting communities where influential members of the community were sought out by schools to be involved in school governance. Currently in both the UK and Australia the emphasis is to broaden representation, thus reducing the focus somewhat on local dignatories and politicians. Sullivan (1998) offers a further change of purpose in the locally elected boards of trustees in New Zealand, where national government policy gave them an employer's role over teachers, in a quest to challenge the previous overcentralized and inefficient educational administration. These examples, while illustrating the dynamic aspect of school governance at local level, serve also to confirm the possibilities of political interference in the running of schools.

The notion that 'localness' can be reflected in the diverse backgrounds of the individuals who make up governing bodies is, at face value, a logical one. Indeed, these very variations in backgrounds are still seen as a key factor in full and fair representation, though there are dangers in regarding this as a guarantee of a workable form of accountability (Farrell and Law, 1999). Likewise, can there be guarantees attached to the idea that devolved lay scrutiny of a school's complex outworkings will result in improvement? Scanlon, Earley and Evans (1999) have assisted this debate by the use of nine illustrative case studies of school governance across school type, age range and locality (*ibid.*, annex 1). They offer some evidence that 'where there's a will, there's a way', and reference earlier in this chapter to the key factors in effective governance makes a useful starting point for governors, their supporters and trainers to consider when assessing their own current performance.

That school governance does attempt to focus upon interactive, joint forms of action (Raab, 1994) can nevertheless be part of a persuasive argument upholding some of the central elements of the democratic *process*. Raab offers a useful insight here:

> Patterns of governance need to be assessed not only in terms of their efficacy in achieving policy intentions, but in terms of their consequences for an array of values that are important to democratic society and politics; values of participation and equity, for example. (*ibid.*, p. 18)

Hence we can consider governance here as a devolved power base offering some 'insights drawn from a variety of theoretical perspectives' (*ibid.*, p. 18). The danger, however, is that the *practical* activities involving governors in the context of schools' effective performance may be expressed as so vital by governments that they outweigh the *principles* underpinning them. This is not to revert to an argument for governance based only upon discursive ramblings at meetings held several times during each school year. It is rather to press for a reassessment of the underlying rationale of governance to enable it to remain in keeping with tangible roles and responsibilities.

Strategic governance: fancy descriptor or political reality?

The quest of governments to encourage the roles of governors to be seen and acted upon as strategic is not altogether clear. As a way of describing a voluntary lay function it may smack more of war than of educational opportunity! In the UK the New Labour agenda for governors, though not massively contrasting in its aspirations from the previous government, has proffered a step-by-step approach towards the encouragement of a strategic view of governance in pursuit of raising standards of achievement. The cynical riposte to this political endeavour has been for governors to ask of others (rarely national politicians, in my view) the actual meaning of acting strategically in the context of governing a school. For example, where governors are methodically checking the overall direction of their school alongside the agreed policies, can this be described as acting strategically? Are the five roles of steering, monitoring, executive, accounting and supporting, as cited above (OFSTED/Audit Commission, 1995), all aspects of the strategic role? Are some roles potentially more strategic than others?

While it is not the purpose of this chapter to provide detailed answers to these important questions, it is likely that further reflection on the strategic role of governors will continue to be encouraged (House of Commons, 1999). At one level this is an attempt to further the role of a democratically constituted body. At another it is no more than a wish to further devolve decision-making to local representatives in order to absolve blame and implication from the national political arena. The issue this predictably begs is one cited earlier: partnership between governors and the professional players *must* be agreed to a measurable extent if *both* the democratic intent *and* the pursuit of excellence for all students are to be attained. Such a presumption demonstrates both a marked naïvety on the part of politicians and framers of educational legislation and a dull appreciation of the realities of putting externally imposed policies into practice.

The voluntary aspect of school governance allows the opportunity for partially excusing ineffective practice. Yet some recent evidence exists to endorse the importance of governing bodies *collectively* considering what they are good at and those which they are not. Scanlon, Earley and Evans's (1999) almost mirror reflection of their previously mentioned positive factors contributing to governors' effectiveness, cite some predictable inhibitors to strategic governorship (p. 30). These include:

- lack of skills and knowledge;
- very demanding workload;
- insufficient contact with the school, fellow governors and school staff;
- lack of funding and resources for the school;
- poor preparation for meetings;
- inadequate administrative support;
- problems with channels of communication;
- training of insufficient quantity and quality;
- problems of recruitment;
- and lack of commitment and involvement.

This exhaustive list may not appear surprising. However, what needs to be examined here is the *impact* these variable inadequacies may have on the desired intentions of governors, LEAs and national governments to carry out their wide-ranging roles and responsibilities.

Consensus on successes and failures is easier to agree than consensus on perceptions of shifting boundaries of expectation and responsibility. In England and Wales a recent press release from the DfEE on governors' training for their role in new pay plans for headteachers (DfEE, 1999) hailed the opportunity for them joining 'school based training in performance management' and their additional involvement in and contact with a ' "training package specifically for governors and a series of guidance documents' (p. 1). One teachers' union's view offers a markedly contrasting opinion. ' "This will shift the role of governors from laying down policy into the actual management of schools," said general secretary [of the National Union of Teachers] Doug McAvoy' (TES, 1999, p. 7).

It is unlikely that this debate will die down. Such a continuation, though to the observer interesting and at times captivating, does little to forge agreement on complementary roles agreed on the basis of a workable partnership. One governors' association's recent survey of its members identified further support for this to be fully addressed:

> Respondents suggest a redistribution of certain responsibilities to what they see as a more appropriate level. They wish to delegate some internal management responsibilities to the head and staff and redistribute some higher management functions to education professionals – primarily those within the LEA. (Governors' News, 1999, p. 4)

In addition, respondents expressed resentment, frustration and anger that they had 'been diverted from the core purpose that they have identified', namely acting in the best interests of children and their education (*ibid.*).

How then might reconciliation be pursued where it is not yet present but is, nevertheless, an aspiration for some? It would be easy to overexaggerate the potential for division at school staff–school governor level. An increasing amount of research (Earley and Creese, 1998) has tended to highlight and expose the positive in contrast to the weak. The key debate remains: what can governments *do*, in practical terms, to assist governing bodies and LEAs in relentlessly pursuing effective governance in the quest for the ever-improving attainment of pupils? Any answers have one major difficulty to face, namely, the navigational rights of passage possessed by democratically elected national governments pursuing their educational policies, against an *ostensibly* local and accountable number of governing bodies who have, above all, *local* agendas. Hence we find further tensions arising from false perceptions, as in the case of school governors not wishing to focus their attentions on the nationally prescribed Education Development Plans (EDPs) of local authorities, since their own focus is that of the school where they serve as a governor. That governors should, in their 'localness', be party to some broader responsibility is up to governors, not the framers of EDPs. While consultation in this area has been a patchwork of variability, ranging from genuine to patronizing, it is a further example of the ever-present and ill thought through tensions that help to mar effective governor practice.

Conclusion

The practical workings of school governance are complex and open to misinterpretation (Thody, 1990). Surrounding the expected roles, and intrinsic to the tensions and traumas, is the principal intention that power – at least some – has been *consciously* devolved to a locally representative body. While it is a relatively simple task to identify factors contributing to both effective and ineffective practice, this does not, of itself, aid the local endeavour at school level. The pursuit of an open and honest approach to governance by the majority of its participants has generally led to some successes rather than none. Sallis insists there is more to it, but not a great deal more:

> My dream is of a school where the governing body has confidently assumed its legal role, where its members are working in harmony with each other and the professional staff. Clear aims are shared by all who work in and with the school, and by the wider community of parents, pupils and neighbours. Management is sure-footed because it rests upon well-debated decisions to which all are committed. Decisions are robust because they take account from the beginning of the questions likely to be asked by the community served by the school. A culture of continuing improvement is strong and durable because of the wide range of interests committed to it. (Sallis, 1999, p. ix)

As a checklist this may be daunting for some governing bodies. As an aspiration it could provide an additional focus for self-review that is so often overlooked in the supposed interests of agendas for meetings and their increasingly demanding requirements.

School governance has long been at several crossroads. They are met when facing policy decisions and imposed when governments attempt to block previously open highways. Essentially, such crossroads emphasize choice of direction and the concomitant responsibility of governing bodies to debate such choices in partnership with the professionals. The extent to which they choose and are encouraged to do so will be reflected in the contribution they make to what is offered to the young people in their school's care.

References

Blackledge, A. (1995) 'Minority parents as school governors in Chicago and Britain: empowerment or not?' *Educational Review*, 47 (3), 309–17.

Corson, D. (1998) *Changing Education for Diversity*. Buckingham: Open University Press.

Creese, M. (1995) *Effective Governors, Effective Schools: Developing the Partnership*. London: David Fulton.

Deem, R. (1993) 'Educational reform and school governing bodies in England 1986–92: old dogs, new tricks or new dogs, new tricks?', in M. Preedy (ed.) *Managing the Effective School*. London: Paul Chapman/Open University.

Deem, R., Brehony, K. and Heath, S. (1995) *Active Citizenship and the Governing of Schools*. Buckingham: Open University Press.

DENI (1997) *Becoming a School Governor*. Belfast: The Stationery Office.

DfEE (1996) *Guidance on Good Governance*. London: DfEE.

DfEE (1997a) *School Governors – a Guide to the Law: County and Controlled Schools*. June edition. London: DfEE.

DfEE (1997b) *From Targets to Action*. London: DfEE.

DfEE (1997c) *Setting Targets for Pupil Achievement – Guidance for Governors*. London: DfEE.

DfEE (1999) Press Release no. 422/99. 24 September.

Earley, P. and Creese, M. (1998) 'School governing bodies: rationale, roles and reassessment'. *Viewpoint*, 8, September, Institute of Education, University of London.

Farrell, C. M. and Law, J. (1999) 'The accountability of school governing bodies'. *Educational Management and Administration*, 27 (1), 5–15.

Gamage, D. T. (1993) 'A review of community participation in school governance: an emerging culture in Australian education'. *British Journal of Educational Studies*, 41 (2), 134–48.

Glatter, R. (ed.) (1989) *Educational Institutions and their Environments: Managing the Boundaries*. Milton Keynes: Open University Press.

Governors' News. (1999) *Research Group Report*. National Association of Governors and Managers, October.

House of Commons (1999) *The Role of School Governors*, vol. 1. Report and Proceedings of the Education and Employment Committee. London: The Stationery Office.

Jones, J. L. (1998) 'Managing the induction of newly appointed governors'. *Educational Research*, 40 (3), 329–51.

Kogan, M., Johnson, D., Packwood, T. and Whittaker, T. (1984) *School Governing Bodies*. London: Heinemann.

Lauglo, J. (1995) 'Forms of decentralisation and their implications for education'. *Comparative Education*, 31 (1), 5–29.

Maha, A. C. (1997) 'Governance of education in Papua New Guinea: the role of boards of governors'. *International Review of Education*, 43 (2/3) 179–92.

Northamptonshire County Council (1999) *Skills Audit of Governors' Effectiveness* [SAGE]. Governors' Services, John Dryden House, Northampton.

New South Wales Department of Education and Training (1998) *School Council Guidelines*. NSW: Executive and Legal Service.

OFSTED/Audit Commission (1995) *Lessons in Teamwork*. London: The Stationery Office.

Raab, C. D. (1994) 'Theorising the governance of education'. *British Journal of Educational Studies*, 42 (1), 6–22.

Sallis, J. (1988) *Schools, Parents and Governors – a New Approach to Accountability*. London: Routledge.

Sallis, J. (1993) *Basics for School Governors*. Stafford: Network Educational Press.

Sallis, J. (1999) *Managing Better with Governors – a Practical Guide to Working Together for School Success*. London: Financial Times/Pitman Publishing.

Scanlon, M., Earley, P. and Evans, J. (1999) *Improving the Effectiveness of School Governing Bodies*. Research Report No. 111. London: The Stationery Office/DfEE.

Scottish Office (1989) *School Boards – Guide to the Legislation*. Edinburgh: Holmes McDougall.

Scottish Office (1996) *Education (Scotland) Act 1996: Guidance on Certain Provisions*. Circular No 8/96. Edinburgh: Education and Industry Department.

Sullivan, K. (1998) (ed.) *Education and Change in the Pacific Rim – Meeting the Challenges*. Wallingford: Triangle Books.

TES (1999) 'Union fearful of governor power'. *Times Educational Supplement*, 7 October.

Thody, A. (1990) 'Governors of the school republic'. *Educational Management and Administration*, 18 (2), 42–5.

Thody, A. (1992) *Moving To Management – School Governors in the 1990s*. London: David Fulton.

CHAPTER

7

Education and Effectiveness

Martyn Roebuck

Introduction

We all share an understanding of educational effectiveness – or do we? Effectiveness in education can be considered at different levels. Scheerens and Creemers (1989) use the term 'educational effectiveness' to refer to the effectiveness of the overall educational system of a country. They use 'instructional effectiveness' to refer to the effectiveness of education at the classroom level and 'school effectiveness' as the effectiveness of the school as an organization and as an educational system. This terminology will be adopted in this chapter which concentrates on international studies of educational effectiveness, and some relationships and parallels with work on school effectiveness. What have the studies been for and how may they be used?

School effectiveness research examines the factors which influence the relative performance of schools. Performance is judged using readily measured output measures such as external examination results and attendance. The linked 'school improvement' movement focuses on the internal processes which operate to move schools forward (see Gray *et al.*, 1999).

International educational effectiveness studies typically are concerned with the relative performance of national samples of pupils on tests administered across several countries, or the proportion of the population reaching particular levels of qualification. Since the early 1960s there have been more than fifteen large-scale international comparative studies conducted by the International Association for the Evaluation of Educational Achievement (IEA) and the International Assessment of Educational Progress (IAEP), using achievement tests, in a range of subjects and involving up to 40 countries.

More recently the OECD (Organization for Economic Co-operation and Development) has reported IEA average achievement scores alongside other national output statistics of education. The OECD has pioneered the use of such data as international indicators of educational performance in reports which explore features of the relative effectiveness of educational systems.

Some sources of interest in comparative performance data

National emphases on the quality and effectiveness of school systems frequently arise following public concern about economic competitiveness. The 1983 report in the USA entitled *A Nation at Risk* (NCEE, 1983) focused the country's attention on issues of quality in education. It became synonymous with concerns for the USA to survive the challenge of international economic competition. It led to structural changes at both state and school level. These included introducing regulations about teacher quality, classroom time, discipline, curriculum standards and pupil proficiency, and school leadership. There was a concern for excellence, focusing on an emphasis on leadership in education. The loss of the USA's competitive edge, with, for example, Japan, was clearly linked to the believed superiority of the Japanese education system.

In Britain, following a 1976 speech at Ruskin College by the then Prime Minister, James Callaghan, there was launched a 'Great Debate' about education. The speech and the debate which followed was given point, to a large extent, by public blame which attributed Britain's lack of economic competitiveness to the quality of its education and training. The debate ultimately probably led to the 1988 Education Act in England and Wales with its emphasis on standards. This Act introduced national testing and a National Curriculum. However, not long after, in 1990, Sir Claus Moser, in a presidential address to the British Association for the Advancement of Science, returned to the concern that shortcomings in British education and training were still affecting the country's economic future. An independent commission on education was set up. Its report *Learning to Succeed* (National Commission on Education, 1993) began by referring to international data which highlighted the very low level of qualifications achieved in England at age 16 and at 18+ compared with countries such as Germany, France and Japan. It acknowledged the limitations of the data available, because of the difficulties involved in ensuring that the measures were equivalent, but at the same time drew attention to the inescapable need for action. The 'vision' of the commission thus begins with two points: (1) in all countries, knowledge and applied intelligence have become central to economic success and social well-being; and (2) in the UK, much higher achievement in education and training is needed to match world standards.

The aims of large-scale international comparative studies

In the Foreword to a report giving the results of one of the first comparative international studies of pupil achievement, a pilot IEA study carried out with

13-year-olds across twelve countries from 1959 to 1962, Dr Saul B. Robinsohn (in Foshay *et al.*, 1962) commented:

> The present study may well be described as an unusual addition to the literature of education. The results of the project here reported suggest that both empirical educational research and comparative education can gain new dimensions, the one by extending its range over various educational systems, the other by including empirical methods among its instruments. In the minds of its authors the project had the double purpose of throwing light on the possibilities of such research, and of obtaining actual results which would, not so much evaluate educational performances under different educational systems in absolute terms, but rather discern patterns of intellectual functioning and attainment in certain basic subjects of the school curriculum under varying conditions. This would be a first step towards bringing into profile the relative merits of various learning processes and procedures. If the results so far, because of limitations on their validity which the authors freely admit, are little more than suggestive, at least they offer real encouragement for believing that such researches can, in the future, lead to more significant results and begin to supply what Anderson has lamented as 'the major missing link in comparative education', which in his view is crippled especially by the scarcity of information about the outcomes or products of educational systems.

The aspirations of that first survey have yet to be realized. The subsequent IEA and IEAP studies have been criticized as weak on explaining their findings (Anderson, 1961), though perhaps not surprisingly so given the type and quality of data which were able to be collected, voluntarily, within the levels of cost acceptable to potential participating countries (Reynolds and Farrell, 1996).

Going beyond reporting test scores and questionnaire profiles, and trying to explain such results through in-depth analyses can be even more difficult and expensive to implement, though as we will see later, after nearly 40 years, some steps forward are being made. During the 1980s, in part because of lack of analysis, but also the cost, several countries were questioning the usefulness of the studies conducted at that time. However, while the IEA was founded initially as a research co-operative, primarily interested in international comparative studies from a research perspective, in the 1980s the growing interest of policy-makers in comparative educational indicators changed the focus and provided a potential funding lifeline. Since then, the IEA has taken on the challenge to serve the interests of policy-makers through its studies. The inclusion of IEA achievement scores in publications of OECD is claimed to indicate that it has started to become successful on this front (Plomp, 1997).

> International comparisons of student achievement have become an essential tool for assessing the performance of education systems. They can serve as measures of accountability that inform key stakeholders in education – such as taxpayers, employers, educators, parents and students – on the effects of their investment in education. (OECD, 1998, p. 25)

Thus the move was made from being a 'research club' to a source of policy advice, with a concern for the outcomes of investment rather than the effect of different 'learning processes and procedures' and, since tables of relative performance on their own have limited interest, a rapidly increasing emphasis on trying to explain why differences occur, not necessarily because of different learning processes.

The development of OECD indicators of educational performance

Over many years the OECD through its Centre for Educational Research and Innovation (CERI) had published qualitative case studies of educational policy in individual member countries. However, there was a growing suspicion that they were viewed by some nations as of tangential interest. Even where focused on initiatives of particular concern, such as the introduction of new technologies in individual countries, they had made relatively little impact on the OECD community, though the process of being involved clearly benefited the country under study. Then, in the early 1990s, a new Director for CERI, with previous experience of OECD's mainstream economic indicators, focused the work of CERI on more 'hard-nosed' issues. Through a network of international working groups, CERI defined and tested wide-ranging sets of quantitative indicators of educational achievement and progress.

Three central purposes were suggested by the OECD for having a comprehensive set of international indicators (MacBeath, 1993):

- To provide information (for policy-makers and for a wider public) on how their own system is performing within an international context.
- To further understanding by providing data rich enough to illustrate the connection and relationships between different kinds of indicators.
- To educate, to stimulate interest, raise questions and define areas for further enquiry.

The OECD began by developing and collecting data for four broad groups of indicators which covered demographic and economic background, educational outcomes, educational programmes and processes, and expectations of, and attitudes to, education.

The collection of the indicator data across OECD countries developed quickly and has enabled the production of the series of authoritative 'Education at a Glance: OECD Indicators' (EAG) reports (now including the latest available IEA survey results). Each EAG report contains comparative tables and commentaries, but is complemented by an *Education Policy Analysis* report which has more in-depth examinations of selected issues. The 1997 *Education Policy Analysis* (OECD, 1997), for example, concentrates on educational expenditure, lifelong investment in education, literacy, failure at school, and on new demands on tertiary education.

By 1998 the EAG report contained seven groups of education indicators:

- demographic, social and economic context of education (including differences in achievement by age and gender, and in relation to parents);
- financial and human resources invested in education (the amounts spent in relation to population and wealth, the sources of funds, and the balance of expenditure);
- access to education, participation, progression and completion (trends in enrolments in the various levels of education and types of educational institutions are shown to indicate how the supply and demand of educational resources have evolved in different countries);
- the transition from school to work (presents a broad picture of the labour force participation of young people 15 to 29 years of age, both while in education and following the completion of initial education);
- the learning environment and the organization of schools (teacher salaries, demographics of the teaching force, the statutory time that teachers are required to teach and students are require to learn, subject emphasis in the curriculum, how decision-making authority is distributed across levels of government, the use of computers in schools); and
- student achievement and social and labour market outcomes of education (IEA Third International Mathematics and Science Study (TIMSS) scores and spread of scores in mathematics, factors affecting variation including students' home backgrounds, links between educational attainment and earnings).

That this shift in focus by OECD/CERI was timely was reflected in the high level of publicity given across nations to the first and subsequent EAGs, and not only in the countries leading the developments of indicators. For example, a 1995 report on evaluating education in Finland highlighted the shift in the management of Finnish education, from regulation and control to delegation and evaluation. It acknowledged that, given the magnitude of educational investments, and the need for organized national evaluation procedures, Finnish officials found it helpful to use aspects of the first OECD EAG as references for setting up their own system. Furthermore they drew some comfort from the difficulty in educational evaluation reported there, of verifying relationships between input and output, even when input and output indicators taken separately are both valid and precise (Yrjönsuuri, 1995). Finland stated that it had already used earlier IEA results to compare its own pupils' performances with those from other countries.

What do the IEA and IAEP surveys cover?

The first point to make about IEA and IAEP studies is their scale. In any given survey the numbers of countries involved usually ranged between ten and twenty. Almost all covered groups of subjects and at two or more age or stage levels. Mathematics and science have been the most frequently chosen subjects but, in addition to other curriculum subjects, there have been surveys of adult literacy and computers in schools. One of the most recent surveys, TIMSS, currently being repeated, tested the mathematics and science knowledge of nearly a half million students in more than 40 countries around the world during the 1995 school year. There is a useful analysis of some of the studies in a review for OFSTED (Reynolds and Farrell, 1996). It tabulates and reports, in relation to England, some implications of the main findings in mathematics and science.

The Third International Mathematics and Science Study has been the largest, most comprehensive, and most rigorous international study of student achievement ever undertaken. Conducted by IEA and co-ordinated by Boston College in the USA, TIMSS tested students in mathematics and science at five grade levels. All countries that participated in TIMSS were required to test pupils in the two grades with the largest proportion of 13-year-olds (seventh and eighth grades in most countries). Many TIMSS countries also tested pupils in the grades with the largest proportion of 9-year-olds (third and fourth grades in most countries) and pupils in their final year of secondary school (covering several grades in some countries). Complementing the achievement tests, TIMSS administered a broad array of background questionnaires. Collecting data from pupils, teachers and headteachers, as well as the system-level information from each of the participating countries, gave TIMSS the potential to examine differences in levels of performance in relation to a wide variety of variables associated with the contexts within which education takes place, including the content and structure of curricula.

While there were criticisms that the same organizations, largely American-based, have increasingly been involved in running the IEA and IAEP studies, with an associated risk of cultural bias in tests and approaches, there are very few institutions in the world which are capable of being contracted to organize such large exercises, or analyse the data sets. The TIMSS organization was sensitive to these criticisms, and tried to address them in the design of its tests and questionnaires. Recently, however, there have been moves by the European Union and the OECD (which has a world-wide membership of more than twenty nations) to commission institutions in other countries, in consortia, to lead such international surveys, thus giving a greater spread of expertise, and an opportunity to counter claims of bias, particularly claims from non-English speaking countries. That major international comparative surveys have a value is underlined by the keenness of such bodies to increase their validity and continue their use.

What are sources of weakness in major comparative studies?

The OFSTED review of international surveys (Reynolds and Farrell, 1996) sets out some of the strengths and weaknesses of IEA-type studies. The authors emphasize difficulties which stem from trying to address two basic problems, the fact that samples of pupils must be compared in their performance on the same skills, or same bodies of knowledge, and the need to try to ensure that the educational causes of any differences between national samples are separated from any other possible non-educational causes.

Devising test items which can be stated with confidence to measure the same skills or knowledge across different countries, with or without translation, is no easy matter and can never be fully achieved. Difficulties arise in choosing aspects of the curriculum to test, given that there can be different content emphases, different methods and types of contexts used for teaching, and different aims in teaching specific topics. While a particular topic may be taught to the same stage across countries, the time of teaching could fall before or after the date chosen for testing. Further, the form of testing can interact with what is being measured, and potentially could affect differences in scores between countries where, for example, pupils are used to completing objective tests within a specific time frame, and those where this is not a familiar method of assessment (as would be the case for Britain).

On the question of non-educational factors, while the range of factors likely to be affecting the test results may be able to be postulated and listed, the relative weighting of these across countries, and the way they operate, cannot be reliably determined. If it were possible (within the constraints of cost) to conduct studies with the same sample of pupils over time, using a 'cohort' design, then allowance might be able to be made for the different starting points in different countries, and statistical analyses used to adjust for background factors.

Reynolds and Farrell (1996) also list a number of research design and sampling issues, some of which were addressed by TIMSS. These include:

- The basic design of the IEA studies, which were concerned to explain country against country variation, may itself have been responsible for problems. Generally, a small number of schools, each possessing a large number of students, were selected, making valid comparisons between schools difficult once factors such as school type, socio-economic status of students and catchment areas were taken into account. Statistics may also be unstable because of the small numbers. (In TIMSS the number of schools were increased and usually sampled about 25 pupils in one class per stage.)
- Curriculum subjects were surveyed separately, making it difficult to provide an integrated picture of schools in different countries. (In TIMSS, however, the same pupils were assessed in both mathematics and science.)
- There is considerable difficulty in designing tests which sample acceptably the curricula in all countries. (Though in TIMSS there was a mapping of the performance of each country against an analysis of its own curriculum, and an analysis of these which indicated that the items were reasonably fair and relevant to the curricula in the majority of countries.)
- There have been very large variations in the response rates across countries. These make interpretation of scores difficult even after statistical adjustment. In the IAEP in 1990, for example, of those schools originally approached to participate, actual involvement varied from 70 per cent to 100 per cent across countries. Pupil participation rates varied from 73 per cent to 98 per cent of those selected. In the IEA Second Science Study, the pupil response rate varied from 99.05 per cent (in Japan) to 61.97 per cent (in England). (In TIMSS there was a strict cut-off response level below which a country could not take part.)
- Sometimes the samples of students used are not representative of the country as

a whole (e.g. Reynolds quotes one of the IAEP studies as using one area of Italy as a surrogate for the whole country).

- There can be variations in the timing of school tests, resulting in students of different mean ages in different countries.
- Choice of certain 'grades' or ages for study may not generate similar sampling populations for different countries. Reynolds refers to the IEA Second Science Study (1990), where the mean ages of the country samples for the 14-year-old students ranged actually from 13.9 to 15.1 years (Reynolds and Farrell, 1996). Given the known relationships between age, length of time in school and achievement, this variation may have been responsible for some of the country differences. (For example, a similar factor might affect the relative performance of pupils in Scotland and England where different regulations for age on starting school mean that, on average, Scottish pupils in a given year stage are on average six months younger than their English counterparts.)
- Policies in different countries concerning 'keeping children down' and 'repeating' or 'putting children up a year' may generate difficulties of comparison.
- Variations in the proportion of children taking part in some studies in each country made it difficult to make comparisons. (Reynolds, *ibid.*, refers to the sampling for the second IAEP study (IAEP2 in 1990), where the restriction of the Israeli sample to Hebrew-speaking public schools meant that the reference 'full' population contained only 71 per cent of Israeli children.)

The Third International Mathematics and Science Study

This is not the place to provide a comprehensive description of TIMSS but it is worth referring to some of the ways TIMSS attempted to address some of the problems set out above and to increase the rigour of the sampling and analysis (Stevenson, 1998). Extreme care went into the co-ordination and preparation, but, because of its complexity, some difficulties inevitably remained. Not all of the nations were able to follow the recommendations for selecting participants. Similarly, it was not possible to ensure that all of the questions in the tests nor all of the items in the questionnaires were equally relevant to all countries. Even so, vigorous efforts were made to obtain the approval of representatives from the 40 countries before items were included.

Despite such problems, the study has been widely commended for the depth and scope of its findings. The task was enormous, not least in the development of relevant and interesting items for the tests and questionnaires which could be applied across different cultures, the translation and checking of these including variants within English, the selection of schools and gaining the co-operation of school authorities, and then analysing and reporting on the results from more than 500,000 participants. Further, because countries participated by choice, and each country had to pay for the collection of its own data, there was no way of requiring countries to participate in all components of the study or even parts of components. As a result, some countries, such as China, chose not to participate at all because of the expense. Others took part in only some population levels or particular components. Local difficulties could be significant in determining the form of participation. For example, in England and Scotland there were concerns over teacher co-operation at the time for administering the tests, and the school and teacher questionnaires. Only slimmed down questionnaires could be used, and these had to be negotiated with education authorities and TIMSS co-ordinators.

Each pupil's test booklet, expected at age 13 to take about 90 minutes to complete, contained a subset of all the mathematics (or science) items. There were eight booklets in all each containing a sample across all aspects being tested. Pupils in the same class sat different booklets. In addition to these 'paper and pencil' tests there were 'performance assessments' (practical tests). The questionnaires, separately administered, gathered details of features such as teaching approaches, school characteristics, resources, pupil and teacher attitudes, and parental expectations.

A key issue in sampling the populations under study was whether participants should be selected on age or number of years in school. Each raised different issues for future comparative analyses. It was decided to go for age-related samples but use existing school structures, and draw single class samples from the grades containing most 9-year-olds, from the grades containing most 13-year-olds and have a sample of those at the end of their secondary schooling. At each population level it meant that sampling could be across one or two grades or stages and, for the third population, several. Thus there were still age differences within samples.

As has been mentioned above, there were explicit criteria for determining whether all parts of a country's data could be used. These were based on the response level from schools and pupils within the chosen sample for that country. For example there was an overall requirement of 75 per cent participation, having allowed some substitution to accommodate schools which dropped out from the original sample. In addition to these rigid rules there were guidelines on within-school selection of classes, which had to be done randomly, assuming pupils were enrolled in appropriate grades. Each country's sampling plan and all details of samples had to be approved by an independent reviewer. Nevertheless it was not always possible to meet all of the sampling criteria, even though there was significant pressure on countries since inclusion in analyses required these minimal levels of compliance. In the final presentation of TIMSS results, countries which could not meet criteria had their results separately displayed. (Scotland missed a response rate cut-off by a small margin and for some data is reported in a separate part of tables.) Significant, however, in determining the level of performance of a country's pupils could be the status given to the testing within the samples, including the encouragement to complete tests and not miss out questions or items. A key determinant of differences between performance by French pupils and their Scottish equivalents in a small comparative study of mathematics in 1994 was the difference in the way the tests were handled by teachers in classrooms. The formal conditions of administration of the tests in France, as part of the national assessment and league tables, contrasted with the relatively informal arrangements within the samples selected from Scottish classes. It is thus likely that, for TIMSS, in some countries the testing might be seen as an intrusion into the work of a class, asking

pupils to answer questions in an unfamiliar format and with no obvious end benefi
to the teacher, class or pupil, or perhaps administered at a time when the value c
'national testing' was a matter of public debate and dispute. This would contras
with other contexts where the format of the tests may not be so unfamiliar, an
where pupils were tested regularly, or where the administration of tests wa
preceded by an encouragement to perform at the highest level for the benefit of th
state, and for the increased status of the school.

Reactions to TIMSS and similar studies

The outcomes of TIMSS were awaited with anticipation across countries, as wa
their incorporation into the subsequent 1998 OECD EAG report.

> The introduction of a national curriculum has failed to arrest England's tumbl
> down the international primary maths performance tables. The latest assessmen
> of how our nine-year-olds compare with their contemporaries in 25 othe
> countries makes fairly dismal reading and will harden the Government's resolve
> to improve numeracy standards in primary schools. (TES, 1997, n.p.)

The reactions in the USA demonstrated the interest and potential value of such
international comparative studies. In a perceptive 1998 review, Harold W
Stevenson looks back at the arguments which flowed in the USA following the
publication of the TIMSS results in 1996. The context and some of the queries
raised about such surveys are described in its foreword (Finn, 1998):

> The results from TIMSS, the Third International Mathematics and Science
> Study, have bombarded America over the past several years. Some of the news
> was cheerful: our fourth graders scored among the best in the world in math and
> science. But our eighth grade scores were mediocre, and our twelfth grade scores
> were downright miserable. The longer our kids remain in school, it seemed, the
> worse they do, at least in math and science, at least in relation to most of the rest
> of the planet. Then came the backlash. From education 'experts' and pundits
> came word that we need not be upset by the TIMSS results. One main line of
> attack tried to invalidate the tests and comparisons on 'technical' grounds. There
> must be something wrong with the tests or how they were administered or how
> their results were analysed. The other major critique – actually more like a dose
> of Prozac – said the country is doing fine so how could the schools have a
> problem? 'Low Scores are No Disgrace' soothed one. 'Stupid Students, Smart
> Economy?' asked another. (p. v)

Stevenson then points out that while a primary goal of international comparative
studies is to assess the levels of achievement of students in various countries, an
equally important goal is to attempt to understand and explain the bases of
whatever differences emerge:

> Is it not time to accept the fact that U.S. students, except perhaps in the lower

elementary grades, experience more serious difficulties in learning mathematics and science than do their peers in many other industrialised countries? Or, stated another way, is there any convincing evidence that students from typical American middle or high schools are as effective or more effective in mathematics and science than their peers in other industrialised countries? There might be reason to answer these questions less confidently if TIMSS were the only study that had been conducted. But this is not the case. A series of both large- and small-scale studies has yielded the same conclusion: U.S. schools are in need of attention and improvement. No one of these studies is perfect, but the accumulation of carefully conducted studies, all yielding similar conclusions and covering several decades, compels the reviewer to reach this conclusion.

Arguing that schools are better now than they were a decade or two ago begs the central question: Are US schools competitive with the schools found in other advanced industrialized nations, such as those of East Asia and Central Europe? TIMSS may make its most useful contribution to US education by demonstrating the dramatic differences that exist among schools throughout the world in their ability to impart information and skills to their pupils. For the US, the major contribution is to point out that, despite a high financial investment in education, US schools are clearly not among the world's most successful. (Stevenson, 1998, p. 17)

Interpreting and using the results of such studies

Beyond creating headlines at the time of publication do the outcomes of surveys such as TIMSS affect policy and practice? It has been a general comment on IEA-type studies that they were too superficial to be helpful in policy-making, in particular lacking the capability of taking on board local cultural and contextual issues (Watson, 1999). Thus while the curriculum analyses were of value for those who constructed the TIMSS tests, a conclusion such as 'Classroom practices really do differ considerably among countries' is itself of little use to policy-makers (Stevenson, 1998, p. 24).

One obvious value of dramatic headlines calling for action is that politicians can sometimes use them to ease the promotion of preferred schemes, whether or not surveys actually bring hard evidence to support the particular approach.

The influence of international comparisons of pupil performance has grown steadily since the First International Mathematics Study was carried out in 1964. By the late 1980s there were continual attempts to use international comparisons to justify a return to 'basics', in terms of both curriculum content and teaching methods. And this trend has continued following the publication of the Third International Maths and Science Study (TIMSS), which tested children aged 9 and 13 and young people in the final year of secondary school.

While I do not pretend that the numeracy of our pupils is satisfactory, some

recent reporting of international comparisons does not even attempt to represen
the facts accurately. But then there was never any doubt that TIMSS, whic
reported its results in the form of an international league table, was a thoroughl
political activity. The results for the 13-year-old sample were known by Ma
1996, but the testing agencies and government officials in each country wer
required to maintain confidentiality until November 20. It was rumoured tha
the delay was to ensure that the poor results of the United States did not affec
the outcome of the American presidential elections. While this may be untrue
the link between international comparisons and British politics is clear. Th
only country to break the agreed embargo on releasing TIMSS results was th
UK, and for political reasons.

On July 3, 1996, by order of British education ministers, the comparativel:
low ranking of England in mathematics was leaked to *The Times* and wa
criticised in a front-page headline, 'English pupils plummet in world math
league'.

Ministers risked incurring the wrath of the international community becaus
they feared teachers' reaction to the introduction of both mental arithmetic anc
calculator-free papers into national mathematics tests, and wanted to provide a
legitimate reason for this action. (Brown, 1998, n.p.)

Links to School Effectiveness

Clearly, neither league tables of countries nor league tables of schools can tell the
whole story or readily lead to practical outcomes. They may be of headline interes
to the press, but for educational practitioners and national policy-makers, of more
critical concern for the long term should be the answers to 'Why?' questions
Relative standing on average national scores is potentially less illuminating thar
the spread of achievement within countries, or the differences between countries ir
the amounts of such variation; particularly if the differences can be related to factors
known to influence the relative effectiveness of schools. In a similar way, research or
school effectiveness and improvement has moved towards exploring the variations
within schools and examining, for example, why some schools do well and others
poorly in similar locations. These studies have usually found answers in the effects
of school leadership and planning, and emphases on quality, school ethos and self-
evaluation as well as on teaching approaches. Are there national equivalents?

For the USA the use of single average figures for the whole country in TIMSS
league tables can be particularly misleading, since the diversity of the school
population and of performance in a country the size of the USA is most pronounced.
Australia and the USA show the same average level of mathematics performance in
TIMSS, but weaker performers in the USA have markedly lower scores than their
counterparts in Australia. On the other hand stronger performers in the USA score
more highly than stronger performers in Australia (OECD, 1998). Further, when
the differences within the USA are examined, even at a relatively superficial level,
one can find that

Asian American students out-score all students in the world in math and science. Advantaged urban students of all races in America score better than students in all but one other nation, Taiwan, and the difference in these scores is insignificant. White students in the U.S. score better than students in all but two other nations, Taiwan and Korea. [But] there are still segments of the U.S. population which are not doing well. In fact, the differences in scores within the U.S. are far greater overall than the differences between nations. (Hitz, 1996, n.p.)

Examples of relatively small within-country variation would be Japan and Korea, where the spread of achievement is much narrower and over 75 per cent of the students in Japan and Korea score above the OECD average. It was the fact that many Pacific Rim countries scored relatively highly in this way that prompted North American and European (British) educators to try to see whether there were school-level practices in those countries which could be transferred, or to hypothesize whether underlying cultural factors might play a subtle but significant role. For example, was the emphasis by teachers on ensuring that all members of a mixed ability group kept up with the work of the class a key factor? The OFSTED review (Reynolds and Farrell, 1996) is an example of such an approach which ultimately involved visits to examine school practices. A Scottish report recommending changes in the teaching of mathematics was a reaction to both TIMSS and Scottish Assessment of Achievement survey data. It followed visits to high-scoring countries in the Far East and Europe (SOEID, 1997).

The size of the IEA data sets appears to lend them to analyses similar to those developed in school effectiveness research. Through such approaches it might be possible to see whether international differences can be explained through different country weightings applied to factors such as those shown to be important in determining school effectiveness in the UK or in the USA. These include educational leadership, classroom processes, and the use of direct instruction. If so, then practices might be transferable and lessons learned.

Studies to date, by leading school effectiveness statisticians, have yet to provide fruitful outcomes. For example, reanalysing the IEA Reading Literacy Study of 9-year-olds found no readily forthcoming explanations of achievement which they could apply across national samples. In trying to use a statistical model of school effectiveness at a country level 'each country appeared to have its own unique "educational production function". Factors that work in some countries do not work in others' (Scheerens and Bosker, 1997, p. 261). This is not to say that such studies could not work but much more control would be needed over the original survey data collection. There may need to be pre-tests with the same samples (with the near impossibility of tracing the samples across years in different countries), increased numbers of teacher respondents and different ways of assessing factors beyond self-reporting by teachers. The organizational and time costs of such extra requirements could make the process prohibitive. Alternative approaches may lie in case studies closely tied to existing surveys, following up pointers consistently derived from the major studies.

Follow-up to international league tables

Differences between England and Pacific Rim countries identified or quoted by Reynolds (Reynolds and Farrell, 1996) as being possible explanations for their relatively superior performances include: cultural features, characteristics of the educational system, school and classroom factors. Some of these, such as length of time in school, seem unlikely to be key factors on their own, though it is of interest to note that there was a national study to examine the use of 'time in school' in the USA. It was set up on the basis that international data showed that 'students in other post-industrial democracies received twice as much instruction in core academic areas during high school' as did American students (National Commission on Time and Learning, 1994, n.p.).

An effective mix of factors influencing performance, however, could well be, as suggested, the combination of cultural features such as the relatively high status of teachers, a high value upon learning and education, high aspirations of parents for their children and high levels of commitment from children who are keen to do well at school, within a culture which puts an emphasis on the role of effort and the importance of an individual's striving and working hard. Having identified this cocktail, however, can it be proven to be the cause? Are there not curriculum or classroom instruction factors at play also? How do they interact? And, if that were the cocktail, could it be transferred to another context? Surely only with a major policy shift in education and society could another country develop similar characteristics and produce significant and long-lasting effects. While such changes might be achievable, they would take longer than the life of an average government, and might therefore, in any event, not be politically viable.

Not many or all of these subtle differences in practices and influences can readily emerge from the main major survey data sets. The very restrictions on the range of questions imposed by financial and organizational practicalities cause factors to be confounded, for example, when teachers self-report on their schools and practices. Most insights come from small-scale separate comparative work. However, this was recognized by the planners of TIMSS and as part of that survey there were parallel case studies and video classroom studies which were carried out in the USA, Germany and Japan. Stevenson explains that this was no mean feat, and not a cheap exercise (Stevenson, 1998):

> The first impulse is to rely on questionnaires as a means of obtaining relevant information. Indeed, questionnaires are an obvious choice when it is necessary to collect large amounts of data on an array of topics at the least expense. How could information from all the participants in TIMSS have been obtained if the organizers had not relied on questionnaires? Case studies, which involve observations, long conversations, and interviews, are much more time-consuming, require more highly trained researchers, and are necessarily more expensive than questionnaire studies. Nevertheless, through the use of relaxed interactions and observations in everyday settings, case studies offer the possibility of gaining a depth of understanding that is difficult to reach with more

impersonal questionnaires, especially when the studies involve different cultures and languages.

Because of the magnitude of TIMSS and the limited amount of time available to conduct it, it was impossible in the case studies to cover all facets of education or to include all of the participating nations. As a result, the project was limited to the four topics and three countries mentioned earlier. As far as we know, this is the largest, most complex cross-cultural project using the case study method that has ever been conducted in the social sciences or education. (p. 19)

Among the findings of the case studies were claims of significant differences, for example in the ways in which teachers' maintained their professional knowledge, in particularly contrasting German and American teachers' lack of interactive updating compared with Japanese equivalents. Another feature reported as influencing scores were the relatively poorly organized revision arrangements for American pupils preparing for examinations compared with their compatriots.

The separate pilot video studies of classrooms, despite being limited by recording only single lessons and not sequences, report illuminating findings:

The viewing group was … asked to determine the quality of the lessons by judging the percentage of lessons that required the students to engage in deductive reasoning. This occurred in 21 per cent of the German lessons and in 62 per cent of the Japanese lessons. It was never found in the U.S. lessons.

[Another] type of judgement made in viewing the tapes was whether the teacher merely stated the principle by which a type of problem could be solved or attempted to help the children develop an understanding of the basis for the solution. It is evident … that vastly more topics in the U.S. than in the German or Japanese tapes contained concepts whose application was simply stated rather than developed logically. [Comparing] … the frequency with which lessons relied on the development of understanding rather than acquisition of routine skills … This occurred nearly three times as often among Japanese as among U.S. and German lessons. (Stevenson, 1998, p. 22)

Thus while the large surveys can provide powerful data of relative levels of performance, and hint at cultural factors such as attitude to school and learning, the more detailed analysis which would be essential to formulate policy at national or school level would seem to require more contextual interpretation. This, at present, relies on case studies and visits. The former are particularly costly, and the latter present problems of validity.

Self-evaluation

Since the early work in school effectiveness lists have been developed of key factors for school success. For example, for primary schools such lists would include: purposeful leadership by the senior school staff, and the involvement of teachers; consistency among teachers; structured sessions involving intellectually challenging teaching; a work-centred environment; limited focus within sessions;

maximum communication between teachers and pupils; record keeping; parental involvement; and positive climate (Mortimore *et al.*, 1988). Many of these are reflected in a set of characteristics published by Her Majesty's Inspectors of Schools (HMI) in England as a follow-up to inspection reports on good practice in schools, and separately by HMI in Scotland in a series of reports on what was judged to be 'effective practice' (SOED, 1988, 1989), and which have led to work on school self-evaluation.

In Britain, interest in school effectiveness and school improvement became intertwined with government moves to change the way in which schools were managed and quality controlled (with suggestions that politicians were quoting research out of context to support their policy ends [Goldstein and Myers, 1997]). The government policy initiatives were characterized, particularly in England, by changing the nature and increasing the frequency of inspection, requiring league tables of school results, diluting the role and power of local authorities, and establishing a National Curriculum and national tests. While in both England and Scotland the government aim was to improve quality and drive up standards, the approaches differed, and have continued to follow separate paths. The emphasis in England has been based on assumption that it is possible to 'improve through inspection', by targeting 'failing' schools, avoiding bottom-up approaches and rejecting self-evaluation as 'soft'.

The Scottish HMI reports specifically encouraged all schools to evaluate their own performance against the examples of effective practice in both academic and social aspects of school life. These reports were followed in 1992 by the publication of a series of performance indicators for schools to use, and then in 1996 by a seminal handbook on school self-evaluation *How Good Is Our School?* (SOEID, 1996), and subsequently performance targets which focused on raising standards of achievement were set for each school. The development of this handbook was part of a strategy to complement the external inspection by HMI with explicit guidance on school-based evaluation and planning. Thus national reports on 'Quality and Standards in Scottish Schools' by the head of HM Inspectorate evaluating the educational system at a national level, based on external HMI inspections, would eventually be mirrored by equivalent reports at school and education authority level, based upon the same or equivalent performance indicators.

European studies of school self-evaluation

It is of interest to note that the European Commission, while exploring ways of providing cross-national data, is also now focusing on educational effectiveness in Europe. It is pursuing an approach based on self-evaluation, drawing heavily on Scottish experience in school effectiveness research and the use of performance indicators. The policy intention is to raise awareness about the need to evaluate secondary education in Europe, to enhance existing national procedures and to give a European dimension to quality evaluation, and to support the exchange of information and experiences (MacBeath *et al.*, 1999). A pilot project with 101 schools across Europe has explored how self-evaluation can be developed in each country, even where there has been very little recent positive experience of evaluation systems; and how the outcomes from such school-based activity can be acted upon to help to raise the quality of national education systems. The intention is not to devise a model which can be applied across the board but to develop approaches, with basically equivalent aims, but reflecting the different national contexts, and the historical, social, cultural and political situation in each country.

Conclusion

There is a tension in international comparative studies between the practicality of complex survey and measurement techniques, and the ability to obtain readily interpretable findings from the data. Surveys to be valid have to be capable of being accommodated on top of existing school and educational system practices, including timetabling, curriculum and workload constraints. As national systems strive to improve in response to the quality concerns the surveys highlight, the demands on teachers and administrations seem to increase.

A report on a recent seminar (OECD/CERI, 1999) which was examining the use of research in education compared with that in other professions, commented:

An underlying question of these CERI discussions has been whether the education sector can produce, disseminate and use knowledge in ways that help transform its productivity. Education systems have often been under fire from policy-makers and others for failing to improve their performance; educational researchers for failing to provide practitioners with the tools to do so. At the present forum the criticism came in a somewhat different form – that of scepticism (from some quarters) about whether educational research and knowledge could ever produce the required solutions, since it is impossible to carry out educational research in a laboratory that replicates sufficiently the complex and context-specific conditions of the classrooms in which innovation has to be applied. (p. 6)

Education systems are complex and multivariate, and clearly difficult to understand using survey instruments alone, but that does not mean that a combination of methods could not provide useful policy advice. At the same time, making policy decisions in the absence of precise knowledge, has not prevented the mounting of major national initiatives in education in the past.

References

Anderson, C. A. (1961) 'Methodology of comparative education'. *International Review of Education*, 8(1), 7–8.

Brown, M. (1998) 'Findings lost amid political jockeying'. *Times Educational Supplement*, 20 March.

Finn, C. E. (1998) 'Foreword' to H. W. Stevenson, 'A TIMSS primer: lessons and implications for U.S. education', *Fordham Report*, 2 (7), July. Available at http://www.edexcellence.net/library/timss.html

Foshay, A. W., Thorndike, R. L., Hotyat, F., Pidgeon, D. A. and Walker, D. A. (1962) *Educational Achievements of Thirteen-Year-Olds in Twelve Countries.* Hamburg: UNESCO Institute for Education.

Goldstein, H. and Myers, K. (1997) *School Effectiveness Research: A Bandwagon, a Hijack or a Journey towards Enlightenment?* BERA Conference paper and Education-Line document available at http://www.leeds.ac.uk/educol/

Gray, J., Hopkins, D., Reynolds, D., Wilcox, B., Farrell, S. and Jesson, D. (1999) *Improving Schools: Performance and Potential.* Buckingham: Open University Press.

Hitz, R. (1996) *Beware International Comparisons of Educational Achievement.* Montana State University College of Education. Available at http://www.montana.edu/wwwpb/univ/hitz.html

MacBeath, J. (1993) 'Developing international educational indicators'. *Scottish Educational Review,* 25 (1), 46–52.

MacBeath, J., Meuret, D., Schratz, M. and Jakobsen, L. B. (1999) *Evaluating Quality in School Education: A European Pilot Project.* Brussels: European Commission.

Mortimore, P., Sammons, P., Stoll, S., Lewis, D. and Ecob, B. (1988) *School Matters.* Wells, Somerset: Open Books.

National Commission on Education (1993) *Learning to Succeed.* Heinemann: London.

National Commission on Excellence in Education (NCEE) (1983) *A Nation at Risk: The Imperative for Educational Reform.* Washington, DC: US Department of Education.

National Commission on Time and Learning (1994) *Prisoners of Time.* Washington, DC: US Government. Available at http://www.emich.edu/public/emu_programs/tlc/toc.html

OECD (1997) *Education Policy Analysis 1997.* OECD: Paris.

OECD (1998) *Education at a Glance 1998: Key Comparisons and Trends.* Paris: OECD.

OECD/CERI (1999) *Measuring Knowledge in Learning Economies and Societies.* Draft report on Washington Forum, organized jointly by the National Science Foundation and the Centre for Educational Research and Innovation, OECD, 17–18 May. Paris: OECD.

Plomp, T. (1997) 'IEA: what it is and does: mission, history', in S. Hegarty (ed.) *The Role of Research in Mature Education Systems.* Slough: NFER.

Reynolds, D. and Farrell, S. (1996) *Worlds Apart?* Office for Standards in Education. London: HMSO.

Scheerens, J. and Bosker, R. (1997) *The Foundations of Educational Effectiveness.* Oxford: Pergamon.

Scheerens, J. and Creemers, B.P.M. (1989) 'Conceptualising school effectiveness'. In *Developments in School Effectiveness Research* (Special issue), *International Journal of Educational Research,* 13, 691–706.

SOED (1988) *Effective Secondary Schools.* Edinburgh: Scottish Office Education Department, HMSO.

SOED (1989) *Effective Primary Schools.* Edinburgh: Scottish Office Education Department, HMSO.

SOEID (1996) *How Good Is Our School?* Edinburgh: Scottish Office Education and Industry Department, HMSO.

SOEID (1997) *Improving Mathematics Education 5–14.* HM Inspectors of Schools. Edinburgh: Scottish Office Education and Industry Department.

Stevenson, H.W. (1998) 'A TIMSS primer: lessons and implications for U.S. education'. *Fordham Report,* 2 (7), July. Available at http://www.edexcellence.net/library/timss.html

TES (1997) 'Maths failure lingers after curriculum revolution'. *Times Educational Supplement*, 13 June.

Watson, K. (1999) 'Comparative educational research: the need for reconceptualisation and fresh insights'. *Compare*, 29 (3), 233–48.

Yrjönsuuri, Y. (ed.) (1995) *Evaluating Education in Finland*. Helsinki: National Board of Education.

8

Education and Training

Christopher Winch

Any explanation has its foundation in training. (Educators ought to remember this.) (Wittgenstein, 1967 p. 419)

Introduction

Training has a very bad press amongst educators. It is often thought of as the opposite of education (Abbs, 1987). This is a harmful belief because it means that many teachers are reluctant to even consider using techniques that may actually benefit their pupils. The unpopularity of training has deep and complex cultural roots, the full uncovering of which is beyond the scope of one article. Briefly these are the belief that training is authoritarian and that authority is harmful, the confusion of training with conditioning and the association of training with very narrow forms of vocational preparation. I will try first to show that training is not the same thing as conditioning and, second, that the belief that either education or training can be accomplished without the recognition of authority of some kind is an illusion. Preservation of that illusion leads to a reliance on *covert* forms of conditioning. It would be better to recognize that the role of the teacher as someone who is *in authority* because s/he is *an authority* (Peters, 1967) on the acquisition of certain kinds of knowledge and skill, would lead to a more clear-sighted perception of what is necessary both for education and for training. In arguing this second part of the case for training I will be making an extended criticism of some of the ideas in Rousseau's *Emile* (Rousseau, 1762), from which I believe that much of the antipathy towards training stems.

Although it is common for liberal educators to warn that education is in danger of being displaced by training of a narrowly vocational kind, comparatively little attention has been given by them to the concept of training. A notable example is

R. F. Dearden. Unfortunately his account of the educational importance of training is flawed by his belief that training precludes understanding, which, I hope to show, is a misunderstanding of the nature of training (cf. Dearden, 1984) and consequently, the role that it plays in education tends to be undervalued. The result of this neglect is that both liberal and vocational education have suffered. Liberal education has suffered from the influence of progressivism which has tended to downplay the importance of training in learning generally and vocational education has suffered by adopting the impoverished model of training that liberal educators have rightly associated with behaviourism (cf. Hyland, 1993). In addition, vocational education in the UK has tended to be based on a narrow training model that placed very little emphasis on the need for workers to understand the processes which they operated. This dismissive attitude to vocational education can be found in the work of Adam Smith, for example:

The first invention of such beautiful machines [clocks and watches], indeed, and even that of some of the instruments of work employed in making them, must, no doubt, have been the work of deep thought and long time, and may justly be considered as among the happiest efforts of human ingenuity. But when both have been fairly invented and are well understood, to explain to any young man, in the completest manner, how to apply the instrument and how to construct the machines, certainly cannot well require more than the lessons of a few weeks; perhaps those of a few days might be sufficient. (Smith, 1981, p. 226)

Smith's idea that vocational education is a matter of training in a few mechanical skills, easily learned, in such a way as to involve little judgement or understanding by the worker, has done much to fix in the minds of educators and the wider public that training is a low-level and almost mindless form of learning.

Training, however, is a complex concept which is important for many aspects of human learning, from early childhood to adulthood. It is to be distinguished from concepts like *conditioning* on the one hand and *discovery* on the other, although it has connections with both. Training is not an alternative to education because the two concepts belong to different categories; education concerns the long-term preparation of an individual for life, training is usually concerned with the shorter-term acquisition of abilities, attitudes and dispositions. But the succesful acquisition of these is an essential aspect of education and so training should have its place at the heart of any worthwhile educational endeavour, whether it be liberal or vocational. On the other hand, a form of training that is sufficiently lengthy and broad in the range of knowledge, skill and understanding that it covers, may well qualify for the term 'vocational education' rather than 'job training'. The point is that although training and education are distinct concepts, the boundaries between the two are not clear in every instance. It is not my aim to argue that training should be a substitute for education, but to suggest that it should be recognized as having an important role to play in education.

One of the major problems inherent in any attempt to deal satisfactorily with the concept of training is its varied nature. Training can be an important aspect of first language learning, of the acquisition of literacy and numeracy, of the acquisition of physical skills, of moral, aesthetic and religious sensibility as well as of vocational education and preparation (Kazepides, 1991). First, however, it is necessary to distinguish training from conditioning.

Training and conditioning

A major item on the charge sheet against training is that it is no better than *conditioning* and thus that it narrows human abilities rather than broadens them. Here is a typical complaint from a well-known contemporary liberal educator.

> We talk about 'potty training', 'dog training', 'training an army', 'training engineers' or 'technicians'. It would seem that training invariably involves a narrowing down of the consciousness to master certain techniques or skills. (Abbs, 1987)

Two highly questionable assumptions are made in this passage. The first is that dog training is comparable with training engineers, and the second is that learning skills and techniques involves a narrowing down of the consciousness. Both these assumptions are wrong and seeing this is one of the keys to understanding that training has far more to offer education than is often dreamed of by the majority of liberal educators. Even the model of animal learning that behaviourist psychologists call 'operant conditioning' is quite inadequate to grasp what an animal learns when it is trained.

Associative learning theory concentrates on the relationship between two events, E1 and E2, and the way in which learners associate the two events. One of these events is known by psychologists as the 'important event' because it is capable of eliciting a response without previous conditioning. Such events are also known as 'reinforcers' because they strengthen other responses. For example, a bodily injury is capable of eliciting a response of flight without there having been any previous conditioning to flight. If an animal has been conditioned to flight by another stimulus, say a loud noise, the reinforcer will strengthen that response.

In *classical conditioning* theory, the important event is preceded by a stimulus, and the typical result is that the signalling stimulus comes to elicit the same response as the important event. For example, a puff of air induces blinking and will do so in the absence of previous conditioning. When the puff of air is preceded by a light, eventually the light will elicit blinking in the way that the puff of air does.

In *operant* or *instrumental* conditioning (Lieberman, 1990, pp. 33–4), the important event follows a response rather than a stimulus and the result is a change in the probability of the response on subsequent occasions. In *reinforcement* the consequence is attractive and results in a strengthening of the response that was instrumental in producing the reinforcement. So, for example, if a child is given sweets each time he cries, he is more likely to cry in the future. When the important event is not attractive, it will tend to diminish frequency of the response. This negative reinforcement is sometimes known misleadingly as *punishment* although it cannot have any of the normative overtones of what we ordinarily mean by 'punishment'.

Conditioning theory concedes that the behaviour of an organism is not completely determined by conditioning, by allowing for unconditioned response. But this should not lead us to think that the processes of either operant or classical conditioning in any way approach the complexity of training. In order to appreciate this, it is necessary to see that the behaviourist tradition on which contemporary associative learning theory is based, models itself on a value-neutral system of observation and description. In order for a theory of associative learning to be built up, it is necessary that investigation of the theory is carried out in such a way that the values and beliefs of the researchers do not intrude on the research and its description. Furthermore, since it is necessary to study the effects of particular selected stimuli and the responses that they evoke, the variety of stimuli available to a subject have to be limited if one is going to find out how it reacts to *particular* stimuli. These imperatives mean that research into associative learning needs to be carried out under experimental conditions, and descriptions of such work tend to be couched in a value-neutral 'data language' (cf. Taylor, 1964, for a critique of the idea of a data language).

These constraints have an important consequence. Since the theory of conditioning is concerned with the repeated application of positive and negative reinforcers, it is necessary to be able to identify and reidentify these on numerous occasions. This means that expressions such as 'the same reinforcer' have to be interpreted strictly so that they can be defined in experimental terms. This is to ensure that findings made in laboratory conditions are *reliable*, that is, can be replicated in future experiments. It does not follow that they are *valid*, that they can serve as general accounts of how the animals learn. In fact, the training of animals, although a much simpler affair than the training of humans, is more complex than the operant conditioning model suggests. To appreciate this, it is necessary to realize that the expression 'of the same type', when applied in non-experimental conditions, has to be interpreted much more loosely than when it is applied in the laboratory. An animal, when trained in a reasonably complex activity, has got to interpret the stimulus or signal to a certain degree and has to exercise flexibility in responding. Neither or these possibilities are allowed for in the operant conditioning model.

For example, a dog that is trained to round up sheep is usually expected to respond to a variety of signals which tell it that certain manoeuvres are called for. These signals are given in contrasting physical circumstances and will vary in volume depending on distance. They will also be related to a context which the dog has to interpret; it is expected to perform a manoeuvre of a certain type in connection with sheep in a certain configuration which will be unique to that occasion; this does not mean, however, that we are committed to saying that it entertains thoughts (cf. Malcolm, 1977). The dog has got to bring the sheep from one place to another efficiently, without causing them harm and without counting on the willing co-operation of the sheep themselves. It has to exercise perception, judgement, patience and audacity. In other words, its mental capacities are employed to the full.

The example shows us that successfully training a dog is a much greater and more complicated achievement than eliciting behaviour patterns in a rat in a maze through the use of operant conditioning techniques. Human training involves far more than dog training in many, if not the overwhelming majority of, cases. Both the training process and the outcome of training are more complex in the case of humans than they are in the case of animals. Perhaps the most important differences are that *language* plays a part in human training and that humans learn according to *rules*, and what they do may be corrected and commented upon. These rules require interpretation and evaluation. They can be taught, but the person trained has got to be able to use them in a wide variety of circumstances as well, in which the associated activities of interpretation and evaluation may well play a key part. There are some activities which we are trained to perform which are like conditioning and which do not require a great flexibility of response; Abbs's example of potty training would be one such. But it would be unwise to conclude that this was in any way typical of a trained response. As we have seen, Abbs's example of dog training could be applied to a dog rounding up sheep, and a closer consideration of this example suggests that training can lead to the exercise of mental and physical abilities of a high order, given the general capacities of dogs.

It would be odd to say of a dog that had been trained to round up sheep that this involved a narrowing down of its consciousness. If a dog that had been trained to round up sheep thereby lost its abilities to do other things which required the exercise of skill and judgement, then there might be grounds for saying it. But there is no reason to suppose this to be the case. The point applies to human training; a trained engineer, for example, has to follow rules, evaluate and interpret them and exercise skill, understanding and judgement in circumstances that are often unique to the occasion of their exercise. This hardly amounts to a narrowing down of the consciousness, particularly when we remind ourselves that, in becoming a trained engineer that individual is not thereby precluded from doing things that s/he already does, or learning things that s/he does not already know. These considerations should make us suspicious of Dearden's claim that training does not involve developing understanding. In many cases it is evident that training does exactly that.

The flight from training

We can now begin to partly answer the question: 'Why is training so unpopular with educators?' The manifest inadequacy of the theory of conditioning as an account of human, or even animal, learning has already been shown, and while it is right to be wary of conditioning as either an effective, or an ethically desirable, way of getting humans to learn anything, it has also been demonstrated that training is a concept quite distinct from that of conditioning and leads to the development of abilities that are more flexible than the responses evoked by conditioning. In addition, it carries no necessary connotations of ethical undesirability. One reason for suspicion of training on the part of educators is, therefore, quite unfounded.

It is now time to look at one of the other major reasons why training is viewed with suspicion, namely the influence of progressivism and the rise of anti-authoritarianism in educational thinking. Rousseau's educational prescriptions, which are to be found largely in *Emile* (Rousseau, 1762), are based on his desire to show how education should both promote, and proceed in accordance with, the maximum possible degree of human freedom. According to his thinking, the overt imposition of one will on another leads to harmful forms of *amour propre* (or self-respect), which in turn leads to resentment on the part of the learner against the teacher (Dent, 1988). By the imposition of the teacher's will, the consent of the learner is sacrificed to the detriment of further learning. Indeed, according to Rousseau, the overt imposition of one will upon another is likely to have detrimental consequences for character formation. Therefore, Rousseau's hypothetical pupil, Emile, learns through a process of discovery in practical situations where he has a need to learn. This rejection of authority in educational processes is crucial to an understanding of the rejection of training as a form of learning and will be returned to later. But, as we shall see, it rests on a fatal confusion of authority with power. Successful conditioning depends on the *power* of the conditioner over the conditioned; in the human case, training involves the recognition by the trainee of the *authority* of the trainer. The trainee and the trainer exist in a relationship bound by a common understanding. In the case of humans training other humans, the trainee understands that in order to acquire a skill he needs to follow the programme of instruction that the trainer provides. Without this consent to the authoritative position of the trainer, training would not work. Conditioning, on the other hand, operates through the power that the conditioner has over his subject, which often involves the use of force.

However, in order to achieve the desired result, Rousseau sets up situations which essentially manipulate Emile into learning what the tutor wants him to learn. There are numerous examples of this in *Emile* and, given that Rousseau does not think that a child fully acquires reason until the age of 12, and given also that he is averse to any use of training techniques, as these involve the submission of one will to another, it is difficult to see how else he could teach Emile anything. Thus the child is taught not to break things by learning what the lack of the thing broken will mean in his life.

He breaks the windows of his room; let the wind blow on him day and night and don't worry about colds; because he's better off with a cold than mad. (Rousseau, 1762, p. 122)

It is noteworthy, though, that if this lesson does not work, Rousseau recommends that the child be put in a room without windows in order to better appreciate what the lack of them means. Although formally the child is still learning through the appreciation of what the lack of something means, *covertly* the will of another has been imposed, since the child has been removed by an adult to a place where he can have this unpleasant experience. A more famous example is the account of how Emile finds his way back to the house, Montmorency. Emile is told that the forest is to the north of Montmorency and the following day he is taken for a walk in the forest without having eaten very much beforehand. Presently he becomes hungry, thirsty and lost; it is midday and Emile begins to cry. The tutor reminds Emile of what he knows in a manner reminiscent of the dialogue between Socrates and the slave boy in Meno (Plato, in Javeet, 1970, pp. 232–5). Under questioning, Emile recalls that north can be found at midday by looking at the direction in which the shadows fall. He works out, under questioning, that if the forest is to the north of Montmorency, then Montmorency must be to the south of the forest. By travelling in a direction opposite to that in which the shadows fall, he realizes that he knows the way back to Montmorency (Rousseau, 1762, pp. 232–5).

The example is meant to illustrate how a natural lack (hunger and thirst) can lead the child to begin to exercise his growing powers of reason in a spontaneous manner, in order to gain geographical knowledge that would otherwise be imparted in didactically. But Rousseau's example will not do the work that he wishes it to do. Emile has already been given information that is vital to his subsequent discovery of Montmorency: that the forest is to the north of it and that shadows fall to the north at midday. There is no suggestion that he finds this out for himself. Second, he is placed in a particular situation by his tutor, he does not spontaneously put himself there; if a human will has not actually been directly imposed on him, he has at least been manipulated into a certain 'learning situation'. Third, Rousseau's style of questioning is designed to elicit from Emile the response that Rousseau desires. Far from demonstrating how learning can be spontaneous, the example of Montmorency illustrates how contrived the situation has to be in order to achieve the desired result of discovery learning, and this is with just one pupil.

Worse though from a Rousseauan point of view, Emile has been already instructed in certain vital pieces of knowledge and it could be said that he is being *conditioned* to put that knowledge to good effect by the manipulation of the situation by one human will effectively, although covertly, controlling another. Rousseau might reply that the *direct* imposition of one will on another is harmful and will lead to resentment. However, resentment might just as well arise from Emile's realization that he has been put into a difficult position by the apparent irresponsibility of his tutor and that he has been conditioned into making a response through the use of negative stimuli, namely feelings of hunger, thirst and fear. Rousseau's examples do not show that learning can most effectively take place without the imposition of rules or authority on a child. In the first case, one human will is imposed on another by the removal of a child to a windowless room; in the second, the tutor arranges a certain situation and Emile's learning relies crucially on knowledge that has been derived from instruction about certain geographical facts, as well as the experience of unpleasant feelings. All this is done in a way that *manipulates* Emile; he is manoeuvred into action through processes that he does not understand himself. One could say that Rousseau has evacuated *authority* from his learning situations and substituted for them a covert form of *power*. It can hardly be claimed that this is morally superior to the traditional exercise of authority by a tutor, which is open and honest and which respects the dignity of the learner by not manipulating him.

Rousseau's own attempt then, to show that learning can take place effectively without either the imposition of one will on another or without the introduction of rules for deriving knowledge, is inadequate; he is constantly smuggling in elements of a kind of pedagogy he himself ought to reject in order to bring about the learning outcome that he desires. Worse still, he appears to be using operant conditioning techniques at times; the window example looks suspiciously like what we would nowadays call aversion therapy. The 'important event' which is to be negatively reinforced is the breaking of windows. Non-repair of the window or, more drastically, confinement, are negative reinforcers introduced to condition out the tendency to break the window. In the Montmorency example, the important event is the experience of getting lost, which is negatively reinforced by feelings of fear, hunger and thirst.

Neither ethically nor pedagogically does this seem to be an improvement on training techniques which aim to treat a person as someone who can understand what is happening to him and what he should be doing. This is all of a piece with Rousseau's reluctance to attribute the full possession of reason to children before the age of 12 (1762, pp. 106, 113). Essentially, what Rousseau describes is a sham possibility; if it is true that human action is rule governed, then learned human action will be rule governed, no matter how it is learned. If engaging in rule-governed behaviour involves the recognition of authority, then the recognition of authority of some kind is a necessary and unavoidable feature of human life (Winch, 1959). The place of authority in human life is unavoidable and we are left with pragmatic judgements as to what is the best way to learn; discovery or training. Rousseau's Utopian proposals do not lead us to Montmorency, but up a blind alley. Given that learning does involve a submission to authority, at least in the minimal form of rule-following, then it cannot be a criticism of learning by training that it involves submission to authority in the form of rule-following. The argument becomes a practical one over which is the best way to teach and learn; does it involve drawing on human institutions and wisdom, or does it involve seeking to re-create them out of nothing? Training can then be considered on its merits as a form of teaching.

The complexity of human training

The training of animals can be a complex affair which results in flexibility of response. This already distinguishes it from conditioning, which involves a rigid response to a single or very limited set of stimuli. There is no clear dividing line between conditioning and training; even some of the training that we give to infants is like conditioning (potty training, to use one of Abbs's examples). Although the experimental conditions required by true operant conditioning are not present, there is a fairly rigid set of responses to a restricted range of stimuli which makes the example closely related to operant conditioning in the strict sense. But the identity of training and conditioning cannot be settled by the use of a few isolated examples.

In fact, the range of activities into which humans can be trained far exceeds the scope of animal training. Training pervades language learning, early childhood and primary education and vocational education, and it takes many different forms according to the stage at, and context in which, it is used. Is there, then, anything in common among this vast range of activities that allows us to label them all 'training'? The very fact that there are borderline cases between training and conditioning suggests that that there is not.

There is, perhaps, a *core* use of the term 'training' which makes it more than just a family resemblance concept like 'game', while remaining a concept with blurred boundaries. This core usage is connected with the idea of learning to do something in a confident way. The emphasis is more on *action* than *knowledge* on the one hand, and on *an unhesitating and confident* action rather than a hesitating and diffident one on the other. Putting it like this is not to deny that successful action requires a degree of knowledge, nor is it to deny that confident action may issue from other forms of learning, like conjecture and testing, for example. It is simply to say that the kind of learning that is associated with training is more closely linked with the development of confident action than it is with knowledge and reflection.

Reflective action is needed in many activities, but is very often most useful when there is effective action to reflect upon. Training may well be, and often is, a stage along the route to quite complex forms of professional activity. Indeed, it is often the case that part of training involves the ability to stand back, reflect and check before carrying on; the concept of training is flexible enough to take account of these cases. We expect a properly trained airline pilot to act confidently, but not to disregard the particular nature of a situation or to take no account of it in his/her actions. We also expect him/her to ponder certain difficult events and to think about how to deal with them better in the future. Indeed, this could be a part of his/her training.

Training and primary education

Because discovery methods of learning are still fashionable in schools (at least in the UK, if not elsewhere), the idea that training has an important part to play in primary education is repugnant to most progressive primary educationists, although the realization has grown in recent years that pedagogic methods which rely more on training techniques can be very effective. It is, nevertheless, important to investigate the role of training in primary education. In the first place, it is necessary to distinguish between the rhetoric and the reality. We know from various studies that the practice of primary teachers is varied and does not all conform to a progressive ideal (see, for example, Alexander, 1992; Galton, Simon and Croll, 1980; Mortimore *et al.*, 1987). Second, because something is a prevalent practice does not guarantee that it is the most effective or even *an* effective practice.

The key question that we need to ask is: 'Does training have something to contribute to primary education and, if so, has it been neglected?'

There can be little doubt that primary education involves initiating children into a range of fundamental skills connected with becoming literate and numerate. In addition, they need to acquire a considerable amount of factual knowledge during the primary years. In learning to acquire these skills they need to engage in rule-following activities of various kinds. The question now arises, 'Does learning to follow these rules best take place through discovery or through training?' Although this is an empirical question, it is not without conceptual overtones. In particular, as in our previous discussion of Rousseau, we need to be careful about the nature of the discovery that is being proposed. If it resembles the kind of operant conditioning that Rousseau resorts to, then this can hardly be a point in its favour. If conditioning is an even more autonomy-denying practice than training, then conditioning masquerading as discovery will hardly escape the criticisms levelled against training, which, to the extent that they are valid, will apply with even greater force in the case of conditioning.

The case against training as an effective and flexible form of learning is certainly not proven. There are also a number of studies of primary school practice which, at the very least, suggest that some aspects of traditional primary teaching are superior to progressive, discovery-based forms of learning (Alexander, 1992; Bryant and Bradley, 1985; Mortimore *et al.*, 1987; Tizard *et al.*, 1988). In addition, comparative international data suggests that countries with more traditional forms of primary education, in which training still plays a significant role, achieve better results in certain subjects, notably mathematics (Prais, 1986).

But the dispute about the role of training, as opposed to other forms of learning in the primary school, has rarely been conducted on the empirical level and empirical findings are always subject to dispute and misinterpretation. In order to understand why training methods have fallen into disrepute it is necessary to look at the ideological opposition to training as a form of teaching and learning. One aspect of this has already been identified, namely the confusion between training and conditioning. But the other aspect relates to the specifically human side of training, namely, that it takes place in the context of a rule system and therefore involves the recognition of the authority of the trainer on the part of the trainee.

As we saw earlier, progressivist forms of education, which ultimately stem from the work of Rousseau, rest on a rejection of authority. The whole moral psychology of Rousseau and the progressivist movement is based on the idea that it causes harm for one human to overtly impose his/her will on another, both to the imposer and to the individual imposed upon. But Rousseau, although he distinguishes between legitimate and illegitimate impositions of the will in adult life, is unable to distinguish between cases where such an imposition is legitimate and cases where it is not in the upbringing of children, and he himself resorts to the covert imposition of will in order to achieve certain learning objectives. But it is the *authority* of the trainer in the human situation which makes training acceptable to the trainee. This authority is nothing if it just derives from being *in authority* by virtue of holding a special position; the trainer is in authority because s/he is *an authority*, that is, s/he has knowledge and skill which command the respect of the trainee, who stands in need of acquiring some of that knowledge and skill (Peters, 1967).

This is true even in the case of mother tongue learning, where a young child relies on and defers to the linguistic knowledge of adults in order to develop competence in communication (Halliday, 1978). A primary school teacher, equipped with the knowledge and skill that children need to acquire, has the moral authority to use training methods where appropriate if s/he feels that this is the most effective way of getting children to acquire knowledge or skill, if s/he is in authority because s/he is *an authority* on the subject matter which s/he is teaching. No doubt this involves the imposition of his/her will on those of his/her pupils, since s/he, not they, is setting the agenda, but to see this as objectionable in itself is to fall into Rousseau's confused position, where it is the imposition of will *in itself* that is harmful. But, as we have seen, given the rule-governed nature of human life it is a confusion to think that this can be avoided. The important thing to ensure is that it is done in a proper way, through the legitimate exercise of authority.

Naturally, decisions about when, and for how long, and with what other methods, training should be used, are a matter of professional judgement. It will suffice to draw attention to the implications of the observation that human life is rule governed. First, if recognition of and submission to authority is not in itself morally harmful to children, then decisions about whether to use training or some other techniques to promote learning can be made on judgements about the efficacy of those techniques and evidence about effectiveness becomes significant rather than just another ambiguous and disputable weapon in an ideological battle. Second, the potential importance of training extends across the curriculum, from activities like learning to read and write, to mathematics, learning to behave morally and learning to create works of art (Best, 1993; Kazepides, 1990). In so far as these are all rule-governed activities, training can be considered as a possible technique for the promotion of learning.

Training and autonomy

I want now to consider the objection that if one of the main aims of education is the promotion of *autonomy*, then the use of training is inimical to that aim, since it encourages submission to authority rather than the growth of independent judgement. This objection might have some weight if it were to be proposed that all that children should be trained to do is to submit to authority. The use of training is best seen as a means to an end and the end can be autonomy. A child who can use his/her mother tongue has more independence than one who cannot, even though learning to speak involves some training and some recognition of authority. An adult who is literate, numerate, reasonably knowledgeable and who possesses a craft skill, is more independent than one who does not have these attributes, even though the acquisition of them involves training at some stage. Training can lead to autonomy if it gives people the skill and knowledge to then act independently and to discover things for themselves. Learning by discovery is not an alternative to training, it is a set of techniques that can emerge from the skills acquired in training. The point is that the decision whether or not to use training or some other teaching techniques is not an either/or matter, it is a question of balance and the balance of techniques may well change through the course of education.

Finally, in learning to follow a rule, one learns *to go on*. A child who has learned how to generate a number series through addition can then go on to generate further numbers in that series, an adult who has learned to use woodworking tools can use his/her training to make and repair things. The very ability to follow a rule involves some degree of independence. In many cases learning to follow a rule involves judgement, interpretation and evaluation. For example, a rule-follower may need to *judge* whether or not some situation is one in which a particular rule applies; s/he may need to *interpret* a sign in order to determine which rule it is an instance of, and s/he may need to *evaluate* how well s/he has succeeded in following a rule. The ability to judge, interpret and evaluate in a variety of different contexts is an essential aspect of autonomy.

Conclusion

It has been shown that training is to be distinguished from conditioning. It is a form of teaching that, if effective, leads to the confident deployment of skill and technique in a wide variety of situations. In the case of human training, it invariably involves the use of language and rule-following, thus making it more complex and qualitatively different from the most complex forms of animal training. It can, therefore, promote independence and autonomy. In so far as the case against training rested on a kind of anti-authoritarianism derived from the work of Rousseau, it has been shown to be confused. In most cases, conditioning rests on power or force and leads to an unthinking response in a limited set of situations; this is certainly the case in experimental psychology. There is a limited, but only a limited, set of situations in which it is morally justified to submit humans to conditioning. The first sort of case is where the conditioning is beneficial to the subject but the subject is unable to give consent through extremities of youth, age or illness; in these cases a legitimate authority is required to consent on behalf of the subject. The second case is where someone in command of his/her faculties and not under duress, consents to submit to a programme of conditioning which, s/he understands, will be for his/her benefit, as in some kinds of medical treatment, for example. These exceptions do not cover any educational or quasi-educational uses of conditioning. Animal training rests on the power that humans have over animals but is capable, with the higher mammals, of leading to a variegated kind of response in a variety of cognate situations. The training of humans invariably involves the recognition of authority based on knowledge and skill, as well as institutional position, and can have a complexity of process and flexibility of outcome that the use of language and rule-following techniques are alone capable of giving.

Human training is, therefore, not merely more complex than animal training, it is of a different order and there is no reason to think that it is, *in itself*, morally unjustified. Indeed, if it is an educator's duty to teach through the most effective means possible, then it can be stated that there are numerous occasions when training *should* be used.

References

Abbs, P. (1987) 'Training spells the death of education'. *Guardian*, 5 January.

Alexander, R. (1992) *Policy and Practice in the Primary School*. London: Routledge.

Best, D. (1993) *The Rationality of Feeling. Understanding the Arts in Education*. Brighton: Falmer.

Bryant, P. and Bradley, L. (1985) *Children's Reading Problems*. Oxford: Blackwell

Dearden, R. F. (1984) 'Education and training'. *Westminster Studies in Education*, 7, 57–66.

Dent, N. (1988) *Rousseau*. Oxford: Blackwell.

Galton, M., Simon, B. and Croll, P. (1980) *Inside the Primary Classroom*. London: Routledge.

Halliday, M. A. K. (1978) *Learning How to Mean*. London: Arnold.

Hyland, T. (1993) 'Competence, knowledge and education'. *Journal of Philosophy of Education*, 27 (1), 57–68.

Kazepides, T. (1991) 'On the prerequisites of moral education: a Wittgenteinian perspective'. *Journal of Philosophy of Education*, 25 (2), 259–72.

Mortimore, P., Sammons, P., Stoll, L., Lewis, D. and Ecob, R. (1987) *School Matters*. Wells: Open Books.

Lieberman, D. (1990) *Learning*. Belmont, CA: Wadsworth.

Malcolm, N. (1977) 'Thoughtless brutes', in N. Malcolm *Thought and Knowledge*. Ithaca, NY: Cornell University Press.

Peters R. S. (1967) 'Authority', in A. Quinton (ed.) *Political Philosophy*. Oxford: Oxford University Press.

Plato, *Meno* in B. Jowett (1970) *The Dialogues of Plato*. London: Sphere Books.

Prais, S. (1986), 'Mathematical attainments: comparisons of Japanese and English schooling', in B. Moon, J. Isaac and J. Powney (eds) *Judging Standards and Effectiveness in Education*. London: Hodder and Stoughton.

Rousseau, J.-J. (1762) *Emile*. Paris: Garnier Flammarion 1986 edition.

Smith, A. (1981) *The Wealth of Nations*, vol. 1 (first published 1776). Indianapolis: Liberty Fund.

Taylor, C. (1964) *The Explanation of Behaviour*. London: Routledge.

Tizard, B., Blatchford, P., Burke, J., Farquhar, C. and Plewis, I. (1988) *Young Children at School in the Inner City*. Hove: Lawrence Erlbaum.

Winch, P. (1959) 'Authority', in A. Quinton (ed.) *Political Philosophy*. Oxford: Oxford University Press.

Wittgenstein, L. (1967) *Zettel*. Oxford: Blackwell.

9

Education and Self-directed Learning

Stephen Brookfield

Introduction

The history of educational discourse surrounding self-directed learning demonstrates, depending on one's viewpoint, either its remarkable conceptual utility or the co-optation and enslavement by corporate capitalism of a once subversive idea. From being regarded as a vaguely anarchistic, Illich-inspired threat to formal education, self-direction is now comfortably ensconced in the citadel, firmly part of the conceptual and practical mainstream. The marriage between self-direction and education seems to have settled into a comfortable and harmonious rut. Epistemologically contradictory approaches to researching self-direction co-exist like partners who know each other's faults but have decided that something flawed is better than nothing at all. We can see a phenomenologically inclined naturalism sitting next to an experimental positivism without any visible rancour between them. What contentiousness exists is mostly confined to debates concerning the reliability and validity of measurement scales.

As with the most idyllic of marriages, however, there are occasional arguments and disagreements. I want to build on some of those moments of dissonance that occasionally have disturbed the equanimity of educators who align themselves with the idea of self-direction. In particular I want to develop the productively troubling elements introduced by Gelpi (1979), Griffin (1983, 1987), Candy (1991) and Hammond and Collins (1991) to the effect that the political context, cultural contingency and social construction of self-directed learning activities have generally been ignored. Ten years ago, Brockett and Hiemstra (1991) wrote that 'concerns about the socio-political dimension of self-direction remain valid today' (p. 97) and they noted as one of their concluding recommendations for theory that 'the political dimension of self-direction continues to be largely overlooked by adult educators and this needs to be remedied' (p. 220). In the years that have passed since their observation, this neglect of the political aspects of the idea has, if anything, deepened.

In this chapter I want to address three issues. First, how can we understand the cultural formation of self-directed learning (SDL) so that its elevation to a position of prominence in educational (especially adult educational) discourse is understood as a political phenomenon? Second, is self-direction an accommodative, domesticating idea (as some critics claim) or can it have an emancipatory force? I think critical educators have made a strategically premature decision to dismiss self-direction as having no role to play in building a critical practice of education or in developing forms of critical pedagogy. Given the popularity and widespread appeal of the idea to contemporary educators, some important consequences could ensue for the field if this idea was reframed with a critical edge. Third, I want to make explicit some political dimensions to the idea of self-direction. If these were acknowledged then self-directed learning could join critical theory, critical pedagogy and transformative learning as complementary elements of a rationale for the critical practice of education.

The cultural formation of self-directed learning

It is no accident that the idea of self-directed learning has engaged the attention of educators, particularly those in the USA. As a representation of how learning optimally occurs, the concept fits very much the American ideology of rugged individualism. Self-directed learning underscores the folklore of the self-made man or woman that elevates to near mythical status those who speak a narrative of succeeding against the odds through the sheer force of their individual efforts. This is the narrative surrounding 'adult learner of the year' awards bestowed on those who pull themselves up by their bootstraps to claim their place at the table of stories and voices. President Clinton's campaign team tapped expertly into this individualistic ethic in their video *The Man from Hope* shown at his nominating convention. That anyone can be President by dint of their own self-directed efforts was celebrated as a prized tenet of American culture. The fact that this takes enormous amounts of money and years of courting, and co-optation by, big business interests remained obscured.

There is a certain irony in the fact that a concept like self-direction that is seemingly replete with ideals of liberty and freedom can end up serving repressive interests. Yet this is precisely what happens when the social and cultural formations of the concept are ignored. For many learners and educators the image of self-direction is of a self-contained, internally driven, capable learner working to achieve her goal in splendid isolation. The self is seen as a free floating, autonomous, volitional agent able to make rational, authentic and internally coherent choices about learning while remaining detached from social, cultural and political formations. This idea of the self is what McLaren (1993) refers to as 'the magnificent Enlightenment swindle of the autonomous, stable and self-contained ego that is supposed to be able to act independently of its own history, its own cultural and linguistic situatedness' (p. 121). As a recent analysis of postmodernism's challenge to adult education notes, the self in self-directed learning is 'the classical scientific self – individualised, undifferentiated, an essentially abstract entity, the "mono-logical" self' (Usher, Bryant and Johnston, 1997, p. 94).

There are many problems with this notion of the self. First, we cannot stand outside the cultural streams within which we swim. Second, the idea of a unitary, unconflicted self – an undifferentiated ego – is a fiction. In making what seem like purely personal, private choices about learning we play out the contradictory cross-currents of ideology and genetics that are inscribed within us. Third, it is but a short step from conceiving self-direction as a form of learning emphasizing separateness, to equating it with selfishness, with the narcissistic pursuit of private ends regardless of the consequences of this pursuit for others. Self-direction that honours only the efforts of the individual self rests on the premise that one's needs and desires exist *sui generis* and have an inalienable right to be satisfied. In education programmes that purport to embody the spirit of self-direction it is not unusual for learners to argue that unless they get from educators whatever learners say they want, then the spirit of self-direction has somehow been compromised.

A view of learning that regards people as self-contained, volitional beings scurrying around in individual projects is one that works against collective and co-operative impulses. Citing an engagement in SDL, people can deny the existence of common interests and human interdependence in favour of an obsessive focus on the self. Such a stance leaves unchallenged wider beliefs, norms and structures and thereby reinforces the status quo. This conceptualization of self-direction empha-sizes a self that is sustained by its own internal momentum needing no external connections or supports. It erects as the ideal culmination of psychological development the independent, fully functioning person. Fortunately, this view of developmental trajectories as leading inevitably towards the establishment of separate, autonomous selves has been challenged in recent years by work on gender (Belenky *et al.*, 1986; Goldberger *et al.*, 1996) and critical psychology (Burman 1994; Fox and Prilleltensky, 1997; Morss, 1996). This work questions the patriarchal notion that atomistic self-determination is both an educational ideal to be pursued as well as the natural end point of psychological development. In its place it advances a feminist valuing of interdependence and a socially constructed interpretation of identity.

Politically, the separatist emphasis of SDL makes an engagement in common cause more difficult for people to contemplate. It severs the connection between private troubles and public issues (Mills, 1953) and makes it harder for learners to realize that apparently private learning projects are culturally framed. As Boshier (1983) has pointed out, policy-makers can use research into self-direction to justify cutting spending on adult education. After all, they can argue, if adult educators tell us that adult learners are naturally self-directed (unlike children who are dependent on teacher direction) then why bother making provision for their education? Won't they self-directedly take the initiative in planning and conduct-ing their learning anyway? But atomistic, divisive interpretations of self-directed learning need not be the end of the story. If we can demonstrate convincingly the political dimensions of an idea that is routinely enshrined in programmatic mission

statements and privileged in professional discourse, and if we can prevent interpretations of SDL from sliding into an unproblematized focus on self-actualization,
then we have a real chance to use this idea as a foundational element in building a
critical practice of education.

Self-directed learning as an emancipatory idea

To critical theorists the predominance of the concept of self-directed learning in the
field illustrates the tendency of humanistic educators to collapse all political
questions into a narrowly reductionist technical rationality. From the perspective of
critical theory, the early free spirit of self-direction has been turned (through the
technology of learning contracts) into a masked form of repressive surveillance –
one more example of the infinite flexibility of hegemony, of the workings of a coldly
efficient form of repressive tolerance. What began as a cultural challenge, a counter-
hegemonic effort, has taken a technocratic, accommodative turn. Griffin (1987)
argues that discourse on self-direction is totally disconnected from questions of
power and control in society and that it shows the misguided inclination of
humanistic educators to depoliticize all questions of practice under the rubric of a
Rogerian concern for 'personal growth'. Similarly, Collins (1988) writes that 'self-
directed learning strategies steer them (students) to a negotiated compromise with
predominant interests which support social conformity' (p. 63). Educators who
subscribe to self-directed learning techniques such as learning contracts are
dismissed as willing collaborators in the sublimation of individual needs to
institutional interests.

Following Foucault's (1977, 1980) analysis of disciplinary power, it is certainly
highly plausible to see the technology of self-directed learning – particularly the
widespread acceptance and advocacy of learning contracts (Anderson, Boud and
Sampson, 1996; Laycock and Stephenson, 1993) – as a highly developed form of
surveillance. By interiorizing what Foucault calls the 'normalizing gaze' (teacher
developed norms concerning what's acceptable) through their negotiations with
faculty, learning contracts transfer the responsibility for overseeing learning from
the teacher to the learner. This is usually spoken of as an emancipatory process of
empowerment in which educators are displaying an admirable responsiveness to
student needs and circumstances. But, using Foucault's principle of reversal (seeing
something as the exact opposite of what it really is) learning contracts can be
reframed and understood as a sophisticated means by which the content and
methodology of learning can be monitored without the teacher needing to be
physically present. That the exercise of disciplinary power can be furthered through
self-directed learning is illustrated in a recent book on SDL for schoolteachers
where the 'self-directed plan of discipline . . . a written plan negotiated between the
teacher and student' (Areglado, Bradley and Lane, 1996, p. 66) is the means by
which 'self-directing behavior becomes self-discipline' (p. 63).

Self-directed learning can also be interpreted as an anti-collectivist force,
preventing the momentum of social movements from developing. In Foucault's
terms, insisting on self-directed learning means that 'a collective effect is abolished

and replaced by a collection of separated individualities' (Foucault, 1977, p. 201). On-line instruction, self-assessment, self-managed and self-regulated learning (Pintrich, 1995) are increasingly urged on educational institutions as learner-friendly, student-centred ways of cutting faculty costs. Lyotard's (1979) vision of education as the efficient consumption of learning packages is realized. This replacement of the collectivity of the class meeting with individually developed programmes of study is the educational equivalent of Margaret Thatcher's infamous declaration that 'there is no such thing as society'. Given that self-directed learning can easily be understood as a way of thinking about learning that underscores isolation, separatism and self-monitoring, it is not surprising that its emancipatory possibilities have been neglected. To Collins, the choice is between 'Self-directed learning or an emancipatory practice of adult education' (1988) with the two posed as dichotomous, mutually exclusive options.

I wish to propose an alternative approach, which is to argue that self-direction can be, and should be, reframed as an inherently emancipatory idea, an oppositional, counter-hegemonic force. In this I build on Foucault's (1980) contention that 'there are no relations of power without resistances; the latter are all the more real and effective because they are formed right at the point where relations of power are exercised' (p. 142). To Foucault the tentacles of sovereign power previously exercised by a monolithic state or monarch are today replaced by local practices of self- monitoring (such as learning contracts) which are exercised as disciplinary power. But the very locality and specificity of these practices means they are more amenable to change and challenge than are large-scale societal edifices. We might be unable to contemplate abolishing broad social mechanisms of economy, law or force, but we can see ways of sliding around and through negotiated learning contracts. It is easier to practise Freire's pedagogy of hope (Freire, 1994) and dissipate radical pessimism when we know that struggles can be local and contextual.

Self-directed learning as a counter-hegemonic practice

Self-directed learning contains within it the seeds of a counter-hegemonic practice. If the powerful political underpinnings to the idea could be made explicit, this might help galvanize the political consciousness of many mainstream educators who currently see little political component to their work. In the specific educational sites in which self- direction is exercised there exists the possibility for reframing its practices to stand as a form of resistance. One of the tactical mistakes leftist educators have made is to dismiss as uncritical lackeys duped by oppressive interests those colleagues who subscribe to the ideas and technology of SDL. This unfairly demeans a great many committed educators who are working towards goals they view as emancipatory.

Of course, it is quite possible to believe one is working in a liberatory vein, only to discover later that one's efforts have bolstered the hegemony one was supposed to be opposing. We can have good hearts, boundless energy and deep wells of compassion, but lack political clarity. After all, the belief that SDL always works to further students' liberatory interests is ideologically sedimented, part of many educators' structures of feelings (to use Williams's [1977] phrase), of what seems to us to be the natural way of understanding the world. To stand outside a culture that has accepted SDL as an unproblematized benefit is difficult, to say the least. To subject the idea and practice of SDL to Foucault's principle of reversal, and thereby contemplate the possibility that one's efforts are having an effect opposite to the one intended, is something most of us would prefer to avoid.

But it is important to remember that most educators who stand behind the concept of self-direction do so because they sense that there is something about this form of practice that dignifies people and respects their experiences. For them self-direction represents a break with authoritarianism and educational totalitarianism. It means that control over the definitions, processes and evaluations of learning rests with those who are struggling to learn, not with external authorities. The belief that through self-direction adults can gain increasing control over their lives (however naïve this belief might subsequently turn out to be) is an emancipatory belief. When asked to justify their commitment to SDL most practitioners invoke concepts of empowerment and transformation. Although these words have been robbed of their political import, they can be reconstituted and rearticulated in a counter-hegemonic way to emphasize standing against oppressive interests. That this is possible is represented in Gelpi's (1979) view that

> self-directed learning by individuals and of groups is a danger for every repressive force, and it is upon this self-direction that we must insist . . . radical change in social, moral, aesthetic and political affairs is often the outcome of a process of self-directed learning in opposition to the educational message imposed from without. (p. 2)

For all the accommodative potential that Collins so skilfully identifies in SDL, there is still something intrinsically critical, oppositional and emancipatory about the idea for many learners and educators. People believe that embedded in the idea is some strain of resistance to dominant values and practices that sets educators' faces in opposition to powerful interests. They know that at the heart of SDL is the rejection of institutions' right to mandate and control what and how people learn. So, like Hammond and Collins (1991), I believe that self-direction can easily and naturally be reframed with a political edge so that it 'fits squarely into the tradition of emancipatory adult education' (p. 13).

Reframing self-direction as a political idea

The case for self-direction as an inherently political concept rests on two arguments. First, that at the heart of self-direction are issues of power and control, particularly regarding the definition of acceptable and appropriate learning activities. Who defines the boundaries of intellectual inquiry is always a political question, and self-direction places this decision squarely in the hands of learners. Second, exercising self-direction inevitably requires certain conditions to be in place regarding access to resources, conditions that are essentially political in nature. Claiming the resources needed to conduct SDL can be regarded as a political act. Let me take each of these arguments in turn.

Power and control

Probably the most consistently predictable element in definitions of self-direction is the importance of the learner's exercising control over the educational decisions any learning project requires. What count as legitimate goals of a learning effort, how these might be accomplished, what resources will be most helpful, what methods will work best and what criteria are most appropriately applied to judging the success of any learning effort are all decisions that are said to rest in learners' hands. Of course, these decisions can be manipulated in the way discussed earlier through the technology of learning contracts, but the procedural distortion this technology represents is not endemic to the idea of self-direction. The emphasis on the learner as the locus of power and control – as the ultimate arbiter of what is right and wrong, of what is a worthwhile or wasted effort – is also central to notions of emancipatory education.

For example, when talking about his work at the Highlander Folk School – a much lauded and venerated radical adult education centre – Myles Horton (1990) stressed that 'decision making was at the center of our students' experiences' (p. 152). Through the experience of making decisions about what was to happen at Highlander, participants learned the democratic process. Horton argued that this process was indivisible, it could not be hedged around with facilitator-imposed constraints: 'if you want to have the students control the whole process, as far as you can get them to control it, then you can never, at any point, take it out of their hands' (p. 136). As with the Highlander process, so with self-directed learning: who controls the ways and directions in which people learn is a political issue highlighting the distribution of educational and political power. Who has the final say in framing the range and type of decisions to be taken, and who establishes the pace and mechanisms for decision-making, reveals a great deal about where power really resides.

So the emphasis of self-directed learning on placing the learner at the heart of decision-making calls to mind some powerful political ideals. In its purest form it implies a democratic commitment to shifting to learners complete control over conceptualizing, designing, conducting and evaluating their learning, and for deciding which resources best further these processes. Self-direction can be seen as part of a populist democratic tradition which holds that people's definitions of what is important to them should frame and instruct governments' actions, not the other way round. This is why the idea of full SDL is such anathema to advocates of a core or national curriculum, and why it is opposed so vehemently by those who see education as a process of initiation into cultural literacy. As Gelpi (1979) observes, SDL is institutionally and politically inconvenient to those promoting educational blueprints that attempt to control the learning of others. Emphasizing people's right to self-direction invests a trust in their wisdom, in their capacity to make wise choices and take wise actions. To quote Horton (1990) again: 'you have to posit trust in the learner in spite of the fact that the people you're dealing with may not, on the surface, seem to merit that trust' (p. 131). His advocacy of learners being in control of their own learning is based on the belief that if people have a chance to give voice to what moves and hurts them they will soon show that they are well aware of the real nature of their problems and of ways to deal with these.

If we place the self-conscious, self-aware exertion of control over learning at the heart of what it means to be self-directed we raise a host of questions about how control can be exercised authentically in a culture that is itself highly controlling. It is easy to imagine an inauthentic form of control where students feel they are taking key decisions concerning their learning, all the while being unaware that this is happening within a framework that excludes certain ideas or activities as subversive, unpatriotic or immoral. Controlled self-direction is, from a political perspective, a contradiction in terms, an oxymoron as erroneous as limited empowerment. Superficially we may think we're controlling our learning when we decide the pacing, resources and evaluative criteria of our learning effort. But if the range of acceptable content has been preordained so that we deliberately or unwittingly steer clear of things that we sense are aberrant or controversial, then we are controlled rather than controlling. We are active agents in our own self-censorship and surveillance, willing partners in hegemony.

Hegemony describes the process whereby ideas, structures and actions come to be seen by people as both natural and axiomatic – as so obvious as to be beyond question or challenge – when in fact these same phenomena serve to preserve the existing order and further the interests of dominant groups. A fully developed self-directed learning project would have at its centre an alertness to the possibility of hegemony. To the extent that it is counter-hegemonic, SDL implies that students are ever aware as to the possibility of self-censorship and hidden surveillance. SDL as a counter-hegemonic moment means that learners stay alert to the possibility that they are unthinkingly excluding some potential learning projects because they think they are too deviant or subversive. A fully adult form of self-direction exists only when we examine our definitions of what we think is important for us to learn for the extent to which these definitions serve repressive interests.

Access to resources

The full exercise of control in a self-directed learning contract cannot be realized simply by wishing it into existence. How much control can be said to exist if the self-directed dreams we dream have no hope of ever being realized because we are simply struggling to survive? Any number of self-directed initiatives have foundered because those attempting to assume control over their learning found themselves in the invidious position of being denied the resources to exercise that control properly. Being self-directed is a meaningless idea if you are too weary at the end of the day to think clearly about what form of learning would be of most use to you, or if you are closed off from access to the resources necessary for you to be able to realize your self-directed learning projects. Being the arbiter of our own decisions about learning requires that we have enough energy to make reflectively informed choices. An informed choice is one where the rationale for our choice can be clearly articulated, and one where the choice has the consequences we intend.

Decisions about learning made under the pressure of external circumstances when we are tired, hungry and distracted, cannot be said to be fully self-directed. The process of making reflectively informed decisions is lengthy, tiring and often contentious. For learners to exercise control in any meaningful sense they cannot be so buried under the demands of their daily work that they have neither the time, energy nor inclination left over to engage in shaping and making decisions about their own development. As Freire (1993) points out, action springing from an immediate and uninformed desire to do something, anything, to improve one's day-to-day circumstances can be much less effective than action springing from a careful analysis of the wider structural changes that must be in place for individual lives to improve over the long term. If the decisions we make for ourselves are born out of a desperate immediate need that causes us to focus only on what is in front of us rather than on the periphery or in the future, and if we choose from among options that are irrelevant to the real nature of the problem at hand or our range of choices has been framed by someone else, then our control is illusory. In this regard, decision-framing is as important as decision-making in a self-directed learning project. Central to a self-directed learning effort is a measure of unconstrained time and space necessary to make decisions that are carefully and critically examined and that are in our own best long-term interests.

An inauthentic, limited form of self-direction is evident when our efforts to develop ourselves as learners remain only preferences because the resources needed to take action are unavailable or denied to us. Exercising control over learning is meaningless if control compromises only an intellectual analysis of one's problems and solutions. As learners we may believe we have a beautifully accurate reading of our condition, and we may secure all kinds of promises from those in power to do something about it when resources are more plentiful, but if this is the extent of our control then we are doing little more than playing an intellectual game. Hence, as well as the resources of adequate time and energy needed to make reflectively informed decisions, SDL also implies that learners have access to the resources needed to act on these decisions.

As a learner, I may come to a clear analysis of the skills I need to develop in order to do or learn something but be told repeatedly by those I approach for necessary resources that, while my plans are good ones, the budget cuts that have just been forced on my organization and community mean that priorities have changed and my plans are now rendered useless. If this is the case then sooner or later I am bound to realize that the problem of blocked access to resources is not one of individual personalities (the myopic, anal-retentive, bureaucratic administrator constantly trying to thwart me) but one of structural constraints. I will come to see that learning something I want to learn is a project that is intimately connected to changing not only the political culture whereby the posting of yearly profits is extolled as the zenith of cultural and community achievement, but also the structures through which wealth, power and resources remain the preserve of an unrepresentative minority. Taking control over our development as learners and requesting resources to act on the development efforts we envisage will bring many of us to a realization of the connections between personal learning efforts and changes in the wider political structures.

It may also be the case that I decide I want to learn something that I consider essential for my own development, only to be told that the knowledge or skills involved are undesirable, inappropriate or subversive. A desire to explore an alternative political ideology is meaningless if books exploring that ideology have been removed from the public library because of their 'unsuitability' or, perhaps more likely, if they have never been ordered in the first place. In a blaze of admirable masochism I may choose to undertake a self-directed learning project geared towards widening my understanding of how my practice as an educator is unwittingly oppressive and culturally distorted. In doing this I may have to rely primarily on books because my colleagues are convinced of the self-evident correctness of their own unexamined practice. Yet I may well find that the materials I need for this project are so expensive that neither I, nor my local libraries, can afford to purchase them. In this regard it is ironic – an example of repressive tolerance (Marcuse, 1965) through which ideas are marginalized even as they are disseminated – that critical analyses of education are sometimes hard to obtain from publishers and often priced well beyond the pockets of those who could most benefit from reading them.

Again, I may need the physical equipment for a self-directed learning effort I have planned and be told by those owning or controlling such equipment that it is unavailable to me for reasons of cost, or because of other prior claims. If I decide to initiate a self-directed learning project that involves challenging the institutional hegemony of a professional group (for example, physicians or lawyers) I may find that medical and legal experts and their professional organizations place insurmountable barriers in my path in an effort to retain their position of authority. So being self-directed can be inherently politicizing as learners become aware that the resources necessary to conduct their learning projects successfully are differentially distributed across society and often in the control of gatekeepers unwilling to relinquish their monopoly on information or facilities.

Self-directed learning, critical practice and American culture

In the contemporary discourse of American critical pedagogy, the most common approach towards developing a critical practice of education focuses on explicating the educational relevance of the work of European critical theorists and political economists, especially Jürgen Habermas and, perhaps less prominently, Antonio Gramsci. As work on this valuable project continues it is important also to try to develop, simultaneously, approaches to a critical practice of education that are framed in terms that are perceived by American adult educators as being more familiar and congenial and that represent what seem to them to be some indigenous American intellectual traditions – even if these traditions turn out to be much more polymorphous than they imagined. If there is one thing that we have learned from activist educators like Horton and Freire it is that we must start (though not stay) where people are; that we must bring them to an uncomfortable and often unsought confrontation with iniquitous political realities, and with their own unacknowledged collusions in these realities, by grounding this activity in terms and processes which look, feel, sound and smell close to home. In Horton's (1990) words, 'if you have to make a choice between moving in the direction you want to move people, and working with them where they are, you always choose to work with them where they are' (p. 112). Horton believed that 'you have to start from where people are, because their growth is going to be from there, not from some abstraction or where you are or someone else is' (*ibid.*, p. 131).

A strong case for the development of indigenous language and forms of analysis to undergird a critical practice of education in the USA has been made by Maxine Greene (1986). Greene writes that

> the sources of European critical theory are to be found in responses to the destruction of the Workers' Councils after the First World War, the decline of the Weimar Republic, the rise of Stalinism, the spread of fascism, the Holocaust, the corruptions of social democracy. (*ibid.*, p. 437)

These memories, she argues, are European, not American. Hence, for Greene, 'a critical pedagogy relevant to the United States today must go beyond – calling on different memories, repossessing another history' (*ibid.*, p. 438). That movements of European critical theory and American pragmatism might not be as separate as some believe has been pointed out by various writers (Antonioni, 1989; Bernstein, 1991; Shalin, 1992). Bernstein (1991), for example, maintains that

> Pervading all of Habermas' writings is his strong and unshakeable commitment to democracy. No less than John Dewey, Habermas is the philosopher of democracy. This is one of the reasons why he has been so drawn to the American pragmatic tradition, especially Pierce, Mead, and Dewey. (p. 207)

Habermas himself declares that 'I have for a long time identified myself with that radical democratic mentality which is present in the best American traditions and articulated in American pragmatism' (1985, p. 198) and he describes Deweyian inspired pragmatism as 'a missing branch of Young Hegelianism' (Habermas, 1986, p. 193) and 'the radical-democratic branch of Young-Hegelianism' (*ibid.*, p. 151). Bernstein (1991) believes that

> Habermas is profoundly right in recognizing that the basic intuition or judgment that stands at the center of his own vision is also central to the pragmatic tradition. Both share an understanding of rationality as intrinsically dialogical and communicative. And both pursue the ethical and political consequences of this form of rationality and rationalization. (p. 48)

Shalin (1992), too, argues that far from pragmatism and critical theory standing in opposition, 'Habermas' *Theory of Communicative Action* can be seen as an attempt to invigorate critical theory by merging the Continental and Anglo-Saxon traditions and bringing the pragmatist perspective to bear on the project of emancipation through reason' (p. 244).

If, ultimately, very little in the American intellectual melting-pot is wholly American in the sense of being free from some form of European influence (after all, those most American of adult educators – Eduard Lindeman and Myles Horton – were both strongly influenced by the Danish Folk High school movement) there are, none the less, certain cultural values that Americans claim as their own.

Perhaps the strongest of these is individualism; a belief that each of us can, with sufficient effort, create a world sensitive to our instincts and desires. As I argued earlier with reference to *The Man from Hope* video, the concept does have its darker side – a narcissistic self-absorption which cuts us off from our collective humanity, communitarian spirit and essential interdependence. Barbara Ehrenreich (1991) writes that in this conception of individualism

> each self is seen as pursuing its own trajectory, accompanied by its own little planetary system of values, seeking to negotiate the best possible deal from the various 'relationships' that come along. Since all values appear to be idiosyncratic satellites of the self, and since we have no way to understand the 'self' as a product of all the other selves – present and in historical memory – we have no way of engaging each other in moral discourse, much less in a routine political argument. (p. 102)

But although individualism can be a divisive, repressive idea, it also contains a strong libertarian streak, a belief that people should control their own environments and destinies rather than have these framed by external authorities. This conception of individualism can be seen in a kind of optimism regarding the contingency and malleability of our personal and political environments. People's belief that by their own efforts they can affect their futures provides a form of moral and civic courage that fuels the fires of change.

In education's interpretation of individualism – that is, in self-direction – the currents of moral and political optimism can flow strongly. By attending to the oppositional elements embedded in these ideas we are able to create some important strategic openings for building critical practice in the field. If issues of power and control are seen as central to an analysis of individualism, and if discussions of self-direction focus on the need for people to be responsible for framing their own choices and taking their own decisions rather than ceding these responsibilities to others, then programmes which espouse self-direction will have to address the politically contentious questions of voice, relevance and authority. Moreover, these questions will be seen to spring from what most Americans would consider to be an appropriate concern with issues of democratic control. For example, taking seriously the pledge of allegiance's call for 'liberty and justice for all' has enormously radical implications, yet one could hardly be regarded as an alien subversive when justifying one's efforts as an activist by these words. In this regard it is interesting to note Greene's efforts to trace the libertarian impulse to individualism back to the republic's founders. Greene writes that 'the founders were calling, through a distinctive critical challenge, for opportunities to give their energies free play. That meant the unhindered exercise of their particular talents: inventing, exploring, building, pursuing material and social success' (1986, p. 430). She turns to Thoreau who, she believes, wanted people

> to reject their own self-exploitation, to refuse what we would now call false consciousness and artificial needs. He connected the 'wide-awakeness' to actual work in the world, to projects. He knew that people needed to be released from internal and external constraints if they were to shape and make and articulate, to leave their own thumbprints on the world. (*Ibid.*, p. 432)

Dewey, too, she argues, was well aware of 'what would later be called "hegemony", or the ideological control, implicit in the dominant view of a given society' (*ibid.*, p. 434).

The constitution, pledge of allegiance, Thoreau, Dewey – to radical educators these may seem like overly romanticized, politically neutered beginnings for critical practice. Yet, it remains the case that mainstream educators will take seriously critical interpretations of their work that spring from such revered – even reified – sources. Clear points of connection between critical theory and adult education can certainly be elaborated in efforts such as Collins's (1991) or De Marais's (1991) interpretations of these ideas in highly concrete ways, and this is crucial to the political project of building a critical practice of education. But, given that so many educators see self-direction as a defining concept for their work, there is also some merit in pursuing concurrently a strategy that reinterprets this familiar idea in a more critical way. If the political dimensions to the idea of self-direction could be made explicit, this could have a powerful effect on the way educators think and act.

Conclusion

One way to politicize practitioners is to confront them with a startlingly different vision of how the world might look. This is why practitioners need to engage with unfamiliar theoretical perspectives that challenge their habitual ways of thinking about practice. But another, complementary, approach is to take the familiar and comfortable and play with redefining it in different ways. This is the approach I am advocating with SDL. If we could make explicit the political dimensions to this idea, then SDL could become one of the most effective Trojan horses in the field of education.

References

Anderson, G., Boud, D. and Sampson, J. (1996) *Learning Contracts: A Practical Guide.* London: Kogan Page.

Antonioni, R. J. (1989) 'The normative foundations of emancipatory theory: evolutionary versus pragmatic perspectives'. *American Journal of Sociology*, 94, 721–48.

Areglado, R. J., Bradley, R. C. and Lane, P. S. (1996) *Learning for Life: Creating Classrooms for Self-Directed Learning*. Thousand Oaks, CA: Corwin Press.

Belenky, M. F., Clinchy, B. M., Goldberger, N. R. and Tarule, J. M. (1986) *Women's Ways of Knowing: The Development of Self, Voice, and Mind*. New York: Basic Books.

Bernstein, R. J. (1991). *The New Constellation: The Ethical-Political Horizons of Modernity/Postmodernity*. Cambridge, MA: MIT Press.

Boshier, R. (1983) 'Adult learning projects research: an alchemist's fantasy?' Invited Address to the American Educational Research Association, Montreal, April.

Brockett, R. G. and Hiemstra, R. (1991) *Self-Direction in Adult Learning: Perspectives on Theory, Research, and Practice*. New York: Routledge.

Burman, E. (1994) *Deconstructing Developmental Psychology*. New York: Routledge.

Candy, P. C. (1991) *Self-Direction for Lifelong Learning*. San Francisco: Jossey-Bass.

Collins, M. (1988) 'Self-directed learning or an emancipatory practice of adult education? Re-thinking the role of the adult educator'. *Proceedings of the 29th Adult Education Research Conference*. Calgary: Faculty of Continuing Education, University of Calgary.

Collins, M. (1991) *Adult Education as Vocation: A Critical Role for the Adult Educator*. New York: Routledge.

De Marais, K. P. B. (1991) 'John's story: an exploration into critical theory in education'. *Adult Learning*, 2 (9–10), 17.

Ehrenreich, B. (1991) *The Worst Years of Our Lives*. New York: Random House.

Foucault, M. (1977) *Discipline and Punish: The Birth of the Prison*. New York: Vintage Books.

Foucault, M. (1980) *Power/Knowledge: Selected Interviews and Other Writings, 1972–1977*. New York: Pantheon Books.

Fox, D. and Prilleltensky, I. (eds) (1997) *Critical Psychology: An Introduction*. Thousand Oaks, CA: Sage.

Freire, P. (1993) *Pedagogy of the Oppressed*. New York: Continuum.

Freire, P. (1994) *Pedagogy of Hope*. New York: Continuum.

Gelpi, E. (1979) *A Future for Lifelong Education: Volume 1, Lifelong Education Principles, Policies and Practices*. Manchester: Manchester Monographs 13, Department of Adult and Higher Education, University of Manchester.

Goldberger, N., Tarule, J., Clinchy, B. and Belenky, M. (1996) *Knowledge, Difference and Power: Essays Inspired by Women's Ways of Knowing*. New York: Basic Books.

Greene, M. (1986) 'In search of a critical pedagogy'. *Harvard Educational Review*, 56, 427–41.

Griffin, C. (1983) *Curriculum Theory in Adult and Lifelong Education*. London: Croom Helm.

Griffin, C. (1987) *Adult Education and Social Policy*. London: Croom Helm.

Habermas, J. (1985) 'Questions and counter questions', in R. J. Bernstein (ed.) *Habermas and Modernity*. Cambridge, MA: MIT Press.

Habermas, J. (1986) *Autonomy and Solidarity: Interviews*. New York: Verso.

Hammond, M. and Collins, R. (1991) *Self-Directed Learning: Critical Practice*. New York: Nichols.

Horton, M. (1990) *The Long Haul*. New York: Doubleday.

Laycock, M. and Stephenson, J. (eds) (1993) *Using Learning Contracts in Higher Education*. London: Kogan Page.

Lyotard, J.-F. (1979) *The Postmodern Condition*. Minneapolis: University of Minnesota Press.

McLaren, P. (1993) 'Multiculturalism and the postmodern critique: towards a pedagogy of resistance and transformation'. *Cultural Studies*, 7 (1), 118–46.

Marcuse, H. (1965) 'Repressive tolerance', in R. P. Woolf, B. Moore Jr and H. Marcuse *A Critique of Pure Tolerance*. Boston: Beacon Books.

Mills, C. W. (1953) *The Sociological Imagination*. New York: Oxford University Press.

Morss, J. R. (ed.) (1996) *Growing Critical: Alternatives to Developmental Psychology*. New York: Routledge.

Pintrich, P. R. (ed.) (1995) *Understanding Self-Regulated Learning*. New Directions for Teaching and Learning, No. 63. San Francisco: Jossey-Bass.

Shalin, D. N. (1992) 'Critical theory and the pragmatist challenge'. *American Journal of Sociology*, 98, 237–79.

Usher, R., Bryant, I. and Johnston, R. (1997) *Adult Education and the Postmodern Challenge: Learning Beyond the Limits*. New York: Routledge.

Williams, R. (1977) *Marxism and Literature*. New York: Oxford University Press.

10

Education and Empowerment

Abdeljalil Akkari and Soledad Perez

Introduction

The purpose of this chapter is to discuss the conceptual framework of Paulo Freire. We begin by situating Freire's political and religious agendas. In the second section, we underscore Freire's main concepts. The current use of Freire's ideas in different regional contexts is addressed in the third section. We conclude by focusing on how we can best use Freire's pedagogical ideas within the classroom setting.

Freire's experiences are deeply embedded within the Latin American political, social and religious contexts of his time. On the religious level, Freire worked with the poor and illiterate *Communidades Eclesiales de Base* (Basic Church Communities) in north-east Brazil. For many Latin American educators, Freire symbolized both the pedagogical arm of the Liberation Theology Movement as well as educators' resistance to political oppression. Freire's early work is liberal-democratic in nature. His book *Education as a Practice of Freedom* reflects the progressive theology of the Brazilian Bishops' declaration of 1963 and the influence of Karl Mannheim, Eric Fromm and Emanuel Mounier (Austin, 1997).

Although his early political agenda was more influenced by Christian ideology, Freire became more radical after his exile from Brazil by the military dictatorship (in 1964). He then embraced a Marxist centred political discourse. In addition, Freire's experiences in former Portuguese colonies in Africa (for example, his experience as adviser to the revolutionary government of Guinea-Bissau in the mid-1970s) contributed to raise his Third World awareness. He identified human exploitation on various levels, which varied from local oppression of poor peasants to the global domination of the South by the North.

In the last period of his activity, Freire (1994) addressed the current neo-liberal discourse, which denies the continued existence of social classes within the context of a post-Cold War world. Freire rejects this assumption by reasserting that the relationship between classes remains a major force in politics today. Freire warns all progressive educators to be wary of the discourse which, as he states, 'masquerades as post-modernity' (*ibid.*, p. 187). Freire remained optimistic that the continued existence of social classes in today's world provides educators with an opportunity to seek 'the socialist dream, purified of its authoritarian distortions' (Freire, 1994, p. 96). From 1963 to around 1985, Freire's epistemology remained impervious to systems of oppression not based on class, in particular gender and race (Austin, 1987). Yet, his collaboration with American critical authors such as Macedo, McLaren and Shor allowed him to enrich his theory by including gender and ethnic perspectives.

Reading through the work of Freire, the informed reader will doubtless find an affinity with Christian, progressive thought. Yet, similarly observable is a constant fluctuation between a critical acceptance of capitalism, coming from a period of *developmentalist ideology* in Brazil at the beginning of the 1960s, and a clear leaning towards socialism and Marxist thought (Araujo Lima, 1990).

Freire's political and religious agendas are characterized by a strong social commitment to the socially excluded (oppressed). His life was centred on the issue of humanization and liberation. For Freire, both politics and education are about liberation.

Freire's philosophies of education

In his early pedagogical work, Freire put no or little hope in formal education. He questioned the apparent discrepancies between schooling's promise and its actual outcomes particularly in Latin America. Freire was very interested in Illich's ideas of a radical de-schooling of society. He visited the centre of intercultural documentation in Cuernavaca (Mexico) and worked with Illich on several seminars discussing various educational issues. Freire's involvement with adult literacy classes and his promotion of revolutionary liberating thought or conscientization revealed the possibilities for a restructured and de-institutionalized education system taking a leading position in social change. This view is clearly linked ideologically as well as personally with Illich and integrated with broader trends in social thought, such as liberation theology (Gould, 1993).

Regarding the relation between teaching and learning, Freire's position is very close to Roger's (1972) assumption about the negative or neutral effects of teaching. Freire (1976) pointed out that the formal educational system is usually a *reproductive structure* that contributes to the interests and needs of dominant and hegemonic groups. Thus, the potential of liberation is limited in formal schooling which excludes the values and cultures of oppressed groups.

Freire (1997) rejected the notion of education as *banking*. The banking model refers to education understood as merely the transfer of pre-existing knowledge from teachers to students. In other words, teachers make *deposits* into the relatively empty mind (accounts) of the students. These deposits take the form of *cultural capital* which when accumulated confers the privileges of traditional formal education. The *pedagogy of the oppressors* is based on an asymmetrical relationship: on one side is the educator who alone holds a knowledge of the truth, and on the other side the learner who receives this knowledge. This traditional conception of teaching is oppressive in the sense that the pupil is considered to be an empty recipient that must be filled without being given the tools with which to gain a critical understanding of the world (Freire, 1974).

Far from being a *final product*, education is for Freire a *process* originating from a socio-historical context. To educate the socially excluded, Freire focused on adult literacy. He observed that any adult can begin to read in a matter of days if the first words he decodes are charged with social and political meaning. Freire trained his educators to move into rural areas in north-east Brazil and to discover the terms which designate current important issues, such as the access to land or interest on the debts owed to the patron. The discussion of these key issues (generative themes) is central in Freire's literacy method. When literacy is embedded in social awareness, learners take reality into their own hands and they are able to write it down and to speak about it critically (Freire, 1970b).

Literacy is central in the work of Freire. It is not a mastering of a script or the acquisition of words, but understanding the connections between disparate elements of the learner experience and his/her social reality in order to control it. Literacy is about the identification of social issues. For Freire, effective learning occurs more outside than inside schools. Until his late nomination as secretary of education in the city of São Paulo in 1989, Freire showed little interest in formal schooling. He basically worked to convert adult literacy into a socially critical pedagogy.

Using a dialectical Marxist perspective, Freire discussed the concepts of alienation and hegemony. The term alienation is derived from Marxist thought and refers to the domination of people by the power élite, material constraints, political structures, culture and thought. Freire also pointed out the physical and symbolic violence linked to hegemony. Oppressed groups are usually convinced of the inferiority of their culture and world. They often accept with resignation to be objects of domination rather than subjects and actors of their own reality. For Freire, the reverse of alienation and hegemony is *conscientization*, which refers to a *critical reading of one's social reality* (Freire, 1973). Conscientization relies on individuals and groups becoming subjects in their own lives and developing critical conscientiousness, in understanding their history and social environment. This process leads them *automatically* to action. Freire's concept of conscientization is broadly similar to the concept of empowerment widely used in anglophone countries.

Marxist criticism in the 1970s condemned Freire for neglecting the class struggle in his analysis of the oppressed. This criticism maintained that Freire utilized a vague concept of the oppressed (Freire, 1994, p. 89), which Freire rejected by asserting that the oppressed do not need to have social classes defined on their behalf. Freire wanted to avoid reducing people 'to a pure reflex of socioeconomic structures' (*ibid.*, p. 89). Freire likewise rejected the presumptions that his pedagogy presents an idealistic or Utopian vision of humanity and social trans-formation. Here, it is important to consider the pragmatic and spiritual aspects of Freire's work.

Freire's pedagogy represents an approach that tries to deconstruct mainstream education; its established faiths and its banking approach. These certitudes were progressively built by transferring a positivist and causal model from physical sciences to the study of human behavior. Deconstructing mainstream pedagogy means also that educators have no chance to be neutral, neither in their methodo-logies nor in their actions. When we speak about neutrality, it is related to our political options and our subjectivity.

In short, we can describe Freire's educational philosophy as *posing problems* on different levels: the learner, the educator and the curriculum. Therefore, teaching is much more than knowing about a subject here and now, but reaching and transforming the beyond. Teaching demands an educational practice that, accord-ing to Freire (1997), respects the following principles: to be aware that learning never ends; to be aware of the conditioning of learners; to respect the freedom of the learner; to use common sense reality; to have humility, tolerance and to advocate for the rights of the learners; to be in touch with reality; to have joy and hope; to have a strong conviction that change is possible; and to foster curiosity. This set of principles combines the notions of citizenship and the autonomy of the learner. Freire argues that educators (teachers) must design educative contexts that accom-modate students towards various forms of participatory engagement.

A dialogical relationship between both educators and learners will ensure that the curriculum content is situated within the masses' *reading of the world* (Freire, 1994, p. 111), and within an environment in which the educator can also offer his or her own analysis of the world. This formulates Freire's defence of adult literacy education, which empowers people to engage in dialectical solidarity through a critical awareness of the world. Moreover, Freire (1994) asserts that the acquisition of language developed through the democratization of education is instrumental to the formation of identity: 'Dialogue is meaningful precisely because the dialogical subjects, the agents in the dialogue, not only retain their identity, but actively defend it, and thus grow together' (p. 117).

Problem-posing education, which is based upon participatory dialogue, is imper-ative to the praxis of education and thus directly relates to the people's assertion of their human rights, their *battle for citizenship*. For Freire (1994), democratic popular education provides the means of empowering people to own their language and thus attain citizenship (p. 39). Thus, the importance of a dialogical relationship, which merges teacher and student, is reaffirmed in *Pedagogy of Hope* through Freire's defence of popular discourse and the democratization of content in education.

Freire allowed us to understand the concept of *problematization* in pedagogy, or how to go beyond an apparent and cognitive understanding of situations. Problem-atization is the antithesis of problem-solving. In problem-solving, an expert takes distance from reality and reduces it to dimensions that are amenable to treatment as though they were mere difficulties to be solved. Problematization recognizes that solutions are often difficult because the wrong problems are being addressed.

Freire opened our minds to the idea of critical consciousness, which is characterized by depth in the interpretation of problems, by testing one's own findings and an openness to revision and reconstruction, by the attempt to avoid distortion when perceiving problems and to avoid preconceived notions when analysing them, by rejecting passivity, by the practice of dialogue rather than polemics, by receptivity to the new without rejecting the old, and by permeable, interrogative, restless and dialogical forms of life (Freire, 1973).

Alienation is oppositional otherness; the simultaneous presence of conflict and distance. When alienation remains beneath the surface of consciousness, it results in ennui, passivity, submissiveness, and anxiety (Freire, 1968). When alienation becomes conscious, it provokes anger, aggressiveness, hostility, frustration, and fear. Self-conscious alienation can also lead to critical reflection on reality and thereafter to action. Action will effectively overcome alienation to the extent that it can reduce conflict either by eliminating the distance through adaptation or compromise, or by increasing the distance through movement outside the sphere of oppositional influence, or by neutralizing the opposition through superior power or force.

Collegiality is one of the original tenets of Freire's pedagogy. Collegiality is a form of social organization based on shared and equal participation by all members of the community. It contrasts with a hierarchical, pyramidal structure, and is represented by a series of concentric circles. Authority resides in the centre-most circle, not over the others, but equidistant from each, so that authority can listen and reflect the consensus of the whole. A collegial model has been frequently associated with liberatory education programmes. Collegiality may be a good model to organize a critical philosophy of education.

Freire's contribution to educational debate in different contexts

The use of Freire's ideas in the educational debate varies according to the era and the regional contexts. In addition, the broader scope of his theory (ranging from literacy classes to macro-social change) as well as his flexible political ideology (an amalgam of Marxism with his early Christian personalism) make the utilization of his pedagogy very diversified. Austin (1997) suggested that Freirian methodology is capable of being absorbed by a reforming *capitalist* regime (Freire's involvement with Goulart's National Literacy campaign in Brazil) and mainstreamed in the name of an intensification of that process amongst the rural population.

In adult education literature, Freire, along with Malcolm Knowles, heads the list of the most frequently cited authors (Coben, 1998). Freire's success as an international reference in adult education is probably linked to the audience present in adult education courses. This audience traditionally comprises people who try a second time to get some cultural capital after being prematurely evicted from the formal educational system. In adult literacy classes, there is no inflation of cognitive examinations or tests to pass. If we consider the three components present in such activity – the adult-learner, the teacher and the content subject – the most important relation between these three components is the one that exists between the learners and the teacher. This points to one explanation of Freire's success in adult education.

In addition, Freirean community-based adult education may provide a working model for resolving the problem of illiteracy in different cultural contexts because it is learning grounded in the day-to-day experience of the people (Heaney, 1989). However, the working model is different in Latin America and the industrialized countries.

In Latin America, the success of Freire's method has given rise to numerous programmes directed towards urban and rural underprivileged populations. The programmes are never politically neutral in the sense that they belong to a perspective of social change that is at both the macro and micro levels. Groups as diverse as rural workers or indigenous groups have used Freire's pedagogy, beginning their work as political action, but with this action being subsequently transformed into a pedagogical one (Preiswerk, 1998).

Perez (1998) suggested that the issue of Indian minorities education brings out several aspects of the right to be culturally different: the right to land, the right to education and the right to culture heritage are among the constant demands of these minorities. For decades, the states have denigrated the native languages (for example, by refusing to recognize Indian first and family names for official purposes).

Clearly, *popular education* in the Latin American context can be understood as an educational practice situated within a wider process that intends to consider that popular sectors (working class, proletarian communities) constitute themselves as organized and conscious political subjects (Garcia-Huidobro, 1983). In Mexico, Freire's contribution has been adopted widely by educators, with particular impact on Indian education and adult literacy. Indeed, Freire's theoretical and methodological principles have influenced the entire national system of education, especially basic-level programmes (Gonzalez Gaudiano and De Alba, 1994).

In the USA and in Europe, the interest in Freire is above all pedagogical. His literacy method has mainly attracted activists teaching literacy to migrant workers and ethnic minorities. Thus, within the framework of a bilingual education project, a team of teachers applied the principles of *popular education* at a Berlin school. Their perspective rested on the idea that culture is an essential instrument in literacy training. The educators based their method on the fact that in German schools, Turkish students were at a disadvantage because of their language. Their culture and daily experiences were ignored. The integration of their daily problems and conflictual situations within the process of classroom learning allowed these disadvantaged students to give meaning to what they were learning (Overwien, 1999).

Freire's contribution in the critical pedagogy movement, mainly in the USA, is ambivalent. On the one hand, Freire brought political struggle to the centre of the debate on multiculturalism. It is a powerful contribution particularly when we see that conservative, mainstream multiculturalism avoids political issues and focuses rather on neutral psychological tools to enhance cultural diversity and minority members' self-esteem. On the other hand, Freire never theoretically or empirically addressed the multiethnic debate. His statements on the subject are general tools on the personal level, while his position as researcher and educator is lacking (Coben, 1998). This is a big limitation of his legacy for multicultural education, particularly if we remember that he initially worked in north-east Brazil, a context historically marked by racism, slavery and ethnic struggles. Austin (1987) rightly pointed out that in his book, *Pedagogy of the Oppressed*, Freire (1970a) failed to address the possibility of simultaneously contradictory positions of oppression and dominance: the man oppressed by his boss could at the same time oppress his wife. By framing his discussion of oppression in abstract terms, Freire slides over the contradictions and tensions within social settings in which overlapping forms of oppression exist.

An analysis of Freire's work is difficult and perhaps even impossible for authors who are unfamiliar with the Latin American context. One can even ask if it is possible to understand his work if one is not Christian, Marxist and Latin American. But the rejection of Freire's work is mainly due to the ethnocentrism of some European and North American educational specialists. We will look at three examples (Coben, 1998; Gur Ze'ev, 1998; Tan, 1999) to illustrate this ethnocentrism and the unwillingness to accept a Third World author as making a major contribution to educational thinking.

Coben (1998) stated that Freire's work is rhetorical, 'At the best, poetic, and at worst, prolix and inaccessible.' However, we can observe that each pedagogical discourse (from Rousseau to Dewey) is a cocktail of principles which intends to combine various components such as psychological research findings, political/ philosophical theory and pedagogical methods. In denouncing Freire's *verbalism*, Coben (1998) misunderstands the status of educational research in the South. A positivist (scientist) educational discourse disconnected from everyday social struggles is not possible in a Third World context. If Freire's writing style appears sometimes strange to northern observers it is because Freire's work is embedded in educational policy which needs a discourse different from a scientific and academic one. Indeed, each educational discourse encounters a powerful challenge in navigating between two alternatives. In one alternative, this discourse can find shelter in the morass of methodological and empirical discussions at the risk of isolating itself in closed *pedagogical laboratories*. The risk here would be to produce *good research* without being able to take it any farther. The other alternative would be to produce an educational discourse centred on action research, which would necessarily result in a political and social commitment. As a philosopher and theoretician of education, Freire never separated theory from praxis. He attempted to implement his educational philosophy on diverse occasions and settings.

Gur Ze'ev (1998) alleged that

> Freire's critical pedagogy is fundamentalist and positivist, in contrast to his explicit negation of this orientation. It is a synthesis between dogmatic idealism and vulgar collectivism meant to sound the authentic voice of the collective, within which the dialogue is supposed to become aware of itself and the world.

The educational links of this synthesis contain a tension between its mystic-terroristic and its reflective-emancipatory dimensions. In Freire's attitude toward Fidel Castro and Che Guevara, the terroristic potential contained in the mystic conception of the emancipated 'group', 'people', or 'class' knowledge is revealed within the concept of a dialogue between partners in the desirable praxis. Che Guevara used a structurally similar rhetoric to that of Ernst Jünger and national socialist ideologues on the creative power of war, blood, and sweat in the constitution of the new man, the real 'proletar' in South America. Freire gives this as an example of the liberation of the oppressed within the framework of new 'love' relations that allow the silenced 'voice' to speak. (p. 467)

This unjustified and undocumented attack on Freire leads us to think that to understand Freire's philosophy, the observer needs to be sensitive to what is the meaning of being powerless. The indecency of Gur Ze'ev's comparison between Freire and the national socialist agenda is similar to a comparison between the Nazi appeal to boycott Jewish merchants and the current legitimate pressure on banks and corporations (Swiss and others) to restitute belongings confiscated by the Nazi regime or lost during the Holocaust.

Gur Ze'ev (1998) seems to believe that we live in a *fair world* where the battle against colonialism lacks legitimacy. Consequently, he cannot understand Freire. Beyond that, his neo-colonial beliefs are so shook up by Freire that he is quick to replace honest debate with slander and ethnocentrism. This is also what Tan (1999) did in his review of *Pedagogy of the Oppressed*. She was disheartened by the flagrant 'anthropocentrism' at the core of Freire's thinking, where animals and the natural world occupy an inferior place relative to human subjects. According to Tan, in the Freirean universe, animals are diametrically positioned against humans to emphasize the superior cognitive abilities of the human race and to justify its existential value. Unlike humans, animals are 'uncompleted beings' and as such, are incapable of reflecting upon the existential world. Tan suggested that such reductionistic imagination of the non-human world led Freire to perceive only humans as possessing and holding the consciousness, intuition and awareness to give meaning to the world. By arguing that animals are nothing more than passive objects to be acted upon and given meaning to by human agency, Freire has unconsciously reinscribed a hierarchical order of the world itself, and indirectly approved the exploitation and subjugation of non-humans by the human race. In Tan's opinion, this points to a contradiction in Freire's rhetoric of love and humility and it is painfully reminiscent of an ugly period in human history where similar world-views have justified the dehumanization and enslavement of certain groups of people. This reading of Freire is the result of a potent ethnocentrism in that it avoids the fact that the *humanization of animals* is not a universally acknowledged belief, but comes from a particular period of occidental thought.

Freire's latter writings often took the form of transcriptions of long interviews, letters or written conversations with other authors within the critical pedagogy movement. This is one explanation of critiques held by academic authors in the North. A second explanation is related to the ethnocentrism of social scientists in developed countries (Gareau, 1986). Yet, consistent as a pedagogue and citizen, Freire gave in his work glimpses of his family life and his friendships while avoiding any academic élitism.

Beyond the ethnocentrism of formal schooling: hearing Freire

When we observe the educational space in the North and South during the last few decades, we perceive that Freire's appeal to abolish *banking education* remained unheard. To some extent, we witnessed the opposite. In the North, the average number of years of schooling is evidently increasing. For instance, in most OECD countries, less than 5 per cent of the age group have left education by the age of 16, whereas between one-half and two-thirds stay on until the age of 18. At age 24, 20 per cent are still enrolled in education in Australia and Canada and over 25 per cent are still studying in Norway (OECD, 1998). In the South, most countries are approaching universal basic education. In other words, every year, more children are going to school for longer periods. We are witnessing an almost universal diffusion of the schooling model.

This diffusion of schooling is not counterbalanced by a reform of banking education. Pedagogical methods and discourses appear to change very slowly. The reproduction of inequalities by schooling denounced by Freire is also still in effect. As suggested by Bernstein (1996),

> Education is central to the knowledge base of society, groups and individuals. Yet education also, like health, is a public institution, central to the production and reproduction of distributive injustices. Biases in the form, content, access and opportunities of education have consequences not only for the economy; these biases can reach down to drain the very springs of affirmation, motivation and imagination. (p. 5)

We would like to point out the existence of two of Freire's powerful legacies: the first is that schooling has no monopoly on effective learning. The second is Freire's analysis of the links between education and democracy. Freire stated that every theory of education is a theory of democracy and that every theory of democracy is a theory of education. Freire's book *Essa escola chamada vida* (Freire and Betto, 1985) illustrates this second legacy quite well.

Resnick (1987) identified several major differences between school learning and other learning: *pure cognition* in school versus tool manipulation outside of school; symbol manipulation in school versus contextualized reasoning outside; and generalized learning in school versus situation-specific competencies outside. The first difference is individual cognition in school versus shared cognition outside of it. It suggests that the dominant form of school learning and performance is individual. Although group activities of various kinds occur in school, students are ultimately judged on what they can do by themselves. Furthermore, a major part of the core activity of schooling is designed as individual work/homework, in-class

xercises, and the like. For the most part, students succeed or fail at a task
adependently of what other students do (except for the effects of grading on a
urve!) In contrast, much activity outside of school is socially shared. Work,
ersonal life, and recreation take place within social systems, and each person's
bility to function successfully depends on what others do and how several
adividuals' mental and physical performances mesh. A second difference is related
o symbol manipulation in school versus contextualized reasoning outside of it.
xtensive use of tools is only one of the ways that out-of-school thinking engages
he physical world more than in-school thinking. Outside of school, actions are
ntimately connected with objects and events; people often use the objects and
vents directly in their reasoning, without necessarily using symbols to represent
hem. School learning, by contrast, is mostly symbol based; indeed, connections to
he events and objects symbolized are often lost. A third and important difference
s the generalized learning in school versus situation-specific competencies outside.
²art of the reason for this isolation may be that schools aim to teach general, widely
asable skills and theoretical principles. This is their *raison d'être*. Indeed, the major
ustification offered for formal instruction is usually its generality and power of
transfer. Yet to be truly skilful outside school, people must develop situation-
pecific forms of competence.

Opposed to this school pedagogy rightly described by Resnick, Paulo Freire
leveloped an educational theory that rests upon a real exchange between educator
and learner to the point that their roles become interchangeable. Students are
onsidered as individuals endowed with a conscience. Thus what is needed is to
nable them to develop the tools which will enable them to understand, to analyse,
and to view the world with a critical eye. Additionally, the teacher no longer sees
him/herself as the holder of the truth, but also as one who is in the process of
earning (Freire, 1974).

At the practical level of pedagogy in the classroom, Freire's work, above all,
allows connections to be made at many levels, not only between learners and
educators, but also between subject matter and the social and daily life of learners
and educators. These connections can contribute to ensure the durability and
permanence of skills obtained by the whole community of learners.

The second strong contribution by Freire is that every educational theory is a
political theory. Compromise and conflict about educational meaning are subject to
more struggles in Third World countries, particularly in Latin America, than in the
North. The status of pedagogical discourse and action is not the same in places
where inequality is obvious and in a context where it is more hidden. It is not an
accident that Freire's philosophy of education is politically centred.

Freire thought out and put into practice an educational theory that works
towards the liberation of the oppressed. His thinking does not concern only
professionals working in education within and outside of the school setting, but
additionally concerns anyone interested in the way that people become aware of
their oppression: unionists, community political activists etc. Democracy requires
dialogue, participation, political and social responsibility, as well as a degree of
social and political solidarity (Freire, 1978). Power relations are central to Freire for

any analysis of society, and this is especially true for education. Power relations are formed in all relations where differences exist. Power for Freire is not necessarily what is commonly meant by this word. Power is something ubiquitous and cannot be reduced to a global duality between those dominating and those being dominated. Freire's position about oppression is close to Fanon's (1968) study of the psychological toll of racism on both colonized and colonizer. In *Black Skins, White Masks*, Fanon (1968) argues that 'As long as the black man is among his own, he will have no occasion, except in minor internal conflicts, to experience his being through others' (p. 109).

Through the development of his theory of education, Paulo Freire succeeded in demystifying the dreams of educators active in the 1960s who expected, particularly in Latin America, that schools do everything: political, economic and social liberation. Distinguishing between *education for domestication* and *education for liberation*, Freire (1972) maintained that one or the other is necessarily used and that a neutral education cannot exist.

Conclusion

In an era marked by the global hegemony of the North on economic and cultural resources (including educational discourses!), the educational debate needs to move beyond its traditional instrumental goals. Freire argued that the ideology of individualism in banking education has dichotomized the individual from the social context. Liberatory pedagogy must inquire into the tension between the individual and social practice. Freire's theory strongly articulates the connection between individual empowerment and democratic ideals. Freire insists that in order to develop an emancipatory education, we must define learning as a critical inquiry.

By focusing on unequal power relationships, Freire's pedagogy may change the minds of learner and educator by acknowledging the political meaning of education. It is urgent to focus the educational debate on interdisciplinary, cross-cultural perspectives. Freire's insightful analyses might serve to transform as well as to inform educational discourses world-wide.

Each exile from his country denoted a clear and productive rupture in Freire's pedagogical thinking. The first exile, caused by the accession to power of the military regime, led Freire to become aware of disparate cultural settings and to undergo new intellectual experiences in several countries. Breaking from his northeast Brazil mentality and *provincialism* (Furter, 1995), Freire was able to debate with a wide range of authors and education specialists. He was constantly searching for new ideas in continuing his successive, intellectual exiles in Chile, the USA, Switzerland and Africa. His return to Brazil (which can be seen either as his last exile or as a return to his roots) allowed him to work once again with Brazilian and Latin American educators. He thus became involved in the reflection on the contribution of teachers to the strengthening of democracy and the preparation of critical citizens. Freire also got involved in the inquiry on how working-class educators could participate in local educational policies.

Debates about educational reform tend to be impassioned, intense and often repetitious. For decades, two modes of education have coexisted in uneasy peace. The traditional school model is based on the idea of teaching as telling. The primary goal is the transfer of information from an expert (the teacher) to novices (the students). The second model consists in active learning approaches. Freire's pedagogy is a radical and socially oriented version of this second model. Despite the popularity of the second model, it has been honoured more in theory than in practice. By bringing theory into practice, Freire contributed to break tremendous barriers impeding the adoption of more active learning approaches.

References

Araujo Lima, M. (1990) 'Paulo Freire e a educação libertadora'. *Debates Sociais*, 47, 49–57.

Austin, R. (1997) 'Freire, Frei, and literacy texts in Chile, 1964–1970', in C. A. Torres and A. Puiggros (eds) *Latin American Education. Comparative Perspectives*. Boulder, CO: Westview Press.

Bernstein, B. (1996) *Pedagogy, Symbolic Control and Identity. Theory, Research, Critique*. London: Taylor and Francis.

Coben, D. (1998) *Radical Heroes. Gramsci, Freire and the Politics of Adult Education*. New York: Garkand.

Fanon, F. (1968) *Black Skins, White Masks*. London: Pluto Press.

Freire, P. (1968) *Acción Cultural para la libertad*. Santiago de Chile: ICIRA (Instituto de Pesquisa e Treinamento em Reforma Agrária).

Freire, P. (1970a) *Pedagogy of the Oppressed*. New York: Seabury.

Freire, P. (1970b) *Cultural Action for Freedom*. Cambridge, MA: Harvard Educational Review Press.

Freire, P. (1972) 'L'éducation: domestication ou libération?' *Perspectives*, 2, 193–202.

Freire, P. (1973) *Education for Critical Consciousness*. New York: Seabury.

Freire, P. (1974) *Pédagogie des opprimés suivi de Conscientisation et révolution*. Paris: Maspero.

Freire, P. (1976) 'L'alphabétisation et le "rêve possible" '. *Perspectives*, 6(1), 70–3.

Freire, P. (1978) *Education for Critical Consciousness*. New York: Seabury Press.

Freire, P. (1994) *Pedagogy of Hope: Reliving Pedagogy of the Oppressed*. New York: Continuum.

Freire, P. (1997) *Pedagogia da Autonomia: Saberes necessários à prática educativa*. São Paulo: Paz e Terra.

Freire, P. and Betto, F. (1985) *Essa escola chamada vida: depoimentos ao reporter Ricardo Kotscho*. São Paulo: Ática.

Furter, P. (1995) 'Paulo Freire et Ivan Illich: Des utopies pédagogiques aux utopies sociales'. *Vous Avez Dit . . . Pédagogie*, 39, 8–25.

Gareau, F. (1986) 'The Third World revolt against First World social science: an explication suggested by the revolutionary pedagogy of Paulo Freire'. *International Journal of Comparative Sociology*, 27, 172–89.

Garcia–Huidobro, J. E. (1983) *Intento de definición de la educación popular*. Santiago de Chile: CIDE.

Gonzalez Gaudiano, E. and De Alba, A. (1994) 'Freire. Present and future possibilities', in P. MacLaren and C. Lankshear (eds) *Politics of Liberation. Paths from Freire*. London: Routledge.

Gould, B. (1993) *People and Education in the Third World*. London: Longman.

Gur Ze'ev, I. (1998) 'Toward a non-repressive critical pedagogy'. *Educational Theory*, 48(4), 463–86.

Heaney, T. (1989) *Freirean Literacy in North America: The Community-Based Education Movement Thresholds in Education*. Available on-line at http://nlu.nl.edu/ace/Resources/ Freire.html

OECD (1998) *Thematic Review of the Transition from Initial Education to Working Life. Interim Comparative Report*. Paris: OECD.

Overwien, B. (1999) 'Apprentissage informel et "educación popular" '. *Education des Adultes et Développement*, 52, 175–89.

Perez, S. (1998) 'Languages and regions in Europe and elsewhere: a revival of regional issues?' *Prospects*, 28(4), 693–706.

Perez, S. and Akkari, A. (1999) 'Educational research in Latin America: the lie of the land'. *Prospects*, 29(3), 365–78.

Preiswerk, M. (1998) *Educação popular e teologia da libertação*. São Paulo: Vozes.

Resnick, L. B. (1987) 'Learning in school and out'. *Educational Researcher*, 16(9), 13–20.

Roger, C. (1972) *Liberté pour apprendre*. Paris: Dunod.

Tan, S. (1999) A review of *Pedagogy of the Oppressed*. Available on-line at http:// fcis.oise.utoronto.ca/ ~ daniel_schugurensky/freire/freirebooks.html

11

Education and Disempowerment

Catherine Matheson and Joanne Dillow

Introduction

This chapter will investigate, first, the assumption that those learners with the greater amount of cultural capital are culturally closer to the centre, that those with the lesser amount are closer to the edge, and that there is consequently less cultural distance between the former and more between the latter and the education system. Second, the processes which lead to certain groups of pupils becoming marginalized within the education system will be examined. Third, we will address the extent to which educational exclusion can be considered an extreme form of marginalization or whether it is a self-inflicted injury.

At a global level the data concerning gender marginalization, that is, how men and woman are situated differently, reveals the extent of gender inequality. Women compose one-half of the world population and perform two-thirds of the world's work hours, yet are everywhere poorer in resources and poorly represented in decision-making positions (Peterson and Runyan, 1993). Unlike sex which is a biological distinction, gender refers to culturally specific and socially learned behaviour and expectations. Thus, the occupations in which women predominate – this is also true for people from the lower social classes and ethnic minorities – tend to have a much lower status than those in which white middle-class males are highly represented (Acker, 1994; Apple, 1999). None the less these occupations are more often than not controlled by white middle-class males. Broadly speaking, through educational marginalization according to gender, social class and ethnicity the education system colludes to a great extent in perpetuating the attribution of a greater value assigned to that which is associated with masculinity, middle class and whiteness and lesser value to that which is associated with femininity, working class and non-whiteness.

An ethnic minority is an immigrant or racial, religious, linguistic, or other, group regarded by those claiming to speak for the cultural majority as distinct and unassimilated, not at the centre but at the edge. People from lower social classes also tend to be perceived as not belonging to the cultural majority and thus as being at the edge and not at the centre. This last point underlines the notion that minority is a hegemonic construct. The number of members of a group is much less important than the power that the group wields. In this respect, people from the lower classes, many ethnic minorities (all of them?) and women have each, in their own ways, aspects of the status of a minority.

The situation of people both from the lower social classes and from ethnic minorities has many similarities with that of women in terms of there being a greater proportion of them and, of course, of women from the lower social classes and from these minorities in low-paid, low-status and/or part-time jobs, that is, in jobs in which there is little or no decision-making, jobs where the power tends to elude you since you do as you are told as opposed to telling others what to do.

Gender, ethnicity and exams

In the UK girls do better than boys in school examinations at all levels. This is, however, not true across all subjects. There is a well-established pattern of arts subjects (especially languages) and mathematics, sciences (other than biology) and information technology that are very gender-typed and boys tend to achieve marginally better results in mathematics, sciences (other than biology) and information technology. This happens to some extent at 16+ external exams (GCSE for England, Wales and Northern Ireland and SCE Standard Grade for Scotland) and to a greater extent at the levels of exams allowing application to higher education (principally A level for England, Wales and Northern Ireland and SCE Higher Grade for Scotland) where boys get nearly all the highest grades. Indeed, in all these exams, more boys perform at the extremes than do girls who cluster much more around the mean. Further, this tendency is more pronounced at the levels of SCE Higher Grade and A level than at 16+ (Mackinnon, Statham and Hales, 1999).

Similar information about ethnic groups and about social class is less available and less reliable than that available for the sexes. When attainment is measured in five or more GCSE passes (grades A–C), at least one A level and beginning a degree, the figures are very similar for white and Asian children (in the UK these are taken to mean people of Indian, Pakistani and Bangladeshi origin) but children and young people of African-Caribbean origin do less well. They achieve lower results in achievement at a third, a half and nearly a fifth of the other two groups. When attainment in measured in terms of people of working age who have no qualifications, the highest percentage is among people of Pakistani and Bangladeshi origin with 60 per cent of women and 50 per cent of men having no qualifications (Mackinnon, Statham and Hales, 1999). There are currently wide disparities by social groups in terms of educational attainment. If we look at those who enter higher education, achieve degrees and other awards the highest percentage is among the higher social classes who have the lowest drop-out rate (Metcalf, 1997).

Feminists and others claim that for girls and women there is equal or better access and equal or better achievement at school, further and higher education (except in certain male-dominated subjects) and that this is due to the influence of feminist movement and to the efforts of the feminists in UK in 1970s and early 1980s. However, these same commentators underline that women are still marginalized in decision-making positions in all sectors of the employment market and that the education system still discriminates against girls and women (Acker, 1994).

Discourses of inclusion and exclusion

The discourse of social exclusion or inclusion which is situated within the dominant discourse of the market or consumerism is a most frequently used term in the UK and elsewhere to describe the situation of people who for one reason or another do not appear to be partaking in mainstream education and training. 'Social inclusion, like social exclusion is becoming a politically attractive concept ... it diverts attention away from the possible need for radical change and encourages compliance with the status quo' (Barry, 1998, p. 5, in Preece, 1999, p. 16). This discourse shapes the measures which claim to address inequality and also diverts attention from particular issues by merging social class, gender and ethnicity or sexuality under one all-encompassing framework which serves to make power relationships less evident, and thus more invisible, and by the same process lowers self-esteem and expectations because the dominant discourse is so culturally embedded that its values have been internalized at the expense of the socio-cultural value systems of the marginalized groups.

According to the Dearing Report (NCIHE, 1997) the problem of under-representation stems largely from attitudes in schools, amongst parents and in local communities where low aspirations and low self-confidence are all too common though financial and other pressures also play their part. With no change in qualifications achieved but with a change in attitude the propensity or likelihood of the middle (skilled non-manual and manual) and the lowest social classes (semi-skilled and unskilled) to apply to enter higher education could be increased to that of the highest social classes (managerial and professional). This would mean that an additional 23,000 students aged 18/19 would enter higher education (17,000 from the middle social classes and 6,000 from the lowest social classes) (Metcalf, 1997).

What may prevent this attitudinal change from happening and keeps various groups such as girls and women, ethnic minorities and lower social classes from not being marginalized has rarely been examined outwith the dominant educational discourse, an example of which is found in the Dearing Report (NCIHE, 1997) which explains the burden of being marginalized in terms of financial constraints, low achievement, low aspirations and low self-confidence. Looking at the life histories of people belonging to marginalized groups, however, shows that socio-cultural marginalization and exclusion is a highly complex process to which all sectors of society contribute. Marginalization and exclusion can be understood by investigating the effects of different power relations and discourses on the learning paths/school experience/experience of the education system, and this might be a better way to address the problem than simply raising expectations so that the marginalized or excluded can become normalized according to the mainstream educational discourse (Preece, 1999).

Cultural distance and marginalization

The following factors interact to produce *cultural distance* towards education:

- socio-cultural background and cultural capital;
- parental influence;
- schooling, experience of learning and, in particular, the attitudes of teachers; and
- influence of educational discourses and influence of the media which reinforce, modify or even create new discourses.

This marginalization or cultural distance in which education is perceived as something 'for people like me' or 'not for people like me' is the consequence of internalized attitudes and values, themselves the consequence of the internalization of societal expectations articulated within the mainstream educational discourse(s). Educational decisions are the joint result of three main processes: what one can do, what one wants to do and, indirectly, the conditions that shape one's preferences and intentions (Gambetta, 1987). These conditions are the powerful societal forces past and present, all the more powerful for being so frequently invisible and subconscious (Benn, 1996).

Marginalization then is caused by the internalization of the dominant discourse which leads to attitudes and behaviour according to the following proposed model. The background, ethnicity or gender of the pupil is not valued or less valued at school or in the wider society. This is seen in the way the curriculum ignores or diminishes or pays scant attention to the specific culture and values associated with gender or ethnicity. It is reinforced by the way teachers and others relate to them. This in turn leads to disinterest and low aspirations, made worse if there is a negative experience of education of the parents and/or of the self. If added to that there is a lack of knowledge about (higher) education and student life, fears and anxieties will lead to a lack of confidence in the ability of the self to perform in examinations, enter higher education and successfully gain a degree (Lynch and O'Riordan, 1998; Reay, 1998; Tett, 1999).

Educational research has hinted at or highlighted this process of internalization of dominant discourses. Robbins (COHE, 1963) found that the disproportionately large Oxbridge intake from public schools was due mainly to the reluctance of grammar school sixth-formers to apply, and only marginally to a preference for public school applicants (COHE, 1963). Willis (1977) suggested that the boys he studied had internalized the working-class ethic of the factory. Griffin (1985) alluded that one of the reasons female academic abilities were used inefficiently was because the girls she studied had internalized the notion that academic success was irrelevant, and at worst a barrier, to more highly valued goals associated with marriage. Heathfield and Wakeford (1991) underlined the importance of the media in shaping the perceptions of university that were held by working-class pupils since these have little or no knowledge of university *per se* whether through their family or the school.

Marginalization, girls and women

The marginalization process is similar for all the groups though girls and women are no longer marginalized in terms of educational access and outcome. They are, however, still marginalized in terms of treatment within the education system and in terms of employment access, treatment and outcome. The way in which girls were expected to internalize the discourse of the ideology of domesticity which prevailed in the UK from the nineteenth century onwards is seen in the way the education of girls was expected to be different from that of boys. When it was found that girls achieved higher scores than boys in the 11+ exams, a fact which could have resulted in more girls than boys obtaining the prestigious grammar school placements, girls' results were weighted differently from those of boys, so that they achieved fewer places than their results demanded, and boys were awarded more places than their results merited. This was justified as a way to make up for the immaturity of boys (Deem, 1981). Norwood (SSEC, 1943), Crowther (ACEE, 1959) and Newsom (ACE, 1963) continued to underline that a girl's place was in the home and a boy's in the workplace. Consequently girls had internalized the ideology of domesticity and until recently, though even today this is not uncommon, placed marriage and motherhood before academic success. Indeed, academic success was perceived as detrimental to marriage and motherhood. The feminist discourse of the 1970s and early 1980s arguably led girls, women and society at large to internalize some of its own values which enabled girls and women to achieve their academic potential to a far greater extent (Acker, 1994). The feminist discourse aimed at reducing female underachievement which replaced the issue of working-class male underachievement dominant during the 1960s and until the mid-1970s (Weiner, Arnot and David, 1997). Feminist research blamed discrimination and male privilege for the underachievement. Mainstream researchers explained it as the consequence of biological and innate gender differences when it concerned mathematics and sciences. The fact that girls were doing better in the humanities was because of hard work and conformism!

Today because girls tend to do better than boys in school examinations at all levels, a new discourse of male underachievement and disadvantage has emerged. Within this discourse female success is viewed as corollary to male failure. While there is little evidence that girls' improvement in examinations has been at the expense of that of boys, this discourse, to a great extent media constructed, has led to a sub-discourse of moral panic especially as black and working-class male disadvantage is depicted as a threat to law and order. The importance and the influence of the media and of its messages is not to be neglected. Girls are portrayed as more industrious and conscientious, better behaved, more passively compliant, and implicitly more unimaginative and boring (Arnot, David and Weiner, 1996; Weiner, Arnot and David, 1997).

There is a multiplicity of ways in which gender inequalities (still) exist in all aspects of schooling and education (teachers' attitudes and classroom practices, teaching resources, school organization and administration). Teachers' attitudes and classroom practices in particular have a primordial influence on maintaining gender inequality. Research has underlined time and time again that boys receive more reprimands and more praise than girls. Teachers select topics that interest boys to establish control in classroom. Boys take up more of the teacher's time and are graded more highly which leads to the teacher's attitudes undermining girls' confidence. Girls are far more likely to underestimate their performance than boys and they interpret failure as lack of ability and not lack of effort as boys do (Acker *et al.*, 1984; Clarricoates, 1980; Deem, 1978; Mackinnon, Elquist-Saltzman and Prentice, 1998; Martin, 1999; Purvis, 1991; Weiner, Arnot and David, 1998).

Female educational experiences are different and unequal to those of males. Present-day schooling (or the education system as a whole) still inhibits women's and girls' confidence, skills and abilities. Females receive and perceive different messages about their aptitudes and abilities from those of males, which has implications for their place in the family and the labour market. Various authors have investigated the discrimination experienced by girls and women in the education system (Acker *et al.*, 1984; Byrne, 1978; Deem, 1980; Paterson and Fewell, 1990; Weiner, Arnot and David, 1997). Others claim that schools benefit boys whatever their social class and that because knowledge is human-made and because of sexism in the curriculum and of the attitudes of teachers girls achieve less than their potential at school (Spender, 1982; Spender and Sarah, 1980). Some go even further and argue that to become men in our society boys have to learn to dominate and control girls. Schools are training grounds for social maleness where boys learn that they will have power over women and they practise that power by intimidating, harassing and putting down girls around them. Schools batter girls into submission to patriarchal values (Larkin, 1994; Mahony, 1985).

This inhibiting of confidence, skills and abilities is also true of ethnic minorities and lower social classes. It is nevertheless interesting to note that when we focus on school exclusion as opposed to socio-cultural marginalization, it is boys who tend to be excluded and not girls, and when girls are excluded it is for similar reasons to boys: abusive behaviour, violence and aggression.

Exclusion: extreme marginalization or self-inflicted injury?

Blyth and Milner (1996a, p. 6) define exclusion as 'the means by which the headteacher of a school can prevent a child or young person from attending school, whether for a fixed period or permanently'. They go on to make the distinction between exclusions, which are school driven, and truancy or school phobia, which is child driven. Exclusion is a highly emotive issue and there is agreed concern from the media, government, parents and teachers about the increasing numbers of excluded children. Concern is evident from headlines such as 'Expulsions spiral as school fights yob culture' (Preston, 1994), 'Out of school and in trouble' (Thornton, 1998a) and 'Expelled – now no-one wants her' (Garment, 1998).

Permanent exclusions have risen dramatically over the past decade following the abolition of the indefinite exclusion category in the Department for Education's White Paper (1992). Garment (1998) suggests that between 1990 and 1995 there was a fourfold increase in the number of permanent exclusions and by 1997 permanent exclusions had reached 12,500, a 13 per cent increase on the previous year (*Special Children*, 1998). There is a general consensus that the official figures underestimate the actual numbers of excluded children. Pyke (1992) and The National Union of Teachers (1992) estimated the total fixed-term and permanent[1] exclusions in 1992 at 25,000 whilst in the same year a MORI poll conducted by the BBC's *Panorama* programme suggested that a figure of 66,000 was more realistic (NUT, 1992).

Sparks (1998) submits that permanent exclusions have risen by a staggering 450 per cent since the early part of the decade and Blyth and Milner (1996a) claim that the actual number of children excluded from British schools is subject to considerable speculation. It is interesting to bear in mind that none of the figures estimating exclusions include those who were excluded in a previous year and had not returned to mainstream education, and 'obviously they do not cover children who are excluded "informally": anecdotal evidence suggests this is not uncommon' (Social Exclusion Unit, 1998, p. 8). These discrepancies highlight the inefficiencies of the systems of reporting exclusions and the need for a more accurate and reliable system.

These factors have induced educational debate concerning exclusion to examine which groups are more likely to be at risk from exclusion and why this is so. Research indicates that there are distinct groups of children who are more likely to be excluded and these will be examined in turn to suggest to what extent this is a problem and the reasons why.

Risk factors in exclusion

The literature identifies many factors that place a child at greater risk of exclusion. If it is the case that there may be other factors influencing why some children are more likely to be excluded from school, these need to be examined further. Figures demonstrate that if you are in Years 10–11, black[2] (predominantly African-Caribbean), male, with special educational needs or living in care, you are at greater risk of exclusion. This needs to be examined to ascertain to what extent educational exclusion can be considered an extreme form of marginalization or a self-inflicted injury. Exclusion from school is primarily a birthright of the disadvantaged, and represents a picture of educational conditions that have changed little over time

(Galloway, 1982). Summaries of the research (Blyth and Milner, 1996b; Lovey, Docking and Evans, 1993; McManus, 1995) identify without exception certain groups of children who are at greater risk of exclusion than others.

Hayden (1997) in her research on primary phase permanent exclusions, surmised that Afro-Caribbean children were over-represented in the figures. Hayden's findings about this over-representation have been confirmed elsewhere. Black children make up 2 per cent of the whole school population. However, 8.5 per cent of all permanently excluded children in 1991–2 were black. It is important to note that not all LEAs record accurate data concerning the ethnic background of their excluded children and the figures are therefore seen as an underestimation. The *Times Educational Supplement* (Thornton, 1998b) conducted its own analysis of UK government figures and arrived at the shocking conclusion that, depending on the area in question, black children were up to fifteen times more likely to be excluded from school than their white counterparts. Nationally (i.e. in England and Wales), 'black pupils were at a 3.4 times greater risk of expulsion than white children in 1996–7' (Thornton, 1998b). This finding caused the Chair of the Commission for Racial Equality to call for 'urgent measures to staunch the flow of ethnic minority children who are being shown the door' (Ouseley, 1998). The sense of moral panic in the broadcast and print media which has accompanied such findings is clearly evident from headlines such as 'Racism fears as exclusions rise' (Pennington, 1998) and 'Black exclusions scandal' (Ouseley, 1998).

Gillborn (reported in Pennington [1998]) claims that African-Caribbean children are six times more likely to be excluded from school than white pupils and believes that this difference is set to grow. He poses the critical question: 'are African-Caribbeans six times more unmanageable than whites, or is there something wrong with the system?' (*ibid.*). The stated position of the UK government is that in these cases 'the education system fails young people' (FCO, 1998, n.p.) and to reverse this failure is one of its educational priorities. It is such a priority that the mentoring schemes to help ethnic minority pupils are seeing their funding raised from a miserable £40,000 per annum to a slightly less miserly £80,000 per annum (DfEE, 1999). These schemes have been widely reported in the media as having a positive and lasting impact on pupils' self-esteem and educational attainment, and yet are subject to financial support that is at best derisory.[3]

We can only wait and see the positive impact of this initiative but its financial levels underline the fact that there is an immediate tension between the rhetoric of social inclusiveness in schools which seeks to validate all pupils and raise their self-worth and the discourse of the market which manifests itself in school league tables (see, for example, http://www.dfee.gov.uk/perform.shtml) which can stimulate a school to divest itself more readily of those pupils whose performance *might* lower its rating.

Stirling (1996), in her research on disadvantaged children, attempts to explain why in the metropolitan authority she studied, African-Caribbean children 'constituted over 40 per cent of recorded exclusions while comprising less than 10 per cent of the total school population' (Stirling, 1996, quoted in Blyth and Milner, 1996b, p. 58). Stirling suggests that in cases where a black pupil has been excluded from school, the race of the pupil very often features as an issue in the background to the exclusion. This frequently takes the form of complaints that the school is racist.

Stirling (1996) highlights the example of a black boy being excluded for fighting as a response to persistent racial taunts. The school's decision to exclude was based upon a view that the child had a 'negative attitude' and yet teachers had been unwilling, or unable to assist when the child had informed them of the racial taunts (Stirling, 1996). It appears clear that in this situation the school believed it was justified in imposing the exclusion and subsequently that it was a self-inflicted injury on the part of the child. Conversely, suggestion can be made that, had the teachers intervened at the request of the black child, the subsequent series of actions may never have occurred.

Stirling (1996) suggests that some teachers' perceptions of black children as a group differed from their perceptions of white children, and yet schools frequently respond to accusations of racism by protesting that they treat all children the same. This fails to recognize that not all children are the same and some have the disadvantage of being subject to additional pressures, such as racist abuse (Stirling, 1996 p. 59). A research review published in 1996 by OFSTED concluded that:

> Qualitative research has frequently pointed to a relatively high level of tension, even conflict, between white teachers and African-Caribbean pupils. Examples quoted varied from teacher complaints about 'troublesome' black pupils, disproportionate levels of criticism and control of black pupils, negative stereotypes, and a 'stimulus-response' situation where pupils identified and responded to expectations of low ability and disruptive behaviour. (Social Exclusion Unit, 1998, 2.18)

It appears clear that 'race' is an influential factor for those at a higher risk of exclusion from school and this could be argued to be a mitigating component in deciding who is to blame for educational exclusion. It already seems to be the case that exclusion cannot simply be explained away as the fault of the child and therefore is not always a self-inflicted injury. Evidence suggests that in some instances the likelihood of exclusion is higher dependent upon skin colour. To suggest that black children are simply more 'naughty' than their white counterparts is naïve and unrealistic in the light of the other factors which undoubtedly play their part.

Gender and exclusion

In an examination of those more at risk of exclusion, statistics suggest that sex is a very important determinant. Boys are four to five times more likely to be excluded than girls (DfE, 1993; Parsons, 1994; Secondary Heads Association, 1992). Hayden (1997) confirms that 90 per cent of the excludees from her research were boys. Figures from the Social Exclusion Unit's report *Truancy and School Exclusion* (1998) suggest that 83 per cent of excludees were male and Cooper, Upton and Smith (1991) claim that although boys (especially African-Caribbean) are over-represented in exclusion figures, the authors also found that white European boy were over-represented in exclusion statistics also. They therefore conclude tha 'gender rather than race factors probably accounted for these results' (Cooper Upton and Smith, 1991, quoted in Blyth and Milner, 1993, p. 259). What is no tackled in this conclusion is the double effect of being black, with the accompany ing teacher/school/peer group/societal expectations, and being male, with th expectations that accompany this.

'Male socialisation processes emphasising aggressiveness and assertiveness a positive male characteristics and reinforcing gender stereotypes' (Blyth and Milner 1993, p. 299) are an influential factor for the high representations of boys ii exclusion statistics. From this stance it could be argued that the aggression that cai sometimes lead to exclusion is the responsibility of socialization through the family and school and not the child. One must be careful with this argument because it ha the scope to become an all-embracing explanation for the behavioural problems of children. One must not forget that although there are good examples of misbehav iour being the result of emotional or even physical difficulties, there is still evidence to suggest that in some instances there are no mitigating circumstances found.

It seems that some children are predisposed (or might we say predestined?) to exclusion, and one could therefore argue that exclusion cannot always be deemed to be simply a case of a self-inflicted injury. 'The behaviour that leads to exclusion doe: not in itself, supply a full or sufficient answer to the question of why pupils are excluded' (OFSTED, 1996, p. 8). A further important issue in the examination of where responsibility lies for educational exclusion is the home background of the child. 'Far too many children looked after by local authorities are excluded (OFSTED, 1996, p. 7) and they are one of the groups most at risk from exclusion.

One survey (Maginnis 1993) calculated that a child living under social service care was 80 times more likely to be excluded from school than a child living in a family home. It is assumed that children 'looked after' have the weight and support of the local authority to secure their rights to equality and opportunity within the education system. Children in residential care have a one in three chance of being permanently excluded from school compared with one in 47 in foster care (Maginnis, 1993). This indicates the importance of having a supportive home background. OFSTED (1996) concludes that the correlation between children who are 'looked after' and children who are excluded is too high. Indeed the Social Exclusion Unit (1998) indicates that this is a serious cause for concern and shows that in England a child in care is ten times more likely to be excluded from school than is his/her average peer.

Firth and Horrocks (1996) suggest that there must be reasons why these children are so disadvantaged educationally. The most popular explanation given for 'looked after' children's lack of achievement focuses around a familiar excuse. 'These young people are deemed to be the products of their early childhood and what should we expect from children who come from such a disadvantaged background' p. 79). Research has shown that children who require local authority placements have experienced various levels of deprivation, and it would therefore be naïve to disregard completely the impact of past experience on a child's ability and attitude towards education.

A common theme for many children who are 'looked after' by their local authority is how children often underestimate their own potential and ability, and do not expect to do well at school. A further mitigating factor for educational deficits and disproportionate exclusions is the low educational expectations of the children by social workers, carers and teachers.

Firth and Horrocks (1996) are adamant of the link between social service care and exclusion from school and this possibility deserves consideration. Government findings would seem to support this (Social Exclusion Unit, 1998). Evidence is clear that those in the care of the social services are more likely to be over-represented in exclusion figures.

It is not only those in social service care who are at a greater risk of exclusion. The frequently made assertion that many excluded pupils have difficult home circumstances is backed up by OFSTED (1996) whose detailed study of excluded pupils' home and family circumstances 'presented a grim catalogue of misery' (n.p.).

Among the problems were: poverty, often related to unemployment; the need to look after a sick or disabled parent; the loss of one or both parents, through bereavement or family breakdown; strained family relationships; absentee fathers; the involvement of older (usually male) siblings in crime or drug abuse, with pressure to follow suit; the inability of parents or carers to exercise control; physical or sexual abuse; and racism fears, perceived or actual, in the area if not in the school (OFSTED, 1996).

The conclusion of many commentators, including the Elton Report (DES, 1989), is that the variation in exclusion rates between schools in socio-economic catchment areas and with similar intakes shows a lack of direct and consistent correlation between these factors. This contrasts sharply with the more intuitive findings from the Secondary Heads Association (1992, p. 19) who found that 'much, if not most ... relates to the nature of the intake of schools'. OFSTED (1996) acknowledges that the socio-economic context of the school is sometimes associated with rates of exclusions. The report goes on to say that children from families which are under financial or emotional stress are more likely to produce poor behaviour which leads to exclusion.

Exclusion and special educational needs

It is clear that factors exterior to the schools have an effect upon the child and these external factors can be detrimental to the educational careers and futures of some children. This is again highlighted by the claim that children with special educational needs are more likely to be excluded. In 1992, children with statements of special educational needs made up between 12.5 and 15 per cent of permanently excluded children although children with a statement only made up approximately 2 per cent of the general school population (Blyth and Milner, 1996b).

Parsons (1996) calculates that for 1993–4, special school exclusions accounted for 0.46 per cent of the total exclusions. However, none of the figures account for children who have special educational needs, but do not have a statement. This again highlights the inaccuracies of the figures concerning exclusion. Even OFSTED (1996) concedes that low levels of literacy are more likely to lead to poor behaviour and exclusions. Hayden (1997) argues strongly that all excluded children should be treated as having special educational needs and/or being 'in need' of an education and should therefore receive support and protection from legislation rather than receiving sanctions such as exclusions. This does, however, throw up certain moral questions, not least of which concerns with whom the responsibility for a child's behaviour actually lies. If a child is marginalized and his/her behaviour is a consequence of that, then the responsibility for the child's behaviour can at least be shared with the dominant discourse which has produced this marginalization. Clearly, in some cases marginalization may be more evident than in others but, none the less, there is still the problem of how and where to draw the line between what is acceptable and what is not, what is excusable and what is not and to do these things in a just and inclusive manner which aims to maximize the educational experience of the child and validates his/her background and culture.

Hayden (1996) states that whether or not a statement of needs is in operation, many children who are excluded because of behaviour are also experiencing difficulties in learning. If learning difficulties are the root cause of the behavioural problems, it is ineffectual to exclude the child on the grounds of the behavioural problems. It would be more beneficial to tackle the original learning difficulty. Argument arises here that having a learning difficulty does not constitute a reason for exclusion, and yet it was this that eventually brought about the exclusion. Hence the need to look beyond the surface of the events leading to exclusion.

Many of the children (more than 20 per cent) in Hayden's study had statements of special educational needs, almost always to provide support for their emotional and behavioural difficulties. This figure is likely to underestimate the true number of children with severe emotional and behavioural difficulties since some authorities did not afford these children the protection of a statement until 1994.

Exclusion: self-inflicted or imposed?

It is important to stress that many pupils face problems which affect their studies. OFSTED (1996) describes a number of these: low attendance; volatility and periodic aggression, sometimes interspersed with periods of more co-operative behaviour; strained relationships with adults, sometimes manifested in verbal abuse; extreme disaffection with school, with exclusions sometimes provoked as a means of leaving school; alcohol, drug and substance abuse; poor mental health; inappropriate sexual behaviour, and difficult relationships with the opposite sex; symptoms of severe emotional disturbance, such as a compulsive fire-raising or soiling (OFSTED, 1996).

Particular circumstances make a child more vulnerable and, as we have shown above, the message seems to be: 'don't be black (African-Caribbean) male; don't have special educational needs; don't be in care; don't be working class; or don't have a difficult home background'. Above all, do not be all five. Clearly the more marginalized one is within the society which is school then the greater one's chances are of being excluded. It is not that, for example, middle-class children do not have difficult backgrounds. Indeed, problems such as child abuse cut across all social classes. Rather it is the case that the middle-class child's background and culture are more likely to be valued and validated by the school. The middle-class child's speech patterns are less likely to be deemed 'slang'. S/he is less likely to suffer from negative stereotypical cultural (as opposed to gender) expectations and so on. In short, the problem which the middle-class child has is not compounded by pre-existing cultural factors. Hence the manner in which the child displays the problem will be different from his/her working-class, black, male peer. The manner in which the display will be seen will also be different and probably more positive.

Exclusion is clearly not just an educational issue but also a social issue, in terms both of the school as a social grouping and of wider society.

Galloway (1982, p. 16) concludes that 'a pupil's chances of being excluded . . . are influenced as much, and probably more, by which school [s/]he happens to attend, as any stress in his [/her] family or any constitutional factors in the pupil himself [/herself].' The government inferred in 1992 that the variation in the numbers of exclusions between individual schools seemed to be too great to be explained by the socio-economic nature of schools' catchment areas. It is evident from research such as this that regardless of behaviour, some children are predisposed to exclusion and they are unable to alter this, because sometimes this may not be through any fault of their own.

Parsons (1997) argues that exclusion occurs in a climate of disaffection and underperformance and that social problems, family and community dysfunction and psychological problems contribute to the scenario. Alternative hypotheses have been identified as possibly accounting for the increase in exclusions. Parsons (1996) attributes the increase to changes in the law, psychological factors, family and social factors, stretched educational resources and a cultural response to alienated and alienating behaviour.

In any discussion of factors affecting school exclusions, consideration must be made of the school policies with which each child was excluded. It may be simply the case that some schools are more willing to exclude children compared with others, or that a particular school has competent measures of avoiding exclusions. These factors can be contributory to some schools having disproportionately higher exclusion figures, as highlighted by Galloway (1982), a view echoed by Social Exclusion Unit (1998).

There can be little doubt that educational exclusions are a worrying phenomenon, although the UK government does claim some recent improvement in England.[4] This recent improvement is, however, the first time that such an improvement has been recorded and, while it is much lauded by government itself, it is perhaps a little early to break out the champagne.

It is relatively easy to place the blame on the children being excluded because ultimately it is their behaviour that leads to exclusions, but this simplistic view of human interaction disregards any attenuating circumstances. Hill (1998), from her research on the child's view of exclusion, highlights the importance of home circumstances in their reasons for being excluded. She claims that the number of children who had experienced parental separation and/or another traumatic life event was staggering and supported Parsons's (1994) findings.

The impact of bereavement, strained family relationships, poverty, prostitution, psychiatric illness, and domestic violence cannot be underestimated. An understanding of the background to these difficulties leads to serious questions about whether exclusion is a realistic solution to some of these problems. It is clear that many of the disruptions in school were triggered by problems that were brought in from outside and manifested themselves in school (Hill, 1998). Recalling Blyth and Milner's (1996b) classification that exclusions are school driven, this overtly appears to be the case. Schools are acting on what in many cases appears to be a child or family driven cry for help.

To suggest that educational exclusion is *simply* a self-inflicted injury is neglectful of external influences. Further research is needed if this area of concern is to be fully understood and further examination of the influence of the school and how it interacts with the child's culture is required. We have suggested that exclusion may have a certain appeal since the advent of school league tables, as argues Chaudhary (1998). This is of significant interest following the government's proposal that schools are to rated in terms of their exclusion rate (Cassidy, 1999).

There will always be those children who, no matter what help they receive, will always be unfortunate in terms of education, but there appears consequential evidence to suggest that there are a variety of factors beyond the control of the child which influence whether or not s/he is at risk from being excluded from school. There are a variety of reasons why exclusions occur and one could argue that this is the responsibility of the child, but one cannot ignore the evidence that some children appear 'destined' to become excluded from school. Perhaps school and society have a role to play in the reasons why some children are more at risk of exclusion than others.

Conclusion

Exclusion from school is often the consequence of an extreme version both of the processes of marginalization and of the attributes boys are encouraged to acquire and have been socialized into within the dominant ideology of patriarchy and the discourse(s) associated with it. It is ironical that rather than questioning these processes and these attributes and taking them to be the problem, structures and processes are maintained that seem to foster the development of educational marginalization and exclusion. Unsurprisingly, male low performance and misbehaviour has been variously attributed to the disappearance of traditional family roles, single-parent families with mothers as the head of the household or the fact that girls are now seemingly outperforming boys or sometimes the disappearance of proper jobs for boys and men (Weiner, Arnot and David, 1997). This last point is as true for traditional working-class employment or for traditional middle-class managerial and professional employment, and it is due to restructuring and downsizing practices which arise from increased marketization and competitiveness within the employment sector (Brown, 1995). If females are forging ahead in the classroom, there are still strikingly different class and gender patterns in vocational education and in the labour market, where males continue to hold the advantage (Weiner, Arnot and David, 1997).

Whereas figures indicate that *general* marginalization in terms of educational attainment is continually decreasing, other figures indicate that the marginalization of *particular groups* is increasing and so is the number of pupils excluded from school who tend to belong to these particular groups. For example, there is a disproportionate representation of male, black, secondary school age children with special educational needs and living in social service care who are being excluded. At the same time, more and more people are entering higher education. In 1944 less than 3 per cent of the age group 18–19, less than 1 per cent for women, were entering higher education in England. At the end of the century 35 per cent of the same age group, more then 18 per cent for women, enter higher education (Matheson, 1999). Yet, Garment (1998) claims that between 1990 and 1995 there was a fourfold increase in the number of permanent exclusions and the trend is still upwards.

As headteachers are becoming increasingly reluctant to accept children who have been excluded from other schools, it has become very difficult in an educational climate governed by the discourse of the market, that is, competition and league tables, for a parent to secure a place in another mainstream school, especially when the pupil has acquired a reputation for disruptive and challenging behaviour. It appears that within the current market discourse 'children appear to be seen in terms of the contribution they make to the school's image, whether in terms of attendance, attainment or behaviour, rather than having any intrinsic value' (Blyth and Milner, 1996b, p. 17). Whereas from the post-war period, and especially from the 1960s to the 1980s, the ideology and thus the discourse of meritocracy dominated, they have now been replaced by that of the market and parentocracy. 'As a consequence, educational selection is increasingly based on the wealth and wishes of parents rather than the individual abilities and efforts of pupils' (Brown, 1995, p. 44).

While girls, pupils from the lower social classes and from ethnic minorities are marginalized by the way they are treated within the education system, boys mainly from ethnic minorities and lower social classes are the ones who are excluded from school. Even if girls do better than boys in examinations, it is worth noting that girls are still marginalized far more than boys are excluded. Staffing structures still present a picture of male and white superiority. Headteachers, heads of department and the school caretaker are more often male and white. Women are seen in the subordinate roles of teaching auxiliaries, dinner attendants, school secretaries and teachers on basic salary. The situation is even more pronounced in primary schools.

School's functions within society are multiple and it seems to carry the blame for many of society's perceived failures, be this teenage pregnancy or economic underperformance. Yet, empowerment of the learner which might help pupils learn to deal more constructively and effectively with their circumstances seems not to figure very highly, if at all. Rather, for a substantial part of the cohort it disempowerment in the form of marginalization, exclusion and generalize attempts at reducing feelings of educational self-worth that figure prominently and all this appears to be in the service of a dominant discourse that favour maleness, whiteness and middle classness over all other markers of identity.

Despite this, girls are still performing better in examinations than boys. I would be too easy to assume from this success that girls' marginalization ha disappeared. As we have seen, it is the very behaviour that is encouraged in boy which, in more extreme forms, leads to exclusion. Such behaviour is still encour aged in boys and the furore which has occurred in the UK over boys' apparen underperformance *vis-à-vis* girls, compared with the general silence when it was th other way round, demonstrates just how little has really changed. Research ha continued to show that the experience of girls and boys in school has changed ver little, with boys continuing to dominate the physical space, teacher time an classroom resources (Lloyd, quoted in Skelton, 1993). This situation is even mor pronounced in subjects more strongly associated with masculinity such as math ematics, science, information technology and craft and design, underlining that th culture and the discourse of education is particularly protected and controlled by it own patriarchal, racial and class power structures. This sets bounds on meaning an the relative worth of both pupils and their knowledge and learning. But such is t deny or diminish the perceived validity of cultures and sub-cultures outwith th dominant discourse and to marginalize them. Marginalization tends to occur i there is no recognition between cultures of new or different values of differen subjective interpretations of meaning (Jarvis, 1992). Perhaps one of the challenge for the school in the coming century is to develop and enhance such recognition.

Notes

1. Pyke (1992) actually refers to children being 'suspended' or 'expelled' but thi terminology is no longer used in the UK. Subsequently, 'fixed-term' and 'perma nent' exclusions will be used to allow for consistency.

2. The term 'black' in this context is used to indicate African and African-Caribbea descended populations. This does not include other minority ethnic groups such a: Indian, Pakistani, Chinese or Bangladeshi which are not over-represented i permanent exclusion figures (Smith, 1998).

3. An example of such a mentoring scheme is KWESI: 'This is a rapidly growing project in Birmingham. It was started after concern about high exclusion rates an low attainment of African-Caribbean children. KWESI largely provides mentoring support to schools. The project has won the support of both schools and the LEA successfully recruited from the community, trained and put in place mentors; anc has seen exclusion rates falling by 23 per cent. Two thirds of this reductior comprises ethnic minority pupils' (Social Exclusion Unit 1998, ch. 2, n.p.).

4. 'Permanent exclusions have fallen by 3 per cent, from 12,700 in the 1996–7 schoo year to 12,300 in the 1997–8 school year. This is the first time that numbers have fallen since the Department for Education and Employment first collected informa tion in 1994/95. Permanent exclusions of black pupils has fallen by 3.5 per cent

compared to a fall of 2.6 per cent for permanent exclusions of White pupils' (DfEE, 1999).

References

Acker, S. (1994) *Gendered Education*. Buckingham: Open University Press.

Acker, S., Megarry, J., Nisbet, S. and Hoyle, E. (1984) *World Yearbook of Education 1984: Women and Education*. London: Kogan Page and New York: Nichols.

Apple, M. W. (1999) 'If teacher assessment is the answer, what is the question?' *Education and Social Justice*, 1 (2), 43–7.

Arnot, M., David, M. and Weiner, G. (1996) *Educational Reforms and Gender Equality in Schools*. Manchester: Equal Opportunities Commission.

Barry, M. (1998) 'Social exclusion and social work: an introduction', in M. Barry and C. Hallett (eds) *Social Exclusion and Social Work*. Dorset: Russell House.

Benn, R. (1996) 'Access for adults to higher education: targeting or self-selection?' *Journal of Access Studies*, 11, Autumn, 165–76.

Blyth, E. and Milner, J. (1993) 'Exclusion from school: a first step in exclusion from society?' *Children and Society*, 7 (3), 255–68.

Blyth, E. and Milner, J. (eds) (1996a) *Exclusion from School*. London. Routledge.

Blyth, E. and Milner, J. (eds) (1996b) 'Exclusions: trends and issues', in E. Blyth and J. Milner (eds) *Exclusion from School*. London. Routledge.

Brown, P. (1995) 'Cultural capital and social exclusion: some observations on recent trends in education, employment and the labour market'. *Work, Employment and Society*, 9 (1), 29–51.

Byrne, E. (1978) *Women and Education*. London: Tavistock.

Cassidy, S. (1999) 'Exclusion toll to be next league table'. *Times Educational Supplement*, 8 January.

Central Advisory Council for Education (ACE) (1963) *Half Our Future* (The Newsom Report). London: HMSO.

Central Advisory Council for Education (England) (ACEE) (1959) *15 to 18* (The Crowther Report). London: HMSO.

Chaudhary, V. (1998) 'School league tables blamed for boom in exclusions'. *Guardian*, 17 March.

Clarricoates, K. (1980) 'The importance of being Ernest . . . Emma . . . Tom . . . Jane. The perceptions of and categorisations of gender conformity and gender in primary schools', in R. Deem (ed.) *Schooling for Women's Work*. London: Routledge and Kegan Paul.

Committee on Higher Education (COHE) (1963) *Higher Education: Report of the Committee under the Chairmanship of Lord Robbins*, Cmnd 2154 (The Robbins Report). London: HMSO.

Cooper, P., Upton, G. and Smith, C. (1991) 'Ethnic minorities and gender distinctions among staff and pupils in facilities for pupils with emotional and behavioural difficulties in England and Wales'. *British Journal of the Sociology of Education*, 12 (1), 77–94.

Deem, R. (1978) *Women and Schooling*. London: Routledge and Kegan Paul.

Deem, R. (1980) *Schooling for Women's Work*. London: Routledge and Kegan Paul.

Deem, R. (1981) 'State policy and ideology in the education of women, 1944 to 1980'. *British Journal of the Sociology of Education*, 2 (2), 131–43.

Department for Education (DfE) (1992) *Exclusion: A Discussion Paper*. London: DfE.

Department for Education (DfE) (1993) 'A new deal for "out of school" pupils'. Press Release 126/93. London: DfE.

Department for Education and Employment (DfEE) (1999) '£140 million to tackle truancy and exclusions'. Press release 445/99 11/10. London: DfEE. Available at http://www.dfee.gov.uk/news/99/445.htm

Department for Education and Science (DES) (1989) *Discipline in Schools* (The Elton Report). London: HMSO.

Firth, H. and Horrocks, C. (1996) 'No home, no school, no future', in E. Blyth and J. Milner (eds) *Exclusion from School*. London: Routledge.

Foreign and Commonwealth Office (FCO) (1998) 'Europe must tackle social exclusion timebomb, warns Blunkett'. Press release 25/6. Available at http://www.fco.gov.uk.

Galloway, D. (1982) 'A study of pupils suspended from school'. *British Journal of Educational Psychology*, 52, 205–12.

Gambetta, D. (1987) *Were They Pushed or Did They Jump?* Cambridge: Cambridge University Press.

Garment, L. (1998) 'Expelled – now no-one wants her'. *Bella Magazine*, 30 June.

Griffin, C. (1985) *Typical Girls? Young Women from School to the Job Market*. London: Routledge and Kegan Paul.

Hayden, C. (1996) 'Primary School Exclusions', in E. Blyth, and J. Milner, (eds) *Exclusion from School*. London: Routledge.

Hayden, C. (1997) *Children Excluded from Primary School: Debates, Evidence, Responses*. Buckingham: Open University.

Hayden, C., Sheppard, C. and Ward, D. (1996) *Primary Age Children Excluded from School*. Portsmouth: Social Services Research and Information Unit. Report 33, University of Portsmouth.

Heathfield, M. and Wakeford, N. (1991) *They Always Eat Green Apples: Images of University and Decisions at 16*. Lancaster: Innovations in Higher Education.

Hill, R. (1998) 'Excluded voices: the experiences and perceptions of excluded secondary school children'. Unpublished MSc thesis in educational psychology. University of Newcastle upon Tyne.

Jarvis, P. (1992) *Paradoxes of Learning*. San Francisco: Jossey Bass.

Larkin, J. (1994) 'Walking through walls: the sexual harassment of high school girls'. *Gender and Education*, 6 (3), 263–80.

Lovey, J., Docking, T. and Evans, R. (1993) *Exclusion from School: Provision for Disaffection at Key Stage 4*. London: David Fulton.

Lynch, K. and O'Riordan, C. (1998) 'Inequality in higher education: a study of class barriers'. *British Journal of Sociology of Education*, 19 (4), 445–78.

Mackinnon, A., Elquist-Saltzman, I. and Prentice, A. (eds) (1998) *Education into the 21st Century: Dangerous Terrain for Women?* London: Falmer Press.

McManus, M. (1995) *Troublesome Behaviour in the Classroom*. London: Routledge.

Mackinnon, D., Statham, J. and Hales, M. (1999) *Education in the UK: Facts and Figures*. London: Hodder and Stoughton (in association with the Open University).

Maginnis, E. (1993) 'An inter-agency response to children with special needs: the Lothian experience – a Scottish perspective', in E. Blyth and J. Milner (eds) *Exclusion from School*. London: Routledge.

Mahony, P. (1985) *Schools for the Boys? Co-education Reassessed*. London: Hutchinson.

Martin, J. (1999) 'Gender in education', in D. Matheson and I. Grosvenor (eds) *An Introduction to the Study of Education*. London: David Fulton.

Matheson, C. (1999) 'Access to higher education', in D. Matheson and I. Grosvenor, *An Introduction to the Study of Education*. London: David Fulton.

Metcalf, H. (1997) *Class and Higher Education: The Participation of Young People from Lower Social Class Backgrounds*. London: The Council for Industry and Higher Education.

National Committee of Inquiry into Higher Education (NCIHE) (1997) *Higher Education in the Learning Society: Report of the National Committee* (Dearing Report). London: NCIHE.

National Union of Teachers (NUT) (1992) *Survey on Pupils' Exclusions*. London: NUT.

OFSTED (1996) *Exclusions from Secondary Schools 1995/6*. London: The Stationery Office.

Ouseley, H. (1998) 'Black exclusions scandal'. *Times Educational Supplement*, 18 December (http.//www.tes.co.uk/fp/900000/PRN/teshome.html).

Parsons, C. (1994) 'The experience of excluded primary school children and their families'. *Social Policy Research*, 63 (Joseph Rowntree Foundation).

Parsons, C. (1996) 'Permanent exclusions from schools in England in the 1990s: trends, causes and responses'. *Children and Society*, 10, 177–86.

Parsons, C. (1997) 'Permanent exclusions from school in England: trends and responses', in C. Martin (ed.) *Absent from School: Truancy and Exclusion*. London: Institute for Studies and Treatment of Delinquency.

Paterson, F. and Fewell, J. (eds) (1990) *Girls in Their Prime: Scottish Education Revisited*. Edinburgh: Scottish Academic Press.

Pennington, M. (1998) 'Racism fears as exclusions rise'. *Times Educational Supplement*, 25 September (http://www.tes.co.uk/tp/900000/PRN/teshome.html).

Peterson, V. S. and Runyan, A. (1993) *Global Gender Issues*. Oxford: Westview Press.

Preece, J. (1999) 'Difference and the discourse of inclusion'. *Widening Participation and Lifelong Learning*, 1 (2), 16–23.

Preston, B. (1994) 'Expulsions spiral as school fights yob culture'. *The Times*, 25 October.

Purvis, J. (1991) *A History of Women's Education in England*. Buckingham: Open University Press.

Pyke, N. (1992) 'Into the exclusion zone'. *Times Educational Supplement*, 26 June.

Reay, D. (1998) ' "Always knowing" and "never being sure": familial and institutional habituses and higher education choice'. *Journal of Education Policy*, 13 (4), 519–29.

Secondary Heads Association (1992) *Excluded from School: A Survey of Secondary School Suspensions*. Bristol: SHA.

Secondary School Examinations Council (SSEC) (1943) *Curriculum and Examinations in Secondary Schools* (The Norwood Report). London: HMSO.

Skelton, C. (1993) 'Women and education', in D. Richardson and V. Robinson (eds) *Introducing Women's Studies*. London: Macmillan.

Smith, R. (1998) *No Lessons Learnt: A Study of School Exclusions*. London: The Children's Society.

Social Exclusion Unit (1998) *Truancy and School Exclusions. A Report by the Social Exclusion Unit*. London: Routledge. Available at: http://www.cabinet-office.gov.uk/seu/1998/trhome.htm

Sparks, I. (1998) 'What's the trouble back there?' *Guardian*, 31 March.

Special Children (1998) 'Possible reprieve for excluded pupils'. *Special Children*, 109, 7.

Spender, D. (1982) *Invisible Women: The Schooling Scandal*. London: Writers and Readers.

Spender, D. and Sarah, E. (eds) (1980) *Learning to Lose: Sexism and Education*. London: The Women's Press.

Stirling, M. (1996) 'Government policy and disadvantaged children', in E. Blyth and J. Milner (eds) *Exclusion from School*. London: Routledge.

Tett, L. (1999) 'Widening provision in higher education – some non-traditional participants' experiences'. *Research Papers in Education*, 14(1), 107–19.

Thornton, K. (1998a) 'Out of school and in trouble'. *Times Educational Supplement, 4* April.

Thornton, K. (1998b) 'Blacks 15 times more likely to be excluded'. *Times Educational Supplement*, 11 December (http://www.tes.co.uk/tp/900000/PRN/teshome.html)

Weiner, G., Arnot, M. and David, M. (1997) 'Is the future female? Female success, male disadvantage, and changing gender patterns in education', in A. H. Halsey, H. Lauder, P. Brown and A. Stuart Weels (eds) *Education, Culture, Economy, Society*. Oxford: Oxford University Press.

Weiner, G., Arnot, M. and David, M. (1998) 'Who benefits from schooling? Equality issues in Britain', in A. Mackinnon, I. Elquist-Saltzman and A. Prentice (eds) *Education into the 21st Century: Dangerous Terrain for Women?* London: Falmer Press.

Willis, P. (1977) *Learning to Labour*. Farnborough: Saxon House.

12

Education in Non-traditional Spaces

Catherine Matheson

Introduction

This chapter draws on retrospective ethnographic explorations of a Scottish secondary school as a space where a multiplicity of educational and political discourses intertwined and intersected. The multi-age and multicultural classroom(s) offered a traditional route for entry to higher education for the pupils and an alternative route for the adults as they were taught together and studied together for the traditional qualifications required to enter higher education. The perspectives of the pupils, adult students, the teachers and the school management team are examined in this chapter, which challenges the notion not so much that pupils and adults learn differently but that they can only be taught together at the expense of one or both groups.

Why do adolescents and adults take part in formal education?

Adolescents' participation in post-compulsory formal education is strongly related to social class. Adolescents take part in order to gain qualifications and perhaps enter higher education. This may be a decision or a non-decision depending on the internalized expectations of self and those of parents, peers and teachers. Insofar as entry to higher education is concerned, the shorter the cultural distance the more it is a non-decision. The longer the cultural distance the more it is a conscious and difficult decision and the more it becomes an existential authentic choice.

Authors such as Courtney (1992), Duke (1987) and West (1996) suggest that adult participation in education is concerned with the management of various kinds of change and crisis situations, including at work, in relationships, in illness and depression. In such situations, education could be an attempt to reconstitute the self, and identity and a life in changing times. Hopper and Osborn (1975) add a further social dimension in arguing that learners are often marginalized people, torn between different social affiliations, wondering who and what they are, and using education to resolve the uncertainties evoked. For women, starting on a journey to learning involves the constant negotiation of multiple identities as mature women balance their studies with the demands of home, looking after children, family, friends and sometimes work (Edwards, 1990, 1993; Pascall and Cox, 1993). A high proportion of mature students return to formal education at a critical stage in their wider life-experience. According to Duke (1987), there is a daunting hidden curriculum to negotiate since the decision to re-enter formal education is often either the consequence of, or the catalyst for, other changes in life patterns such as the break-up of long-standing relationships or unemployment.

How the spaces and discourses of adult education have evolved

The reasons adults have for taking part in formal education, especially the hidden curriculum of education as therapy, reflect adult education's long history of interest in the development and transformation of the self and its belonging to the 'technologies of the self' identified by Foucault, which consists of 'taking care of oneself' in order to transform oneself to attain 'a certain state of happiness, purity, wisdom or immortality' (Foucault, 1988, p. 18). Adult education is thus more than simply adults being educated. Houle (1972) gives a broad definition of adult education as 'the process by which men and women (alone, in groups or in institutional settings) seek to improve themselves or their society by increasing their skill, their knowledge or their sensitiveness' (p. 229).

The defining report on Scottish Adult Education, The Alexander Report, proposed a narrow concept of adult education as 'voluntary leisure-time courses for adults which are educational but not specifically vocational' (SED, 1975, para. 1). This narrow definition of adult education implied that at that time traditional adult education spaces were either extra-mural classes offered by a Department of Adult and/or Continuing Education in an institution of higher education, or further education, or what was on offer within community education, and this could take place in school buildings or in any other building either during the day or, more often than not, in the evening. Foucault's and Houle's notions focus on adult education as a process and do not imply any particular space.

Adult education was and still is based on the often generalized assumption that *all* adults learn differently from *all* young people *all* of the time. The adult education literature generally and Knowles (1970) in particular claim that teaching adults should be approached in a different way from teaching children and adolescents. Instead of pedagogy, adults require what has been known as andragogy (Donaldson, Flannery and Ross-Gordon, 1993; Knowles, 1970). The assumptions of the pedagogical model are that: (a) the learners are required to learn; (b) their previous experiences are unimportant; (c) they are still developing psychologically;

l) they are subject-oriented; and (e) they are externally motivated. The assump-
ons of the andragogical model are that: (a) learners choose to learn; b) their
revious experiences are valuable and validated; (c) they have reached their full
sychological development; (d) their learning is life-oriented; and (e) they are
nternally motivated (Knowles, 1984).

Other theorists believe that adult education is essentially the same process as
ducation generally; that it does not require a separate teaching approach and that
: should primarily be responsive in nature (Garrison, 1994; Tennant, 1988).

Brookfield (1986) and Tennant (1988), among others, have questioned the
videspread notion of self-direction in adults and its implied absence in children.
ater, Knowles (1998) himself, who popularized the notion of pure andragogy,
noved from his earlier perspective in which the two models were mutually
xclusive to admitting that 'the pedagogical model is an ideological model that
xcludes andragogical assumptions. The andragogical model is a system of assump-
ions that includes the pedagogical assumptions' (Knowles, 1998, p. 72).

This change in perspective within the mainstream discourse of adult education
way from pure andragogy arguably happened as a consequence of developments in
he educational field from the late 1970s onwards, when higher education can be
aid to have welcomed mature students for reasons of social justice and also to
ompensate for a predicted demographic decline in the traditional clientele
Matheson, 1999). The UK saw older mature students and especially women
nature students enter higher education in ever-increasing numbers. This was
nelped by the popularization of Access courses, first introduced in England in the
ate 1970s (later in Scotland), which provided an alternative entry route in higher
·ducation for adults without formal qualifications and have now become a tradi-
ional adult education space. Access courses are considered more of a traditional
dult education space than higher education or traditional qualifications – such as
A-levels or Scottish Highers undertaken in further education or in secondary
chools – because Access courses are student-centred rather than subject-centred
nd do not mix adult and younger learners (who are less than 21 years old).

A decade after higher education set out to widen access to mature adults,
econdary schools in Scotland set out to attract adults for exactly the same reasons.
Adult students, by their numbers and the consequent funding which followed
hem, could make a substantial difference to a school just as they could to a higher
·ducation institution. Schools – that is, educational spaces which had been the
·raditional preserve of adolescents and possibly, but not necessarily in the Scottish
:ase, very young adults (as school leavers) – either began to open their doors to older
oeople or opened them more widely in the case of the few community schools that
nave existed in Scotland since the late 1970s. In certificate courses, the pupils and
:he adults were taught in the same educational space. This did create some ripples
of concern.

In 1988 the Scottish Community Education Council (SCEC) had moved from a
narrow definition of adult education to a far broader one that took into account the
ever-increasing number of adults in higher education. The Carnegie Report,
prepared under the aegis of SCEC, underlined that the aims of adult education were

to 'enable people to improve and make continuing use of their *capacity to learn*; help people acquire *confidence* in themselves' (SCEC, 1988, p. 14, original emphasis).

While this definition is more in line with the broader definitions of Houle (1972) and Foucault (1988) rather than the narrow one of the Alexander Report (SED, 1975), the Carnegie Report (SCEC, 1988, p. 15) also stated that 'it is a good idea to provide separate adult classes, for adult returners to secondary schools, wherever possible'. The Carnegie Report acknowledged the existence of adults in secondary schools in Scotland, but the declared 'good practice' was that adults and pupils had different educational needs and expectations which may not be compatible, and that it was better that they be taught separately. The practicality of the situation, however, meant that, except for leisure classes, there were rarely sufficient adults and/or staff to justify separate spaces and thus separate classes. None the less, some schools not only welcomed adult students but deliberately targeted them as potential students, creating new offerings and even modifying existing provision to attract them. In a number of cases, this modification went as far as the offering of free crèche facilities (but not bursaries as these were only available for Access courses and in further education), thereby further blurring age and role boundaries. This meant that secondary schools, some more than others, saw adults crossing its threshold not only in the role of learners but also as parents of small children, thus becoming not only a non-traditional adult education space but also a non-traditional pre-school space. The very presence of small children in secondary schools (being taken from the crèche to the student common room and to the school canteen for lunch) as well as the presence of adults, women in particular, in secondary schools is of course worthy of consideration. How adolescent learners might be affected by it seems a fascinating field of enquiry, since it is at school (among other places) that they learn what is expected of them as adults and that these expectations are still not the same for both sexes despite efforts to achieve equal opportunities (Acker *et al.*, 1984; Acker, 1994; Arnot, David and Weiner, 1996; Clarricoates, 1980; David, 1980; Deem, 1980; Martin, 1999; Spender, 1982; Weiner, Arnot and David, 1997, 1998). However, space precludes examining this further in this instance.

The Access course and the secondary school as adult learning spaces are underpinned by opposing ideological assumptions. The latter is based on the assumption that adults and adolescents can and do learn in rather similar ways. The former is based on the andragogical assumption that school pupils and mature adult students require radically different kinds of educational provision. Opening the doors of secondary schools to adults provides at one and the same time a traditional qualification and both a traditional and a non-traditional pathway to subject-centred higher education within a non-traditional adult education space – unlike Access courses which provide a student-centred experience (Parry, 1986; Weil, 1986). Scottish secondary schools were consequently placed in direct competition with both non-traditional and traditional adult education spaces. The former were colleges of further education (non-traditional adult education space) offering either A-levels or Scottish Certificate of Education (SCE) Higher Grades[1], that is, a traditional qualification and a traditional pathway. The latter were Access courses in institutions of higher and further education (traditional adult education space) offering a non-traditional pathway to a traditional provision: in other words, a student-centred preparation for a subject-centred experience (Parry, 1986; Weil, 1986). Secondary schools in Glasgow, especially those situated in socially deprived areas, provided free crèche facilities well before many colleges of further education and institutions of higher education even started to offer paying crèche facilities. As McGivney (1994) has shown, the findings of countless previous research indicate categorically that some form of childcare is essential to assist women's access to education and their educational progression. In that respect, some secondary schools in Scotland were even more non-traditional adult education spaces and this because they offered what traditional adult education should have provided but did not!

In contrast to the non-traditional adult education space that is the secondary school classroom, traditional adult education spaces are rarely free of charge to the consumer. Adult students in secondary school did not qualify for a local authority grant but were taught free of charge, though some schools charged them for sitting Highers or other external examinations. Unlike students studying for Highers in a secondary school, students on full-time Access courses and those doing at least three Highers in a further education college were until recently eligible for a local authority grant, but not those doing these courses part-time. Extra-mural courses were never free, except for those unemployed or on very low income. Reflecting the limited amount of public funding available to it, adult education is, according to Mason (1992), the most blatantly market-driven segment of education, a situation much deplored by Rittenburger (1984) and Beder (1992).

Scotland is unique in Europe in the degree to which it promotes provision for adults within the secondary school system, with 80 per cent of secondary schools providing for adult students and 4 per cent of the secondary school population being made up of adults, most of whom attend part-time (Blair, McPake and Munn, 1995). Most of the adults who attend secondary schools are either retired or at home caring for small children and, occasionally, unemployed. They participate for a wide variety of reasons. The range and levels of courses are such as to appeal to learners of all ages, but most especially to women (Blair, McPake and Munn, 1995; MacIntosh 1990). Because of the large numbers involved, some leisure classes are sometimes offered to adults only, but certificated classes at the level of National Certificate modules (called Scottish Vocational Education Council (SCOTVEC) modules in Scotland[2]) as well as Scottish Certificate of Education (SCE) Standard Grades or Higher Grades tend to be mixed, usually with a majority of pupils and a minority of adults. In these classes, most if not all the adults are women, more often than not with small children (Blair, McPake and Munn, 1995; MacIntosh 1990).

The secondary school as a non-traditional adult education space

The learning experiences of mature students in Access courses and/or in higher education have been investigated qualitatively by Ainley (1992), McFadden

(1995), West (1996) and Lea (1996). Mature women students have similarly been researched by Weil (1986, 1988), Edwards (1990, 1993), Pascall and Cox (1993) and Lunneborg, (1994) while Woodley (1984), Smithers and Griffin (1986) and Woodley *et al.* (1987) have carried out larger-scale quantitative studies of the experience of mature students. Whereas most of the British research on the experience of adult/mature (women) students has been largely anglocentric, the larger-scale Scottish studies have tended to look at Access courses rather than adult (women) students in secondary schools. Munn, Johnstone and Robinson (1994) have investigated the effectiveness of access courses in Scotland, Karkalas and Mackenzie (1995) undertook a long-term study of the effectiveness of Access courses offered by the University of Glasgow, and Powney and Hall (1998) examined the experience of former Scottish Access students in higher education. Only MacIntosh (1990) and Blair, McPake and Munn (1995) have looked in some depth at the experience of both providers and adult students in Scottish secondary schools.

Unlike Access courses, the secondary school classroom has not yet become a 'traditional' learning space either for adults or for pupils. Indeed, adults in schools is a topic which does not even figure in the literature concerned with alternative routes into higher education in Scotland. It is ignored, for example, by Osborne and Gallacher (1995), while Bryce and Humes's (1999) attempted overview of the entirety of contemporary Scottish education, from cradle to grave, equally fails to include adults in schools as a field of enquiry.

Methodology of the retrospective ethnographic study of a non-traditional educational space

Spanning a decade from the late 1980s to the late 1990s, the present study draws on autobiographical life history, informal discussion and formal semi-structured interviews. Printed documents from the school and from the local authority (Strathclyde Regional Council) as well as minutes from the School Board were used. I was an adult student in the Scottish Catholic secondary school under investigation and which I attended on a daily basis for nearly two years, studying for three Higher Graders and attending various leisure classes (sewing, swimming and art). Following on from that, I attended the school on a weekly basis for three years as I undertook three SCOTVEC (Scottish Vocational Education Council) modules in word-processing. From 1989 to 1993 I was also a co-opted member and treasurer of the School Board, regularly wrote the minutes of its meetings and attended meetings once a month, more in times of crisis. In the late 1990s I returned to the school to conduct interviews with the School Management Team and other staff. I also interviewed former students. The resultant scripts were given to those involved for them to comment on their validity and representativeness of how things were. The underlying methodological assumption is largely based in part on critical autobiographical recollections of the researcher and in part on the recollections of others – a sound epistemological base if treated critically (Griffiths, 1995). It is still unusual for researchers to be explicit about autobiographical dimensions, although eminist writing (Griffiths, 1995; Mies, 1993; Patai, 1988) and writers such as Linden West (1996) and Malcolm Tight (1998) have tended to challenge this silence. While critical autobiography can both liberate and restrict, in the sense that it can 'appropriate the data to the researcher's interests, so that other significant experiential elements which challenge or partially disrupt that interpretation may also be silenced', it can also become a means to empower participants by highlighting differences (Opie, 1992, p. 52).

Background to the non-traditional educational space

Historical context

The school opened in 1937 as the second Catholic co-educational secondary school in the city of Glasgow. It is now closed and is used as a community centre. The building is situated at the heart of an area of multiple deprivation in Glasgow, once a thriving centre for the shipbuilding industry, but since the late 1970s an area of multiple deprivation extensively redeveloped and increasingly depopulated.

The school was built in the same red sandstone as the tenements that surrounded it. Additional buildings were added and in the late 1980s the school included a swimming pool, football and hockey pitches, extensive gymnasia and a small theatre. As was the case with many of Glasgow's secondary schools, the building was used by various community groups during the evenings and at weekends. Since opening its doors to adults in the mid-1980s, and especially since the opening of the free crèche in 1987 and until its closure in 1998, the school served the whole community, though it was never accorded the official status and corresponding funding of a community school.[3]

Educational and political contexts

It was arguably in part as a consequence of urban redevelopment that the school opened its doors so widely to adult learners. Other factors to be taken into account are the demographic decline in the 1980s and the Parents' Charter (1980) which, by introducing parental choice, induced a steady haemorrhage of pupils to other Catholic schools in more socio-economically advantaged areas but still within easy travelling distance by bus or car. For about a decade until it was finally closed the school, with the help of its School Board (in existence since 1989 and which had a say in the appointment of senior staff), successfully fought to remain open chiefly on the grounds of the services it provided the local community and, more especially, on the grounds of the number of adults who were regularly attending the school and then progressing on to higher education and finally to graduation.

The political context of the continuing threat of closure by the local authority was the decline in the number of pupils attending the school. The Catholic Church was asked its opinion by the local authority and complicated the situation by advocating the closure of the school and the relocation of Catholic secondary school provision to a more middle-class area of the city. The situation was compounded by

the interest taken in the school by the candidate for the Labour Party, who was d
to contest the local parliamentary seat at the next General Election to be held
1992. The Labour candidate incorporated saving the school into his electi
manifesto and this brought him into direct conflict with the Church. T
incumbent MP was from the Scottish National Party: he had captured tl
traditional Labour stronghold in a by-election and did not want to be drawn ir
the fight. This engendered a large amount of ill-feeling between the vario
authorities, religious, political and educational.

Simply delaying closure until the General Election was not enough an
following the recapture by Labour of the seat in 1992, the Chairperson of the Schc
Board (a single mother with children at the school) took the local authority
Scotland's highest civil court, the Court of Session in Edinburgh, to preve
another threat of closure being carried out. This delayed the school's closing f
another six years.

Socio-cultural context

Most if not all the pupils were from working-class backgrounds, that is, from tl
lower socio-economic groups. According to both the Headteacher and the Depu
Headteacher who were interviewed in October 1998, the school not only welcome
adults from the mid-1980s onwards but eventually, due to both increasing pressu
for closure and damaging press speculation, actively sought to recruit them n
only for leisure classes but more especially for SCE O Grades (later Standard Grade
and Higher Grades. Indeed, many women adult students, myself included, partic
pated in these recruitment drives. The main focus of publicity was the full-tin
crèche, which enabled many mothers to progress to further and higher educatio
Between 1990 and 1998, when the school closed, no less than 13 women, most
mothers with young children, moved on to full-time higher education aft
attending the school and gaining the required qualifications to enter. Most of the
graduated, myself included. Between 1988 and 1998, only two men (one in h
sixties and the other in his late seventies) each obtained one Higher at grades
(Geography) and A (Art and Design) respectively.

In the late 1980s and early 1990s, middle-class women from adjacent area
seemed to be over-represented among the adults studying for Higher Grades. Late
working-class local women became increasingly represented and eventually mac
up the majority of the returning adult group. Three of the most recent adu
participants in higher education – three mothers, two of whom were single – wer
recipients of a scholarship worth £3,000 per annum, which was applied for throug
the school and which aimed at assisting individuals from areas of multipl
deprivation to enter and remain in higher education. These women, unlike the
middle-class predecessors, tended to be drawn towards the sciences rather than th
arts and humanities and also tended to enter the new universities in the Glasgo
area to study engineering and biochemistry as opposed to the older universities t
study humanities.

While it could be argued that all these women were 'empowered' throug education, it should not be forgotten that they operated within a framework shaped to a very large extent not by themselves but by the all-male Senior Management Team of the school who wanted it to remain open come what may. The women did not campaign to get a crèche or to get bursaries for further study. This was done by the Senior Management Team and by local councillors, but for whose ultimate benefit? Whether this matters or whether one is less empowered because the space and discourse is shaped by others is another issue.

The Scottish secondary school classroom as a non-traditional multi-age and multicultural educational space

How did the pupils, adult returners and teachers experience the multi-age learning and teaching experience within a non-traditional educational space?

The pupils on the adult women students

The pupils seemingly did not mind being taught alongside adult students. They were very aware that adults would be highly likely to feel awkward in a class of teenagers, afraid of 'making a show of themselves by returning to school' especially at the beginning. The adults and pupils tended to have relatively little to do with each other outside the classroom. Interestingly, the adults were perceived by the pupils as studying 'part-time' as opposed to 'full-time' even though, in some cases, the adult women and the pupils were studying for the same number of Highers.

The pupils were of the opinion that adults were treated the same as 'ordinary' pupils, insofar as they had to answer in class and do their homework. The only difference was, as they good-naturedly remarked, that 'adults do not get punishment exercises for talking too much'. Along with the rather surprising empathy for the problems faced by adult students, there was also a feeling, with a hint of resentment in a few instances, that the adults were more privileged than the pupils as they may miss classes and get flexible deadlines for their work. What could have been a situation potentially fraught with difficulties was handled very well by the teachers – though in a variety of ways. Some pupils said that this was because, under the watchful eyes of the adult students, the teachers were on their 'best behaviour', for example better prepared, less dictatorial, less patronizing and more even-tempered.

The adult women students and the pupils

Most of the women adult students in the secondary school in question, though anxious and lacking confidence in their learning abilities, had a sense of their own greater ability to take advantage of educational opportunities. They felt like those of MacIntosh (1990) and Edwards (1990, 1993) that their experience gave them a clear advantage over younger students. Relationships with the pupils seemed less

problematic than those of former Access students in higher education with young(
students, as was investigated by Elsey (1982) who identified a culture clash whei
younger students were regarded as a minor irritant due to their refusal t
participate in tutorials.

The staff on adult students

Apart from a small minority of teachers who were completely opposed to the idei
the staff enthusiastically accepted the whole notion of having adults in the schoo
It was generally felt that as a result of having adults there the pupils were bett(
prepared, better behaved and keener to learn. The main reason for opposition by th
small minority was a fear of having their teaching scrutinized by the potentiall
more critical adults. Over the years, many staff meetings were spent debating ho'
adult students should be treated and the implications of treating them one way c
another. The staff thought that initially adults were anxious and had low expecta
tions of themselves but very soon integrated well in the class and with the othe
pupils. They were perceived as being highly motivated. Indeed, it was highlighte
that 'the competition created is beneficial to both adults and pupils; the latte
however, can sometimes sit back and let the adults do all the work in class' and ':
the teacher is not careful, adults can dominate the classroom'. Most teachers, eve
those who were sceptical at first, found that they really liked to teach adults becaus
there were 'no discipline problems' and because the majority of adults had 'a matur
writing style which made marking a pleasure'.

The adult women students and the teachers

I will not write about Mr M(athematics)'s class where I was the only adult studen(
and the only female out of nine people and one of only two members of the class wh(
obtained a Higher Grade in Mathematics. I will only write about Mr H(istory)'
class to say that he had 16 pupils and two adult students and that he was perceivec
as very aware, willing, responsive and flexible. He met the needs of both groups i)
his class while being careful to make sure that neither adult students nor the pupil
monopolized his time or the classroom participation/discussions. He was in hi
early forties and was able to motivate adult students by fostering enthusiasm an(
confidence and by addressing individual concerns with great tact and sensitivity
He was an authority (very impassioned about his subject) but not authoritarian
especially not with adults with whom he shared his power. He always welcomec
direct or indirect personal experience in classroom discussions. He was the teache
as facilitator *par excellence* and yet had no previous experience of teaching adults.

The staff (and this includes Mr H and Mr E(nglish)) were viewed very positivel
by both the women and the men, especially Mr H who was also responsible for th(
welfare of the adult students within the school. The fact that so many adul(
students, all women apart from the two men mentioned earlier, took certificat(
courses speaks for itself.

I will now discuss the experiences of myself and others in the Higher Grad(

English class. The teacher was in his early sixties but looked much younger. He had experience of adult students as he taught in a college of further education one or two evenings a week. However, in the secondary school classroom, he followed to a greater extent than did Mr H the model of the teacher who is an authority and is authoritarian. In the English class there were eight adult students and 16 pupils. The women were all in their late twenties apart from one in her late thirties. They were all married with children, except one who was separated. Most of them were taking one or two Highers though some were taking three. Apart from two women who lived locally and were from a working-class background, the others all came from adjacent areas and were from middle-class to lower middle-class origin, including four women of Pakistani origin and a European of francophone origin (myself).

Just as Johnson and Locke (1990) found that mature students reported lecturers in higher education who were unsure about dealing with mature students and who unconsciously discriminated against them, so were adult women in the English classroom critical of a particular aspect of what went on in this non-traditional educational/learning space, which was in some respects a rather traditional teaching space for the following reasons. The adult women students were critical (to varying degrees ranging from outrage to puzzlement) of what was perceived to be a lack of sensitivity on the part of Mr E who insisted, unlike any of the other teachers, that both pupils and adult students should not just quietly walk into the class when late, but instead that they should knock at the door and wait for Mr E to signal when they could enter without disrupting the flow of the lesson. If anyone forgot this exigency and just walked in, they were asked to go back out and wait until they were asked to come in. The waiting could last several minutes and was felt to be a rather unpleasant experience (totally humiliating for some) both for the person standing outside the class behind the glass-panelled door and for those inside the class watching, especially since the lateness (a rather rare phenomenon) was due to childcare issues and to the morning traffic as six out of the eight women drove to the school.

What made things even more embarrassing and awkward for us was that the class was at 9 a.m. and that A, the Pakistani woman who lived the furthest away, was late three days out of four each week, often up to 20 minutes. The dramatic tension would become nearly unbearable. Our attention would be mostly focused on A as she would knock and patiently wait to be waved in. The flow of the lesson may not have been disrupted for Mr E but we were certainly distracted as a consequence of the theatrical and totalitarian gate-keeping of the educational space. We all thought that it would have been better to let adults *and* pupils come in quietly without knocking if late, as happened in all the other classes. Unfortunately for Mr E, this all too frequently recurring scenario tended to be perceived as sexism and racism when it may not have been. Mr E's attitude was viewed as: (a) symptomatic of both some discomfort in having to deal with adult women; (b) suggesting a certain reluctance in having adults at all in the class; and (c) perhaps a rather morbid fear of not wanting to appear to treat the two groups adults and pupils differently. Yet Mr E, who was also the head of department, had decided to

take *all* eight adult women (who formed one-third of the class) in his High
English class rather than suggest that they attend the other Higher English cla
taught by a much younger woman (who did not seem very student-friendly).

In the English classroom, the power relation of male teacher/female adu
students was clearly and overtly defined in the teacher's terms (though A
behaviour may have indicated perhaps subconsciously or unconsciously or eve
consciously a certain level of resistance against the authority of the teacher – a kin
of silent protest or power struggle. Arguably, by not directly challenging h
behaviour (which was found to cause extreme discomfort and embarrassment in a
the women and in most of the pupils), we were adopting a submissive role both a
women and as learners. Indirectness, such as complaining to Mr H or th
Headteacher so that they would speak to Mr E about changing his gate-keepin
ways, however, which at least showed a certain degree of resistance or protest, wa
totally unsuccessful. The situation was quietly brought to the attention of both th
headteacher and Mr H, whose remit included responsibility for the adult student
Mr E, who had considerable teaching experience and was not long afterwards to b
awarded an MBE for his services to teaching, was tentatively spoken to about th
issue by the teacher in charge of adult students but refused very politely to alter i
any way his particular exigency.

Paradoxically, Mr E did not refuse to acknowledge the adult status of the wome
in any other way or completely fail to take into account their domestic responsibili
ties. He accepted that the women adult students, who all had several youn
children, sometimes had to miss classes. He offered to comment on essay drafts i
this was needed and was not inflexible with assignment deadlines. He eve
successfully appealed for the two Pakistani women who had failed the exam
Whereas he was showing some degree of responsiveness to the needs of his learner
and whereas his absolute enthusiasm for the subject which he passed on to us mad
it a worthwhile learning experience, Mr E would be unfortunately for eve
remembered for the negative effect of his inflexible gate-keeping, whereby one ha
to be granted the privilege of entering the sanctity of the learning space.

Studies show that students in Access courses or in higher education wanted thei
teachers to value their past experience, but the adult women in the secondary schoo
classroom had no particular expectations about it. They were rather surprised tha
it did not occur 'only rarely' as shown by Weil (1986), Johnson and Locke (1990
and Edwards (1990, 1993), who looked at mature students' experience in highe
education. Mr H, who taught history and instilled great enthusiasm for his subject
always welcomed direct or indirect personal experience in class discussions. Mr E
apart from his particular exigency concerning accessing the teaching and learning
space after the class had started, encouraged the adult women to write about thei
own life-experiences whatever these may be and, like Mr H, welcomed the sharing
of experiences in class discussions. This last point seemingly contradicts the
findings of Edwards (1993) in higher education and Weil (1986) in both higher
education and an Access course. The former's respondents said that lecturers were
willing to accept contributions based on experiences within certain areas of their
lives but not others. The experiences of the public sphere were more acceptable than

those of the private sphere. While none of the women students in the secondary school had much experience of the public sphere, they did not feel a difference between how their experience of the public sphere of work and the private sphere of home was perceived and valued by the teachers.

Weil (1986) found that students repeatedly expressed disappointment over what they regarded as a denial of the voice of their experience. This arose from aspects of experience related to gender, race and/or class being made invisible or redefined in the teachers' terms. Interestingly, this very last point was indeed found to occur, but in relation to pupils and not to the adults. The socio-cultural background of a particular pupil was in a dramatically unforgettable manner (yet again) redefined in the teacher's terms. One memorable morning in the second term, we were reading *The Crucible* by Arthur Miller. I had been assigned to read the part of Abigail Williams and one of the boys in the class, P, who was 18, was reading the part of John Proctor. At one point, after I had cried out 'Oh! Heavenly Father, take away this shadow!' (the stage directions indicated that at this point he had leapt at me and was grabbing me by the hair), he was meant to snarl at me 'How do you call Heaven! Whore! Whore!' (Miller, 1984, p. 97). Unfortunately, P was unable to say this word according to Mr E's idea of how it should be 'properly' pronounced and could only exclaim 'Hoor, Hoor'. We had to go through this scenario more than half a dozen times, me saying my line and P saying his line and with Mr E desperately attempting to have him say 'whore' and not 'hoor' in between each attempt, by enunciating the word very slowly and very carefully to him in his best Received Pronunciation but, alas, without any success whatsoever, his elongated vowels and aspirated 'r' contrasting markedly with the truncated vowels and hard 'r' of the pupil. While the whole drama caused much hilarity every time we heard 'hoor, hoor', the women and to a lesser extent the pupils felt, at one and the same time as we were uproariously laughing at this incongruous situation, increasingly uneasy about the fact that Mr E should have insisted so rigidly and for so long upon the 'correct' pronunciation. It was embarrassing for P, who was arguably made to be an object of ridicule by the teacher and who had turned bright red, and for me to be repeatedly called such a word even in role-play!

All this showed that it is easier to make pupils and adult women knock and wait before they are 'allowed' to enter the teaching and learning space than to attempt to impose 'correct' pronunciation of a word that is not part of the everyday classroom language, especially since the word in question is so emotionally charged. Whether this was done consciously or otherwise, it could be said that P was engaged in a form of cultural resistance by refusing to have his socio-cultural background redefined in the teacher's terms.

The cultural hegemony of the teacher was seen in his refusal to acknowledge our status as adults but not our socio-cultural background. However, it was this latter that he refused to acknowledge in the case of the pupils. In Mr E's class, our status as learners superseded our status as adults or as women. Ironically, our rather dramatic experiences and incidents in the English class, the very theatricality of the teacher's own peculiarities or fixed ideas, drew our (the adult women's) attention to the hidden curriculum that is taught alongside the subject-centred curriculum in terms of power relationships within the educational space and cultural hegemony within the education system.

Conclusion

Multi-grade classrooms, in which teachers teach across several curriculum levels, were common in the past and are still common in developing countries and many rural areas in industrialized countries. However, the non-traditional educational space that is the multi-age and multicultural classroom poses many paradoxes. The way in which teachers attempt to come to terms with or resolve the paradoxes is shaped by teachers' perceptions of the non-traditional educational space and reflect academic and professional hierarchies and ideologies.

Mr E was a more traditional example of the teacher as an authority and in authority (Peters, 1966), and this was symbolized by his wanting to be the only one who had the privilege of granting access to the teaching and learning space. Mr H accepted that the teaching and learning space was an educational space in which he was an authority and not *obviously* in authority but he did not need to remind people of this all the time, and he was more of a facilitator since he was less authoritarian as far as the control of space was concerned. Both teachers had a passion for their subject, however, and welcomed and valued personal experiences from the adult women both in written work and in whole-class discussions.

Bourdieu and Passeron's (1990) main proposition is that 'every power which manages to impose meanings and to impose them as legitimate *by concealing the power relations* which are the basis of its force, adds its own specifically symbolic force to those power relations' (p. xv) (original emphasis). Education in the broadest sense encompasses more than formal schooling, while formal schooling is defined as the 'imposition of a cultural arbitrary by an arbitrary power' (*ibid.*) and hence a form of symbolic violence. Mr E's exigencies were perceived as a form of symbolic violence. Mr E did not conceal power relations. We were constantly reminded of these. Arguably, Mr H, by not insisting on controlling the teaching and learning space, did attempt to conceal power relations by sharing his power but not his authority.

> I don't see where evil is in the practice of someone who, in a given name of truth, knowing more than another, teaches [them] . . . The problem is rather to know how you are to avoid in these practices the effects of domination. (Foucault, 1988, p. 18)

Learners as participants in the discourse of teaching and learning are never completely without power and agency and thus have the potential to show resistance and/or to initiate change. P, by refusing to have his socio-cultural background redefined by using the 'correct' pronunciation, and A, by highlighting the strictly controlled access to the educational space, showed resistance to Mr E's refusal to share power.

On the whole, the teachers promptly and seemingly effortlessly acquired and put into practice some of the background notions to the andragogical model and this, largely, without even knowing that they were doing so.

Teaching adults and pupils together draws attention to the fact that adults re-entering formal education can benefit from returning to a familiar subject-centred setting where the teacher leads the proceedings, rather than being dropped directly into a student-centred situation where the teacher is a resource to be tapped (Matheson, 1995). Also, having a subject-centred learning experience in a multi-age classroom can arguably be a better preparation for higher education than a more student-centred Access course where the learner is interacting only with other mature students. This may give a false impression and a false sense of security regarding what higher education is going to be like.

As Duke (1987) has highlighted, class discussions or seminars may be dominated by a group of more self-confident mature students, whilst the more inhibited 'traditional' students may be intimidated, subjugated and silenced. This is not, however, a problem linked to the age/experience differential but to gender, ethnicity and culture. In any case, it cuts both ways since mature students may also be intimidated by confident school-leavers. While Duke was referring to higher education, his points apply also to the secondary school classroom as a non-traditional educational space. Looking at it from this perspective, it would seem that the needs and expectations of adult students and school pupils are indeed not so incompatible. The age difference appears certainly less of a problem than the tendency for males to dominate and females to be held back in discussions, and the same point can be made with ethnic minorities (Duke, 1987) and other culturally dominated groups. As Garrison (1994) has underlined, teaching, at whatever level, should be primarily responsive in nature and the ultimate quality of a good teacher is directly proportional to her or his level of responsiveness to students' needs within or outwith an authoritarian framework and this with respect to whatever group(s) the students belong to.

What really matters though is that adult students, and adult women students in our particular case, found that 'the acquisition of new forms of knowledge introduced them to other ways of interpreting and understanding their own worlds' (Lea, 1996, p. 10). Consequently, and as both some of the teachers in the school and MacIntosh (1990) have observed, women who finish a course show an observable increase in self-confidence because of learning, sharing, meeting other learners, relating to teachers in different ways and expressing themselves as individuals. For some, the secondary school classroom became the most important thing in their lives because their success in examinations, for example, turned it into an intoxicating experience, even though some people's attitudes to them changed and went from curiosity to downright disapproval and even mockery (MacIntosh, 1990). *Educating Rita* is, in the words of Duke (1987, p. 59), 'in some respects uncomfortably near the mark'.

Like other adult returners, women returned to formal education in the secondary school in question for a variety of motivations, some to prove to themselves and to others that they had ability which they felt had not been recognized, some to prove their worth through 'second-chance' education by 'settling old scores' (McFadden,

1995), some to escape from their daily routines and some to gain qualifications to enter higher education. Although Access courses count more women participants than men, there is far less of a discrepancy than is the case in the participation patterns of adults returning to school. The adult women, like the adult/mature students of MacIntosh (1990), Edwards (1990, 1993), Ainley (1992) and Blair, McPake and Munn (1995), were very positive about their educational experience as adult returners, though sometimes the nervousness of returning to education and of having to relate to teachers as adults was overwhelming. As MacIntosh (1990) underlined, the younger adults tended to drop out after a week or two. In the secondary school in question, this was sometimes the case. What tended to happen more frequently though, was that some adult women regardless of age simply vanished when the exams were approaching even after having attended the class regularly for months. The very few men below retirement age who started Standard Grade or Higher classes *all* disappeared without a trace after a week or so. As MacIntosh (1990) has pointed out, the reasons for this are far from clear. She suggests that perhaps men are more under the influence of the accepted conventional patterns of school, training, job, though they are socially and economically freer than women. She further remarks that, although education is still to a great extent slanted towards men and their linear career path, boys are paradoxically more constrained by a rigid system which leads them to believe that education is something you leave behind you. They are thus less likely to take advantage of later opportunities to broaden and extend their education, especially if this means returning to school as opposed to undertaking an Access course. According to her, men seemed to have a more instrumental view of education and also find it difficult to admit to areas of ignorance or lack of knowledge, whereas women do not tend to have this hang-up.

Long before the Green Paper *The Learning Age: a Renaissance for a New Britain* (DfEE, 1998) the Scottish secondary school classroom as a non-traditional educational space had espoused the principles of lifelong learning. Having adults in the class helps the pupils to realize that it is never too late to learn. The presence of adults and, to a great extent, the presence of small children in the school is powerful evidence that education is for life (Blair, McPake and Munn, 1995) and demonstrates that it is possible to teach multi-age and multicultural classes since teaching should be primarily responsive in nature (Garrison, 1994). The experience of the women in the secondary school in question was equally an example of lifelong learning, in practice rather than just in theory. It also negates McGivney's (1994) claim that women in the 1990s were still experiencing constraints in adult education through lack of childcare provision for daytime courses, though it concurs with her other claim that the structures of the adult education space, whether traditional or non-traditional such as the secondary school, remain firmly in the control of men.

Afterword

Ironically, the secondary school in question was highly successful as a non-traditional adult education space, which seemingly encouraged and motivated women adult learners not only to pursue their own education (and in many cases obtain a degree) but also, in some cases, to pursue community involvement. However, it was less successful as a traditional educational space. Because of the introduction of market mechanisms in education and also because of local political reasons, it did not attract pupils and was decidedly unsuccessful in its ostensible role as a traditional secondary school and this despite the excellence of the teachers. By the time of its closure, it was virtually deserted by most of its pupils. None the less, it did provide a potentially valuable role model for Glasgow City Council's current attempts to transform a number of its secondary schools in areas of multiple deprivation into community schools.

Notes

[1.] In Scotland, the traditional qualification for entry higher education is the Scottish Certificate of Education (SCE) Higher Grade. It is equivalent in academic attainment to a half A-level but the work is generally done in around a third of the time that would be devoted to an A-level.

[2.] SCOTVEC has now joined forces with the Scottish Examination Board (SEB) to form the Scottish Qualification Authority (SQA).

[3.] Unlike Lothian Regional Council which counted several community schools, Strathclyde Regional Council policy never favoured such initiatives. LRC and SRC fulfilled until 1996, when the Regional Councils were dissolved in favour of much smaller unitary authorities, the function associated in England with Local Educational Authorities (LEAs).

References

Acker, S. (1994) *Gendered Education*. Buckingham: Open University Press.

Acker, S., Megarry, J., Nisbet, S. and Hoyle, E. (1984) *World Yearbook of Education 1984: Women and Education*. London: Kogan Page, and New York: Nichols Publishing.

Ainley, P. (1992) *Degrees of Differences: Higher Education in the 1990s*. London: Lawrence and Wishart.

Arnot, M., David, M. and Weiner, G. (1996) *Educational Reforms and Gender Equality in Schools*. Manchester: Equal Opportunities Commission.

Beder, H. (1992) 'Adult and continuing education should not be market driven'. *New Directions for Adult and Continuing Education*, 54 (2), 69–75.

Blair, A., McPake, A. and Munn, P. (1995) *Adults in Schools*. Edinburgh: Scottish Council for Research into Education.

Bourdieu, P. and Passeron, J.-C. (1990) *Reproduction in Education, Society and Culture*. London: Sage.

Brookfield, S. (1986) *Understanding and Facilitating Adult Learning*. San Francisco: Jossey Bass.

Bryce, T. and Humes, W. (eds) (1999) *Scottish Education*. Edinburgh: Edinburgh University Press.

Clarricoates, K. (1980) 'The importance of being Ernest ... Emma ... Tom ... Jane. The perception and categorisation of gender conformity and gender deviation in primary school in R. Deem (ed.) *Schooling for Women's Work*. London: Routledge and Kegan Paul.

Courtney, S. (1992) *Why Adults Learn: Towards a Theory of Participation in Adult Education*. London: Routledge.

David, M. (1980) *Women, Family and Education*. London: Kogan Page.

Deem, R. (1980) *Schooling for Women's Work*. London: Routledge and Kegan Paul.

Department for Education and Employment (1998) *The Learning Age: a Renaissance for a New Britain*. London: The Stationery Office.

Donaldson, J. F., Flannery, D. and Ross-Gordon, J. (1993) 'A triangulated study comparing adult college students' perceptions of effective teaching with those of traditional students'. *Continuing Higher Education Review*, 57 (3), 147–65.

Duke, F. (1987) 'Degrees of experience: are the needs and expectations of mature adults and school leavers compatible?' *Journal of Access Studies*, 2 (1), 54–63.

Edwards, R. (1990) 'Access and assets: the experience of mature mother students in higher education'. *Journal of Access Studies*, 5 (2), 188–202.

Edwards, R. (1993) *Mature Women Students: Separating or Connecting Family and Education*. London: Taylor & Francis.

Elsey, B. (1982) 'Mature students' experience of university'. *Studies in Adult Education*, 14 (3), 69–77.

Foucault, M. (1988) 'Technologies of the self', in L. Martin, H. Gutman and P. Hutton (eds) *Technologies of the Self: A Seminar with Michel Foucault*. Amherst: University of Massachusetts Press.

Garrison, D. R. (1994) 'An epistemological overview of the field', in D. E. Garrison (ed.) *Research Perspectives in Adult Education*. Malabar, FL: Krieger Publishing.

Griffiths, M. (1995) *Feminisms and the Self: the Web of Identity*. London: Routledge.

Hopper, E. and Osborn, M. (1975) *Adult Students, Education, Selection and Social Control*. Milton Keynes: Open University Press/Society for Research into Higher Education.

Houle, C. (1972) *The Design of Education*. San Francisco: Jossey Bass.

Johnson, C. and Locke, M. (1990) *Experiences and Views of Mature Students*, CIS Working Paper no 61. London: East London Polytechnic.

Karkalas, A. and Mackenzie, A. (1995) 'Travelling hopefully: access and post-access experience of adults who do not proceed to higher education'. *Journal of Access Studies*, 10 (1), 20–39.

Knowles, M. (1970) *The Modern Practice of Adult Education: Andragogy versus Pedagogy*. New York: Association Press.

Knowles, M. (1984) *Andragogy in Action*. San Francisco: Jossey Bass.

Knowles, M. (1998) *The Adult Learner*. Houston, TX: Gulf.

Lea, M. (1996) 'Narratives and identity: adults negotiating higher education'. *Scottish Journal of Adult and Continuing Education*, 3 (2), 5–18.

Lunneborg, P. (1994) *OU Women: Undoing Educational Obstacles*. London: Cassell.

McFadden, M. (1995) ' "Second chance" education: "settling old scores" '. *Journal of Access Studies*, 10 (1), 40–59.

McGivney, V. (1994) 'Women, education and training: a research report'. *Adults Learning*, 5 (5), 118–20.

MacIntosh, M. (1990) 'Second-time pupils: the return of women to school', in F. Paterson, and J. Fewel, (eds) *Girls in Their Prime: Scottish Education Revisited*. Edinburgh: Scottish Academic Press.

Martin, J. (1999) 'Gender in education', in D. Matheson, and I. Grosvenor (eds), *An Introduction to the Study of Education*. London: David Fulton.

Mason, R. C. (1992) 'Adult and continuing education should be market driven'. *New Directions for Adult and Continuing Education*, 54 (2), 77–83.

Matheson, C. (1999) 'Access to higher education', in D. Matheson, and I. Grosvenor (eds) *An Introduction to the Study of Education*. London: David Fulton.

Matheson, D. (1995) 'Adult education in Suisse romande'. *Compare*, 25(2), 115–36.

Mies, M. (1993) 'Towards a methodology for feminist research', in M. Hammersley (ed.) *Social Research: Philosophy, Politics and Practice*. London: Sage.

Miller, A. (1984) *The Crucible*. London: Penguin Books.

Munn, P., Johnstone, M. and Robinson, R. (1994) *The Effectiveness of Access Courses: Views of Access Students and their Teachers*. Edinburgh: Scottish Council for Research in Education.

Opie, A. (1992) 'Qualitative research, appropriation of the "other" and empowerment' *Feminist Review*, 40 (1), 52–69.

Osborne, M. and Gallacher, J. (1995) 'Scotland', in P. Davies (ed.) *Adults in Higher Education: International Experiences in Access and Participation*. London: Jessica Kingsley.

Parry, G. (1986) 'From patronage to partnership'. *Journal of Access Studies*, 1 (1), 43–53.

Pascall, G. and Cox, R. (1993) *Women Returning to Higher Education*. Buckingham: Society for Research into Higher Education and Open University Press.

Patai, D. (1988) 'Constructing a life story'. *Feminist Review*, 14 (1), 143–66.

Peters, R. S. (1966) *Ethics and Education*. London: Allen and Unwin.

Powney, J. and Hall, S. (1998) *Scottish Access Students in Higher Education*. Edinburgh: Scottish Council for Research in Education.

Rittenburger, T. L. (1984) 'Is the marketing concept adequate for continuing education?' *Lifelong Learning*, 8 (1), 21–3.

Scottish Community Education Council (1988) *Adult and Continuing Education in Scotland: Then . . . and Now?* Edinburgh: SCEC (The Carnegie Report).

Scottish Education Department (SED) (1975) *Adult Education: The Challenge of Change*. Edinburgh: HMSO (The Alexander Report).

Smithers, A. and Griffin, A. (1986) *The Progress of Mature Students*. Manchester: Joint Matriculation Board.

Spender, D. (1982) *Invisible Women*. London: Writers and Readers Co-operative.

Tennant, M. (1988) *Psychology and Adult Learning*. London: Routledge.

Tight, M. (1998) 'Lifelong learning: opportunity or compulsion?' *British Journal of Educational Studies*, 46 (3), 251–63.

Weil, S. (1986) 'Non-traditional learners within traditional higher education institutions: discovery and disappointment'. *Studies in Higher Education*, 11 (3), 219–35.

Weil, S. (1988) 'From a language of observation to a language of experience: studying the perspectives of diverse adults in higher education'. *Journal of Access Studies*, 3 (1), 17–43.

Weiner, G., Arnot, M. and David, M. (1997) 'Is the future female? Female success, male disadvantage, and changing gender patterns in education', in Halsey, A. H., Lauder, H., Brown, P. and Stuart Wells, A. (eds) *Education, Culture, Economy, Society*. Oxford: Oxford University Press.

Weiner, G., Arnot, M. and David, M. (1998) 'Who benefits from schooling? Equality issues in Britain', in A. Mackinnon, I. Elquist-Saltzman and A. Prentice (eds) *Education into the 21st Century: Dangerous Terrain for Women?* London: Falmer Press.

West, L. (1996) *Beyond Fragments*. London: Taylor & Francis.

Woodley, A. (1984) 'The older the better? A study of mature students' performance in British universities'. *Research in Education*, 32, 32–50.

Woodley, A., Wagner L., Slowey, M., Hamilton, M. and Fulton, O. (1987) *Choosing to Learn: Adults in Education*. Milton Keynes: Open University Press.

13

Education and Lifelong Learning 'Systems'

David Matheson

Introduction

It is probably difficult to move very much in the literature on education and/or training without encountering terms that refer to learning throughout the lifespan These terms have been thrust very much into the public, as opposed to the academic, domain especially since the mid-1990s.

The purpose of this chapter is to examine education and lifelong learning, to look at the ways in which the latter term has been construed and to situate lifelong learning in the various contexts which exist in the world today.

The concept of lifelong learning

There is a strong element of tautology in the term lifelong learning. Does it simply mean learning that takes place in the course of one's life? If so, then there is, at one and the same time, a lot to it and a little to it. There is a lot since clearly we learn from the cradle to the grave. There is little since most of the learning that occurs in our lifetimes is arguably incidental and consequently unstructured. This is not to detract from its value: the lessons that life teaches may well be those that have the most lasting impact and which act to form us into the characters that we are. However, lack of structure and lack of definable purpose imply a certain serendipity. None the less we have to be careful here. Purpose in education can easily get entangled with institutions. After all, educational institutions usually have curricula, often concerned with the pastoral aspects of learning as well as with the academic. What we have to bear in mind as we go along is that purpose in education in a lifelong learning sense can apply equally to communities as to individuals, to the autodidact as to the learner in the classroom. This apparent vagueness can have its disconcerting aspects and may require some suspension of disbelief on the part of the reader whose experience is largely or exclusively that of the teacher in the class telling the learners what they ought to know.

Taking *purposeful learning* as a starting point, we can enlarge the field of education and learning to encompass a multitude of domains, be they formal, non-formal or informal or pass from one area to another.

A problem which arises out of any discussion of learning is whether it might be termed 'education'. Education, as is well known, is fundamentally a contested concept. The questions of who it is for, what it is for and when it is for are determinant to a great extent in deciding what it actually is. It is potentially a worthwhile exercise for the reader to pause here for a moment to consider his/her own personal conception of education and then compare it with those that evolve in the following discussion.

As regards learning, we can define it in terms of outcomes, competencies and/or in terms of process. Our whole view of learning will change whether we focus on the product or the process. Indeed close to the heart of the lifelong learning debate, which was relaunched with Faure *et al.*'s (1972) report *Learning to Be*, lies the question of whether it is the end that counts or the means. It is of course arguable whether the process can be separated at all from the product. Learning, like baking, is not just a matter of throwing in the right ingredients and waiting for something to emerge. The circumstances make a difference. Minor changes to the process can make a difference too. The same ingredients, mixed in the same manner, can give you either a sponge cake or a raised *pâte brisée fine* that you might use as the base of a tart. The difference is how you put the mixture into the cake tin and the type of tin that you use. So it is with learning: little changes can have big effects, the process is inseparable from the product. What is open to dispute is which of the two has greater value.

Since Faure *et al.* (1972), the debate over lifelong learning has continued to gather, slowly at first and then faster, increasing momentum. Within the UK, for example, commentaries and critiques on the concept of lifelong learning and perceived need for it appeared not only from academics but from political parties, both opposition and government, from the Confederation of British Industry as well as the Trades Union Congress.[1]

Learning: The Treasure Within (Delors *et al.*, 1996) attempted, among other things, to synthesize the developments in the debate though its success in this is open to question. Yet the impact of this publication and the responses to it underlined the essential point that however we choose to define learning, the notions of lifelong learning, lifelong education, the learning society and the learning age have caused more ink to be spilled over the last few years than possibly any other topic of educational theory. A common thread which runs through all the terms used to describe learning throughout the lifetime is the sense of optimism which seems to imbue them all. There have, however, also been a few voices in the wilderness who have questioned the wisdom, or even the motivation, which lies behind this popularization. Tight (1998) considers that, especially in the vocational domain, there is a strong sense of compulsion. There is nothing new in this notion.

As James Lynch (1979) put it, lifelong learning 'may offer unlimited scope for th further subjugation of [wo]man to the world of work' (p. 6).

These warnings arise in part from there being at least two competing discourse of lifelong learning: the emancipatory and the utilitarian. It is interesting t contrast the generalized optimism of most of the writings stemming especiall from the former with the ever-frequent complaints by industrialists the world ov that recruits do not possess sufficient skills of basic literacy and basic numerac' There is a tension between this perceived lacuna and the idea that all skills can b picked up at any stage in life, unless of course one has some physical impedimen that precludes certain activities.

As Duman (1999) states, 'the idea of [a] learning society is quite fashionabl among educationalists, politicians and businessmen [*sic*] despite the fact that it i extremely debatable whether [the/a] learning society is an attainable target fc human societies or not' (p. 127). Duman goes on to contrast a number of theorie of what a learning society might look like and produces models which range fron those wherein the whole learning experience is driven by the logic of the marke and economic relevance to those in which the main goals are personal well-being active citizenship and personal empowerment in the sense of becoming capable o making authentic choice. Clearly there is much space between such models and thi space only adds to the complications surrounding the discourses on lifelong learning.

Fundamentally we can distinguish two poles in the lifelong learning debate anc a multitude of intermediate positions. On the one hand we have the older axis o conscientization whose main inspiration is the work on literacy and thence cultura development which was undertaken and recorded by Paulo Freire. For Freire ai essential point is that individuals come together to move themselves forward a communities as well as moving forward as individuals. Economic growth may happen but it is not a *sine qua non* of Freire's approach. Rather it is a likely consequence of personal and community empowerment (Freire, 1967). With thei emphasis on social justice, social difference and social transformation, Freire's idea: are often termed 'critical pedagogy' (Mayo, 1999, p. 58) and demand an entirely different role for the educator to that most often associated with formal learning and, especially, school.

In the light of postmodernism's description of the death of the Grand Narrative and its assertion of the end of social class, we find the opposing pole of lifelong learning: that of learning for economic necessity. This posits an idea that one's learning is most worthwhile when it is linked to gaining or retaining employment. It is not that liberal education is deemed worthless but it is seen as being of somewhat limited utility. An example of such utilitarian lifelong learning is seen in the UK government's Green Paper *The Learning Age: A Renaissance for a New Britain* (DfEE, 1998) whose launch was accompanied on UK television with an advertise-ment campaign showing how additional qualifications might lead to better employment.

Jary and Thomas (1999) comment that

not only is . . . the promotion of lifelong learning now populist, associated with what Sanyal (1987) has called the world-wide expansion of the 'social demand' for education, it is today increasingly receiving the backing of governments, funding bodies and international organisations. (p. 3)

And this they are doing with a view to equalizing access to cultural capital between individuals and between states. 'Knowledge means power, power in the form of cultural capital' (Jary and Thomas, 1999, p. 3). This fuels the two competing discourses over lifelong learning and the discourse over what counts as education.

Evans, Jarvis and King (1999) propose that education 'has come to suggest that enlightened persons do something to the underdeveloped or incompetent' (p. 107) and consequently favour using the more neutral term *learning*. Their stance is disputable and ignores self-directed learning which fits all the criteria usually ascribed to education. It also ignores the flexible relationship between learner and educator which Freire's (1967) theories of education advocate whereby the educator and learner swap roles and the one learns from the other. Let us, however, bear in mind the limitations of the term *learning* as we proceed.

Nodes on the lifelong learning web

Lifelong learning is a process and as such, since our lives appear linear, is arguably linear itself. However, if we begin to consider the *how*, *when* and *why* of our learning we begin to realize the extent to which we revisit areas of learning. We do not simply learn once and for all. We forget; skills get rusty. We might then endeavour to re-remember, to relearn, to reacquire skills thought forgotten. We have to delve into our personal past, into our memories to do these things. Yet all the while we have gone on learning more and more. The metaphor of the lifelong learning web enables us to see our learning as not simply cumulative with one layer piled atop another. Rather it is a multidimensional tapestry which we can reach on to and into. Some parts may be beyond our grasp and require to be focused upon but all the parts are there, even if some are showing signs of decay or neglect. The web allows an image of us having high skill/knowledge levels in one domain and being total debutantes in another in a manner that the ladder does not. My relative competency at baking has no apparent dependency on my competency on the fiddle or incompetency in German. These skills and the accompanying knowledge grew independently of one another, although they grew side by side and they will make links as the need arises. The ladder metaphor would imply otherwise.

For much of the last three decades, an apparent difficulty in the lifelong learning debate has come from its growing very much from the debates surrounding adult education in the 1970s. It seemed fashionable among adult educationists of that time (and more than one since then) to consciously ignore formal school. This meant that a large amount of the rhetoric and the literature which was produced took as its starting point the end of formal education. The debate has since moved on and it is increasingly accepted that lifelong learning is exactly that: it begins in the cradle, or even before, and ends at the grave. None the less the language used by politicians reveals much about the internalized attitudes towards learning and education. When we hear politicians discuss 'the education system' and only mean *school* (as does David Blunkett, the current Secretary of State for Education in the UK), when philosophers of education do the same (as do Winch and Gingell, 1999), then we begin to realize the limited impact of the discourse of lifelong learning. Education is frequently equated with school as is learning. That this still occurs even at this juncture demonstrates just how slowly changes are occurring in the discourse of learning, as opposed to lifelong learning.[2]

This creates a difficult backdrop against which to discuss lifelong learning systems and indicates that perhaps an important step to be taken along the road to creating real and worthwhile systems of lifelong learning consists of changing the language ever so slightly so that school is equated to a type of formal education and not to education and learning as a whole. Perhaps when learning is seen to be an active part of *life* then lifelong learning systems can be really developed.

Organization and policies

Despite the fact that the very concept of lifelong learning can be viewed from any point along at least one axis, ranging from personal and group enlightenment (however defined) to economic development on a personal or group basis, it is not unreasonable that governments expect (or at least hope for) some financial return on their investments, and the sooner the better. This return can be in the form of, for example, increased productivity/worker flexibility or indeed in increased community involvement. Financial gain for a government may be direct in the former case or indirect in the latter case.

Education's effects on individuals and communities are not to be underestimated and even the World Bank has come to recognize the diverse manners in which it can affect people's lives, their communities and their country's economy. Education can serve to develop human capital and hence productivity. It can impact on health and nutrition, develop social capital and strengthen social cohesion and equity. It can expedite growth and development at the macro level (World Bank, 1999).

Especially in the economic sphere, these benefits are widely recognized and throughout the world there is a clear drive towards maximizing access to and uptake of primary education and increasing the 'school life expectancy' of young learners. Whether this last point is, in itself, wise is open to debate. The Western school/college/university paradigm was developed in very particular circumstances and depended, according to King (1999), on fixed careers, lifetime jobs and more or less fixed competences. That the West is having such problems in adapting its learning and teaching patterns to accommodate a globalized economy in which these assumptions are decreasingly true demonstrates the inadequacy of that thinking, even in those areas that spawned it. On the face of it, it would seem reasonable to argue that the Western model is even less appropriate for industrializing countries as these have to fit into a very different economic climate from that which pertained when the model was developed, essentially in the nineteenth century.

None the less a glance through the UNESCO statistics on this and related topics shows an almost consistent year-on-year increase in the numbers of young persons in primary level education. However, major disparities remain between the regions of the world and this is demonstrated most vividly when we compare the least developed countries with their developed cousins and see that in 1996 70 per cent of children in the least developed countries[3] attended primary school (79.1 per cent of boys, 61.4 per cent of girls) compared with 103 per cent (102.8 per cent boys, 103.2 per cent girls) in the developed countries (UNESCO, 1998). Repetition, early enrolment and late leaving account for the figures over 100 per cent.

Starker differences emerge across lower and upper secondary school. In lower secondary, the developed countries still exceeded 100 per cent of both boys and girls in 1996 while the least developed enrolled 18.8 per cent of the cohort (23 per cent boys, 14.5 per cent girls). At upper secondary, the least developed enrolled a mere 3.1 per cent of the cohort (4.6 per cent boys, 1.7 per cent girls) with the developed countries attaining 50.5 per cent of the cohort (46.8 per cent boys, 54.4 per cent girls) (UNESCO, 1998).

It is striking in the data above that there is a gender balance (more or less) in the developed countries and a stark gender disparity in the least developed countries. Obviously within each group of countries there will be variation. Afghanistan shows 68.4 per cent male participation at primary level compared with 34.1 per cent female participation, and Somalia 11.1 per cent male participation and 5.8 per cent female participation. The most extreme disparity at primary level is Yemen with 99.9 per cent male participation compared to 39.9 per cent female. All the developed countries put their participation at first level close to 100 per cent for both males and females (UNESCO, 1998). In sum, it is clear that at the level of the primary school, there are far too many young people who simply do not figure in the formal educational process. This is not to suggest that these young people do not receive any learning. Such would be absurd. However, the odds are stacked against any person successfully achieving literacy if this is not done at an early age. If the societal expectation is that a person need not achieve literacy on grounds of social class or gender or both, then the demand for schooling is less likely to exist, and still less to be met.

In terms of adult (il)literacy, there is again gender imbalance in terms both of the world and of the least developed countries. In 1995 22.6 per cent of persons aged 15 and over were deemed illiterate, 16.4 per cent men, 28.8 per cent women. In the least developed countries, this rose to 51.2 per cent of the population, 40.5 per cent men, 61.9 per cent women. In the developed countries, 1.3 per cent of the population could not read, 1.1 per cent men, 1.6 per cent women (UNESCO, 1998).

It would be reasonable to suppose that those with the financial means to pay for the schooling of their children are likely to do so, unless they have some major religious or cultural reason for not so doing. It is therefore not a wild extrapolation to suggest that poor women are doubly marginalized in terms of literacy (and, of course, the whole formal educational experience) through being both poor and women.

Illiteracy is also a contested concept since there is no general agreement as what constitutes being able to read, although UNESCO speaks in the following terms:

> Adult literacy rate is defined as the percentage of population aged 15 years and over who can both read and write with understanding a short simple statement on his/her everyday life. Adult illiteracy is defined as the percentage of the population aged 15 years and over who cannot both read and write with understanding a short simple statement on his/her everyday life. (UNESCO 1998, n.p.)

Such a statement is certainly better than none at all but it is so loaded with value judgements that its worth is limited indeed. What is a *simple statement*? And why lump together reading and writing? Are they the same or similar skills? Such questions require answers in the course of deriving a more complete definition of (il)literacy.

The acquisition of literacy can of course be seen, following Freire, as the first step towards *éducation permanente* for adults (Ndimurukundo, 1994). It does of course require support in order that the new skill does not fall into disuse. Jones (1997) asserts that 'universal literacy and basic education is within reach' (p. 368) and goes on to argue that:

> Providing literacy, numeracy, and useful knowledge to mothers in rural areas can have a profound effect on birth rates, the health of their families, the learning potential of their children, and the cultural cohesiveness of their communities (p. 369)

This is exactly the stance which the World Bank has now taken (World Bank 1999) and shows much development from that which Jones (1997) attributes to it whereby mass education and primary education were 'off limits'. In developing countries the discourse of gender, education and development was first established in 1995 by the World Bank statement of priorities in educational policy in which basic education, especially that of girls, became the first priority. This discourse sits firmly within the framework of classical liberal economics. Women's empowerment has become a central concern of projects that are planned from the bottom up with women themselves directly participating in planning projects to improve their lives in place of the top-down approach where projects emanate from professional developers. The discourses of gender, education and development are shifting and are being redefined by a wide range of interest groups with empowerment as an increasingly important objective (Heward and Bunwaree, 1999).

There is, however, the problem of the actual worth of literacy when one has nothing to read and there is the question of how to measure *functional literacy*. Perhaps a good indicator of functional literacy is the circulation level of daily newspapers. This, of course, is dependent on newspapers being available *and* having access to them. There are also cultural attitudes to newspapers to be taken into account and a low circulation might merely mean that readers access their newspapers in public places such as cafés or libraries. With these caveats in mind, the UNESCO data on daily newspaper circulation make interesting reading. To within a couple of exceptions (e.g. Portugal at 75 sales per 1000 inhabitants) every developed country sees sales in excess of 100 newspapers per 1000 inhabitants and this regardless of the common habits of the inhabitants of some countries (such as France and Switzerland) to read newspapers in cafés. In some cases, the circulation figures reach into several hundred per 1000 inhabitants. Indeed the highest rate belongs to Iceland with 535 (UNESCO, 1998). The incidental (and some purposeful) learning taking place in this manner is not to be understated. Regardless of the political stance taken in a newspaper, any which falls short of pure polemic will have an educative function in terms of articles on world affairs, politics, lifestyle and so on. It would not be too strong to suggest that access to newspapers and the ability to read them are potentially important nodes in the lifelong learning web.

It is certainly an aim of primary school to teach basic literacy and numeracy, but it is at the lower secondary level that preparation for employment may be said to begin in earnest. At this level, we begin to see most clearly just how much distance there is in terms of formal education between the developed countries and the least developed countries. The differences in participation rates between the least developed countries and the developed are even greater, the gender imbalances in the least developed likewise. Recognition has to be given, however, to the efforts being made in most developing countries to widen participation in general and to widen participation by females in particular.

Leaving school and going to work

Arguably one of the most important nodes to be made in the lifelong learning web is when the learner goes from formal education to the world of work. The manner in which the new worker enters the job market, the types of work available, the attitude towards further study are all, in great measure, influenced by the experience which was school. Clearly in the light of the growing massification of higher education in the developed countries, the transition will be increasingly from university into work but, throughout the world, for the majority of learners the transition will be from school to work. As developing countries strive to increase the 'school life expectancy' of young people, the lessons which might be gleaned from countries who already have experience in this particular transition become all the more important. These can give not only lessons to follow (with appropriate adaptations to suit a country's particular circumstances) but, as importantly, lessons to avoid.

The transition into the labour market is one which clearly varies across the world. In those areas where parents depend on child labour in order to survive, there is clearly no transition from school to work in the same manner as this occurs in more prosperous areas. This is not to say that in developed countries children do not work. Indeed in the UK there has been repeated concern over the last few years over the number of adolescent and pre-adolescent children who are working for wages of less than a third of the National Minimum Wage. The transition in developed countries tends to consist of moving from a phase of life where formal education is the focus (at least in theory) to one where work is the focus.

The clear and distinct separation between school and work which was long evident in schools, especially in academically oriented streams and classes, is now somewhat attenuated:

> A general trend in many of the EU states has been to try to find ways to bring education and work closer together, both in terms of the relevance of the knowledge and skills imparted through education, and in terms of the organisational links between education and work organisations. (Green, Wolf and Leney, 1999, p. 246)

An example of this was the Transition to Adult Life Pilot Project (TAL) which ran under EU funding in the Castlemilk area of Glasgow, Scotland, from 1984 until 1996. The aims of TAL were multiple and included creating links with secondary schools in other parts of the EU and organizing pupil (and staff) exchanges. Of present interest is the creation within TAL of various mini-enterprise projects where pupils, under the guidance of a teacher, set up and ran small businesses for profit. In the latter years of the project, this consisted, in one Castlemilk school, of restringing badminton rackets. Profits were used to help fund the exchange trips. The pilot project created links with the local community and, through its good offices, initiatives to encourage adults to return to school, in some cases to learn alongside young people, were undertaken (see Monasta, 1995). Occurring in a multitude of secondary schools throughout Scotland, this blurring of the boundaries between those for whom school is intended is potentially an important aspect of developing a lifelong learning system. In the Scottish experience, it has crossed boundaries of social class and encouraged people, especially women, to benefit not only from academic subjects at school level but also courses aimed at improving quality of life. Chapter 12 in this present volume, for example, presents an examination of how the class and gender dynamics operated and evolved in a secondary school in an area of multiple deprivation in Glasgow.

Staying with Scotland, this country has seen over the last decade an immense growth in the range of vocational-type courses and modules available in secondary schools. This is set to continue with the advent of the Higher Still programme which has set itself the task of reducing to a minimum the gap between academic and vocational subjects and courses at upper secondary level. This is an uphill task as I found whilst responsible for the overall administration of modular courses in a secondary school in Glasgow, teachers did not take the modular courses as seriously as they took 'traditional' courses and this was despite groupings of particular modules carrying the same value for university entrance as did the 'traditional' qualifications in the same domains. The same problem was found when I spent a week on industrial placement in a nuclear power plant: the manager in charge of training at the plant simply did not understand the modular courses and referred back to older style qualifications. The transferability so dear to the hearts of the architects of the modular courses was simply not borne out in practice. A basic problem, highlighted by Davies (1999), is the apparently semantic nuance which distinguishes 'having a qualification' from 'being qualified' (p. 39): tradespersons tend to refer to themselves (and be referred to) as 'qualified' whereas those who have followed 'traditional' qualifications tend to refer to themselves (and be referred to as) 'having a qualification'. 'Having a qualification' seems to imply that one has undertaken a terminal examination whereas as 'being qualified' has echoes more of having learned a skill. Crossing the Rubicon that appears to separate these perceptions is a mammoth shift in how things are viewed but attempts are being made.

The advent of the Higher Still has sought to effectively modularize the entire upper secondary curriculum, creating multiple entry and exit levels, allowing pupils to mix levels between subjects in a manner hitherto unknown. Whether this gets over any remaining teacher reticence as to the value of modules and lack (or absence) of terminal examinations remains to be seen. However, this initiative aims to be inclusive and to cater in a meaningful fashion for candidates of all abilities. There is also the problem of how employers will view the new qualifications and how they will articulate with studies undertaken upon entrance to work. Scotland does have a clear advantage in this domain in that the same organization which sets (or validates) school-level qualifications also validates the majority of vocational (including the advanced vocational) qualifications. Indeed the Scottish Qualifications Authority (SQA) was formed through the merger of the former Scottish Examinations Board (school level) and the Scottish Vocational Education Council (principally vocational) in order that the non-university qualifications ladder in Scotland be a seamless robe (SQA, 1999).

Tchaban (1998) terms Scotland's move as 'more flexibility through modules' (n.p.) but while flexibility is certainly an advantage there is the danger of atomization of module provision (where a cohort loses its identity in a manner that is less likely where everyone in a class is following the same overall course) and, as mentioned above, employer ignorance.

However, modular schemes do give learners the possibility to change direction if they have a change of heart. Such is the case with the Ontario Youth Apprenticeship Program which 'gives students who are at least 16 years old and who have completed Grade 10 the opportunity to complete high school while working part-time as a registered apprentice' (Ministry of Education and Training, 1999, n.p.). Further, students who find that they are not suited to the trades can return to the regular school programme with no penalty. The American School to Work Opportunities Program tries to entice possible apprentices into actually making the move by setting up work experience programmes and work placements in such a manner that the learner can effectively have a foothold in both the world of work and school. As Haimson, Hershey and Silverberg (1999) put it:

Whether learning by doing and in context is accomplished at school, in a work setting, or both, School-to-Work seeks to improve career prospects and academic achievement in high school, and thereby boost enrolment in post-secondary education and increase the likelihood of obtaining high skill, high wage employment. (n.p.)

Across the majority of developed countries, skills shortages are increasingly being encountered. Consequently, attempts are being made to revitalize (or reinvent) apprenticeship systems and systems of vocational qualifications which are credible in the eyes of both the general public and employers. This implies a need to re-examine existing systems of vocational preparation in the light of the need for flexible and adaptable workers. The apparent rigidity of some of the dual systems is being questioned and pathways considered for the misoriented as is the case in Austria where, in addition, schools are increasingly introducing vocational courses into the curriculum.

However, while the concern over skills shortages is widely felt, the self-examination needed to address this issue is not apparent everywhere and the academic–vocational divide is, in places, a long time dying. Perhaps the most important place in which it needs to die is in people's heads.

Of course, it is not only in developed countries that this divide is alive and kicking. In former European colonies there is all too frequently the colonial legacy whereby those who work with their heads are seen as doing a superior job to those who work with their hands, regardless of the real employment potential and real earnings potential (Matheson, 1996). It seems clear that until there is a clear parity and progression between the vocational and the academic, lifelong learning will risk simply reinforcing stratifications and divisions between learners.

Higher education in the lifelong learning web

Across the developing countries, we see since the Second World War progress towards mass systems of higher education. The least developed and many developing countries still nestle in the realms of higher education being very much the reserve of an élite. The extent of provision is overall more limited than has been seen in many parts of Europe since the nineteenth century. It is worthwhile, however, considering just what higher education is for and for whom it is intended. In the West we might well regard such low participation rates as a problem to be solved. This would risk losing sight of the context within which this low participation takes place.

Part of this context is the employment possibilities for graduates. It is hard to see much economic sense in spending scarce financial resources in a manner perhaps guaranteed to more or less waste them. Even from a social justice point of view, various objections can be raised to increasing spending on higher education to beyond a point that the economy can sustain. After all, budgets are limited and questions have to be posed as to which investments bring the greatest returns.

As the experience in many rural areas of the developed world has shown (e.g. the

Highlands and Islands of Scotland, the canton of Valais in Switzerland), there is the further quandary of how to avoid the creation (or sustenance) of a brain drain where the most highly qualified persons emigrate and take the investment that has been made in them with them. This creates a dilemma for poorer regions of the world (and not just in developing countries) although a few attempted solutions do emerge.

It is now quite common to sponsor (or to support the sponsoring of) post-graduate students and faculty members to study abroad and then return home and disseminate their new knowledge. This is certainly cheaper than importing academics to whom internationally competitive salaries would have to be paid. The émigré can be placed in what is identified as a centre of excellence.

The principle disadvantage in temporarily exporting one's talent is that it may never come back and while the expatriate may be a good advertisement for the talent which exists in the home country, it is none the less no longer in the home country and hence the financial investment made in him/her has gone, possibly for ever. There is also the problem of the host country being seen as having an educational situation (and accompanying culture) which is viewed as superior to that of the home country. As has historically been the case in many rural and mountainous regions of Europe and elsewhere, the value of the home culture becomes an object of nostalgia but the economic imperative is irresistible.

Alternatives which are currently being promoted by diverse agencies including the World Bank involve the use of the Internet and other distance learning media to teach teachers and other learners, but there is the fundamental question of cost and access to equipment. In this light, initiatives such as the Global Distance Education Net (DistEdNet) and the African Virtual University (AVU) do not seek to be available to the general public. DistEdNet is a 'knowledge guide distance education designed to help clients of the World Bank and others interested in using distance education for human development which exists to help create and help sustain distance learning courses at all levels' (DistEdNet, 1999). Especially via the Internet, DistEdNet makes available materials which cover all levels from adult basic learning through to postgraduate.

Far more ambitious in its use of technology is the AVU which arranges video-conference teaching, live Internet links for academics and other parties such as journalists across Sub-Saharan Africa (SSA). The AVU brings together academics from developed countries with their colleagues and their students in SSA. Its use of information and communications technology (ICT) provides

the flexibility and cost-effectiveness of a virtual academic infrastructure . . . The AVU can thereby contribute to overcoming the existing barriers of declining budgets, too few faculty, outdated equipment, and limited space and facilities that prevent increased access to higher education for a significant majority of students in SSA. The increase in the number of scientifically and technologically literate professionals will, as a consequence, better position countries in SSA to be part of the global information age and the new knowledge economy. (AVU, 1999, n.p.)

The AVU as a distance learning initiative is bold indeed. What is remarkab
however, is that it does not attempt to reach the general population and is therefc
not be confused in any way with the various high-technology open universiti
(such as the UK's Open University or Germany's Fernuniversität von Hagen) whi
one finds in various parts of the world and which depend on high-cost communic
tions equipment being available to students in their homes. Rather the AV
harnesses the ambience of the traditional university and the communicative pow
of the new technologies to deliver its courses. It still runs the risk of students seei
academic excellence as being 'elsewhere' but this perception depends in lar;
measure on the manner in which the AVU is presented to its students and tl
manner in which it presents itself. If it is sensitive to the cultural diversity of i
students, if it is presented as a complement to the standard face-to-face fare whi(
is the mainstay of the traditional university, then the possible problems will ter
to be diminished.

An initiative which avoids many of the cultural difficulties of the AVU is tl
University of Highlands and Islands in Scotland:

The UHI Project is an academic network of 13 existing colleges of furth
education and other specialist institutions supported by a small Executive Offi(
team which is making extensive use of advanced information communicatic
technologies. (UHI, 1999a)

What makes UHI interesting is not only its use of ICT but also its research in
ways of reducing the costs involved in Internet access. In addition, it builds c
existing resources and physical infrastructures to deliver to its primary clientel
scattered across the sparsely populated Highlands and Islands of Scotland, cours(
which are, for the most part, developed for them and by them. Most of the colleg(
forming the UHI have subsiduary 'learning centres' with ICT facilities and throug
these students in all but the most remote areas can study a wide range of subjec
up to degree level by means of distance learning packages, video-conferencing ar
the Internet (UHI, 1999b).

Potentially highly pertinent from the viewpoint of developing countries an
minority cultures is that UHI offers a number of its courses through the mediu
of the indigenous Gaelic language (which counts less than 50,000 speakers i
Scotland), following on from the example set by the successful Sabhal Mòr Ostai;
a Gaelic-medium business school on the Isle of Skye in the Inner Hebrides. Cours(
such as BA Gaelic with North Atlantic Studies and BA Gaelic Language an
Culture are offered through the medium of Gaelic and are clearly tailored to me(
demands from the indigenous population (UHI, 1999b), although nothing pr(
cludes non-natives from applying to enter. The UHI has yet to receive its universit
charter and so, at present, its courses are validated by the UK Open University an
the SQA.

Adult and non-formal education and learning

'Adult and non-formal education have in almost every country at all times been the Cinderella of education provision' (Dodds, 1994, n.p.) and this is as evident in developed countries as in developing ones. Adult and non-formal education are very frequently seen, or so it would seem, as soft targets when budgets are being squeezed. Part of the problem is that adult education, especially in developed countries, is often perceived as non-essential. It may even be seen as a leisure, rather than an educational, activity (Matheson, 1995). The teachers within adult and non-formal education rarely receive the status of 'teacher', which is to say that the salary they receive may bear no resemblance to the salary paid to an 'official' teacher. For example, in the UK, there are few full-time adult educators for the simple reason that there are few full-time posts as adult educators. The salary paid to these educators is generally of the order of £15 to £30 per hour of teaching. This may sound a lot in the UK context but if one only has three or four hours of teaching per week then one earns just enough to be effectively disqualified from most social security benefits. Therefore adult education is generally a part-time activity, even for the adult educators. None the less non-formal education plays a major role in the preparation of skilled workers throughout the developing world. The International Labour Organization (1998) gives the example of Senegal where non-formal technical and vocational training occupy an important place in the preparation of the workforce, especially the female part of it, although, in a manner echoed in Maldonado (1987), the trainees have to put up with situations of little more than servitude.

In the developed countries the non-formal vocational training sector is limited. The developed countries, with a few exceptions, seem to have caught the 'diploma disease' (Doré, 1976). There seems to be less and less attention paid to what one can actually do. Rather the focus is on the certificates that one possesses which in effect demonstrate that at some point in the past one was capable of accomplishing a particular set of tasks.

This contrasts with the ideas of Freire who rejected what he termed the banking concept of education wherein the teacher deposits knowledge in the learner's head for the learner to then withdraw on the day of the examination. This stance brings us to two points which, in the light of Freire's ideas, have a certain irony.

The first is the concept of the 'learning account'. This is an idea gaining ground in the developed countries and accords learners a sum of money (to which they can add) that they spend on what they perceive as their educational needs (Standish, 1999). Effectively what this means is a literal 'learning bank'. Standish (1999) questions how likely is it that 'those from the lowest socio-economic groups will avail themselves of such opportunities' (p. 647).

An answer may well come from another kind of 'learning bank': the Grameen Bank. The Grameen Bank extends credit to those judged to be among the least creditworthy and its 'borrowers make a commitment to a set of social priorities including education, sanitation, and family planning' (THES, 1995). The Grameen Bank aims to:

Reverse the age-old vicious circle of 'low income, low saving, low investment', into a virtuous circle of 'low income, injection of credit, investment, more income, more savings, more investment, more income'. (Grameen Bank, 1999, n.p.)

The vestiges of the old imperial legacy in many developing countries are a long time dying and there is still a tendency in the developed countries to see the developing countries as 'problems'. This is not helped by the media in the developed countries in which 'developing countries only ever figure in the news when disaster strikes' (Matheson, 1996). The Grameen Bank, with its 94 per cent repayment rate and its increasing role in community development, including education (THES, 1995), shows a lesson for breaking the cycle of poverty from which community developers in developed countries might well learn valuable lessons. Equally important in Grameen's strategy is that so many of its borrowers are women. It is therefore acting to reduce marginalization not only in terms of social class and income but also in terms of gender. The transferability of Grameen's approach is witnessed by the growth in microcredit-based banks built around the Grameen model which now number over 150 (Grameen Foundation USA 1999).

Perhaps the Grameen is a learning bank much closer to the ideals of Freire than the notion proposed by, among others, the UK government. It is one where the borrower takes his/her own destiny in hand and learns what can be done with it in a positive sense.

Older adult learners: the U3A

It is common enough to hear expressions such as 'you can't teach an old dog new tricks' and arguably these have become so deeply embedded in daily language that they have effectively entered the discourse of lifelong learning to diminish, if not preclude entirely, the idea that adults can learn effectively. Such is the force of this and other similar adages that it is all too easy to assume that they carry truth with them. In effect, they act to mythologize the ages and stages at which one can learn purposefully. The growth of the 'grey' population, still fit and active and mentally competent, has increasingly challenged this paradigm. Certainly there are activities which the developmental process that is ageing render more difficult to learn as we get older. Joints stiffen and particular degenerative diseases become more common. Yet just how many learning activities depend on suppleness, or physical stamina? Probably very few indeed.

In an attempt to provide mental stimulus and, among other things, companionship in our society which tends to flee old age and worship youth, the University of the Third Age (U3A) made its appearance in France following the upheaval of May 1968. The term 'Third Age' was adopted by dividing the human lifespan into four ages:

1. childhood and adolescence; 2. occupational and wage-earning activity; 3.

retirement from the 'world of work'; 4. dependency on others. The Third Age was emphasised because a good third age can minimise the adjustments and deficits, and indeed the duration, of the fourth age. (Glendinning, 1985, p. 121)

The U3A is an

independent movement of older adults, organising itself, producing its own tutors from its own ranks, developing interesting educational methods suited to their own circumstances . . . In a spirit of self-help and mutual aid the University of the Third Age is beginning to use the knowledge and expertise of its members, which might otherwise go to waste, as the members learn and research and engage in their own educational gerontology. (Shea, 1985, p. 78)

The homepage of the Australian U3A sums up the organization quite neatly:

U3As think of themselves as being universities in the original sense of the term – communities of people who come together to learn from one another – rather than as degree-granting institutions; and so U3A is a learning co-operative of older people. It encourages positive ageing by enabling its members to share many educational, creative and leisure activities. (U3A online, 1999)

This is, of course, just one of many openings for older learners but it is worth highlighting since it challenges several paradigms at once. It challenges the ageist assumptions so prevalent especially in developed countries. It challenges the very nature of the 'modern' discourse of learning which posits itself increasingly on the notion of the qualification. The U3A demands no entrance qualification, gives no qualification on exit (or at any other moment). In these respects, it resembles the Danish Folk High Schools. However, the U3As are self-help organizations. It is generally members who teach each other. In true Freirean fashion the roles of teacher and learner interchange readily and regularly.

The U3A was a product of the generation who lived through the Second World War and who brought to their retirement the attitudes and aspirations of that generation. Whether the current generation of workers will enter their Third Age with the same kinds of notions as their predecessors, we can only wait and see. Perhaps there will be sufficient of the present Third Agers still around to convert the newcomers to their ways.

A problem inherent with the U3As is that they are closed to younger persons. In this respect, they run the risk of becoming educational ghettos for senior citizens. They are also quite difficult to detect in many cases. Their advertisements are few. Few younger people (and relatively few older people) have ever heard of them. And yet they are present in the majority of the countries of the developed world and it would not be too far fetched to suppose that, as increasing numbers of university-educated persons reach retirement in developing countries, more will appear there.

Perhaps the U3As are another symptom of our age of paradoxes. Postmodern discourse describes and discusses how various barriers are coming down, how previous distinctions are fading. Yet a cursory glance will reveal many barriers that are reinforced and new ones that have come into existence. It would, in my view, be regrettable if the U3A served as yet another barrier between youth and older persons. The problem is to find a way to enhance learning opportunities for the older persons without shutting out the younger or being swamped by them.

Conclusion

The concept of lifelong learning has been increasingly at the forefront of political rhetoric for the last couple of decades. In this brief sketch, we have seen that there are major disparities in participation in formal education and that even universal primacy school is an ideal yet to be attained as is universal literacy. Disparities in gender have largely diminished or disappeared in the developed countries and yet remain powerful in the least developed. For lifelong learning to become more than a soundbite it will require reorientation of ideas concerning the so-called academic–vocational divide; it will require moves to reduce disparities and to improve access. Until these things happen, it would be difficult, except in the most rare cases, to talk of a 'lifelong learning system' as anything other than an aspiration. None the less when the will is there to make real this dream, there is much 'good practice' in the world which can be drawn upon and, as suggested with the Grameen Bank, this exchange need not be in one direction only.

As it is at present, lifelong learning as presently conceived does not appear anywhere as anything near a seamless robe. Learning throughout one's life is another matter for we construct our learning web and choose, or are obliged, to move on to particular strands and seek out and strengthen particular nodes. All the nodes in our learning web are joined to all the others. Indeed it is this aspect which makes humans such effective learners: not only do they learn but they make connections, sometimes in the most unexpected ways.

Perhaps what is needed in lifelong learning is the breaking down of categories. In our societies, work is separated from play, education from leisure, the rich from the poor, increasingly the old from the young. Initiatives such as allowing adults to learn alongside youngsters in secondary schools weaken some of these barriers and challenge their legitimacy. It goes likewise for the adoption of the philosophy and practice of the Grameen Bank in developed countries. Unfortunately the tenacious grip of the Western paradigm of what education is, what it is for and who it for holds sway over all other models, regardless of appropriateness.

Lifelong learning has mutated as an ideal. It has spawned variants of itself, some of which are effectively in opposition to the ideals which seemed to drive it from the 1970s and before. This raises the question of whether a learning society is attainable under the present economic and political climate. Does it make any sense to talk of such things when there is such illiteracy in the world? Such imbalances of power?

One set of variants, utilitarian lifelong learning, appears a limited notion

osited on the current economic structures and dedicated to their sustenance. It
lepicts an ideal of lifelong learning not so much in terms of what you do but in
erms of what gets done to you: i.e. you keep your job or get another one *if* you have
lone the appropriate course. You may even get promotion. Could a society with
uch a vision of lifelong learning at its heart call itself a learning society?

One hope on the horizon comes via the World Bank. If such an organization can
hange tack to encompass in its vision of education not only human capital
levelopment but social development, social cohesion, health care and so on, then
perhaps those governments in developed countries who seem so in love with
economic advancement might one day do the same.

While we wait for this to happen, the discourse of lifelong learning may slowly
out surely lose its emancipatory side, lose its notions of quality of life. Let us hope
not. For if it does, it will also lose its humanity.

Notes

1. See Ranson (1998) for a selection of the writings on lifelong learning from the
   1990s.
2. It is perhaps noteworthy that many British politicians and commentators on
   education equate England with the UK (as in *National* Curriculum which does not
   apply to Scotland, as in talking about the British education system when there are
   three in Great Britain and four in the UK). Equating education and learning with
   school, in the face of all evidence to the contrary, is just a step along a similar
   path.
3. Least developed countries: Afghanistan, Angola, Bangladesh, Benin, Bhutan, Bur-
   kina Faso, Burundi, Cambodia, Cape Verde, Central African Republic, Chad,
   Comoros, Democratic Republic of Congo (formerly Zaire), Djibouti, Equatorial
   Guinea, Eritrea, Ethiopia, Gambia, Guinea, Guinea Bissau, Haiti, Kiribati, Lao
   People's Democratic Republic, Lesotho, Liberia, Madagascar, Malawi, Maldives,
   Mali, Mauritania, Mozambique, Myanmar, Nepal, Niger, Rwanda, Samoa, Sao
   Tome and Principe, Sierra Leone, Solomon Islands, Somalia, Sudan, Togo, Tuvalu,
   Uganda, United Republic of Tanzania, Vanuatu, Yemen and Zambia.

   The least developed countries are the poorest countries in the world. They are
   officially designated as 'least developed' by the General Assembly of the United
   Nations, i.e. by the world community as a whole, on the basis of a number of agreed
   criteria. There are currently 48 of them, and they have a combined population of 570
   million (*Source*: http://www.unctad.org/en/subsites/ldcs/aboutldc.htm).

References

African Virtual University (AVU) (1999) available at http://www.avu.org/
Davies, P. (1999) 'Mickey Mouse or Michaelmas: a false dichotomy for an inclusive
framework of qualifications'. *Widening Participation and Access*, 1 (2), 33–40.
Delors, J. *et al.* (1996) *Learning: The Treasure Within*. Report to UNESCO of the Inter-
national Commission on Education for the Twenty-First Century (chaired by Jacques
Delors) Paris/London: UNESCO/HMSO.

Department for Education and Employment (DfEE) (1998) *The Learning Age: A Renaissa* *for a New Britain*. London: The Stationery Office.

DistEdNet (1999) available at http://www.globaldistancelearning.com/about.html

Dodds, A. (1994) 'Distance learning for pre-tertiary education in Africa', in M. Thorpe a D. Grugeon (eds) *Open Learning in the Mainstream*. Harlow: Longman Group. Available http://www.globaldistancelearning.com/Teaching/Design/con-02.html

Doré, R. (1976) *The Diploma Disease: Education, Qualification and Development*. London : All and Unwin.

Duman, A. (1999) 'The demise of local government adult education in England and Wa and the idea of learning society'. *International Journal of Lifelong Education*, 18 (: 127–35.

Evan, K., Jarvis, P. and King, E. (1999) 'Notes and comments'. *Comparative Education*, (1), 107–8.

Faure, E., Iterrara, F., Kaddoura, A.-R., Lopes, H., Petrovsky, R. and Ward, F. (197 *Learning to Be*. Paris: UNESCO.

Freire, P. (1967) *A Pedagogy of the Oppressed*. Harmondsworth: Penguin.

Glendenning, F. (1985): 'Education for older adults in Britain: a developing movement', F. Glendenning (ed.) *Educational Gerontology: International Perspectives*. London a Sydney: Croom Helm.

Grameen Bank (1999) *A Short History of Grameen Bank*. Available at http://www.gramee info.org/bank/hist.html

Grameen Foundation USA (1999) *Grameen Bank Replication Program*. Available at http www.grameenfoundation.org/replications/grameenpage.html

Green, A., Wolf, A. and Leney, T. (1999) *Convergence and Divergence in European Education a Training Systems*. London: Bedford Way Papers.

Haimson, J., Hershey, A. and Silverberg, M. (1999) *Analysis and Highlights: Report to Congr on the National Evaluation of School-to-Work Implementation*. Princeton, NJ: Mathemati Policy Research, Inc.

Heward, C. and Bunwaree, S. (eds) (1999) *Gender, Education and Development*. London: Z Books.

International Labour Organization (ILO) (1998) *Les Femmes dans les Filières techniques professionnelles: Situation des Enseignantes dans quatre Pays ouest-africains (Bénin, Côte d'Ivoi Mali et Sénégal)*. Rapport de synthèse des travaux de recherches et des ateliers nationau Genève: ILO.

Jary, D. and Thomas, E. (1999) 'Editorial: widening participation and lifelong learning *Widening Participation and Lifelong Learning*, 1 (1), 3–7.

Jones, P. (1997) 'The World Bank and the literacy question: orthodoxy, heresy an ideology'. *International Review of Education*, 43 (4), 367–75.

King, E. (1999) 'Education revised for a world in transformation'. *Comparative Education*, 3 (1), 109–17.

Lynch, J. (1979) *Education for Community*. London: Macmillan.

Maldonado, C. (1987) *Petits producteurs d'Afrique francophone*. Genève: ILO.

Matheson, D. (1995) 'Adult education in Suisse romande'. *Compare*, 25 (2), 115–36.

Matheson, D. (1996) 'Imperial culture and cultural imperialism'. *European Journal Intercultural Studies*, 7 (1), 51–6.

Mayo, P. (1999) *Gramsci, Freire and Adult Education*. London: Zed Books.

Ministry of Education and Training (1999) *What Is Apprenticeship?* Toronto: Ministry Education and Training.

Monasta, A. (ed.) (1995) *Master Magister*. Lenzie: Japhet.

Ndimiurukundi, N. (1994) 'Alphabétisation conscientisante comme base d'une éducation permanente'. *International Review of Education*, 40 (3–5), 325–3.

Ranson, S. (ed.) (1998) *Inside the Learning Society*. London: Cassell.

Sanyal, B. C. (1987) *Higher Education and Employment: An International Comparative Analysis*. London: Falmer.

Scottish Qualifications Authority (SQA) (1999) *The Structure of National Qualifications*. Dalkeith: SQA. Available at http://www.sqa.org.uk/higher-still/

Shea, P. (1985): 'The later years of lifelong learning', in F. Glendenning (ed.) *Educational Gerontology: International Perspectives*. London and Sydney: Croom Helm.

Standish, P. (1999) 'Adult and continuing education in Scotland', in T. Bryce and W. Humes (eds) *Scottish Education*. Edinburgh University Press.

Tchaban, A. (1998) *Towards More Flexibility in Training. A Review of Some Experiences to Rationalize the Provision of Vocational Qualifications. Abstract*. Geneva: ILO. Available at http://www.ilo.org/public/English/60empfor/polform/publ/publ-a.htm

Tight, M. (1998) 'Lifelong learning: opportunity or compulsion?' *British Journal of Educational Studies*, 46 (3), 251–63.

THES (1995) 'The new bank that likes to say yes'. *Times Higher Education Supplement*, 8 September.

U3A Online (1999) Available at http://www.u3aonline.org.au/whatare.html

UNESCO (1998) *Unesco Statistical Yearbook*. Paris: UNESCO.

University of Highlands and Islands (UHI) (1999a) 'Megaconference'. Press release, 13 October. Available at http://www.uhi.ac.uk/project/Press_Releases/Megavideoconf.html

University of Highlands and Islands (UHI) (1999b) *Prospectus 2000*. Inverness: UHI. Available at http://www.uhi.ac.uk/prospectus_2000/webintro.html

Winch, C. and Gingell, J. (1999) *Key Concepts in the Philosophy of Education*. London: Routledge.

World Bank (1999) *Education Sector Strategy*. Washington, DC: World Bank Group. Available at http://www.worldbank.org/html/extpb/educat.htm

CHAPTER

14

Education and the Third Wave[1]

Trevor Corner

Introduction

In 1921 the Manchester *Guardian* commented on Albert Einstein's first lecture on relativity to an audience in the University of Manchester as follows:

> Not a single sentence did [Einstein] allow himself to touch on the philosophical implications of his discovery, though that would, no doubt, have been appreciated by his audience. [Einstein] stopped short of pointing out the scientific consequences of his discovery.

Quite clearly Einstein was not communicating with his audience in the way they wished him to. A discussion on education has to be more fulsome, not least because it is a subject that does not easily submit to simple definition. Indeed, it is difficult not to arouse associated philosophical implications and practical consequences in the listener's mind.

This chapter's title comes from Toffler's book of 1980 *The Third Wave*, which had followed on from his earlier publication *Future Shock*. Whilst Toffler's first book had tried to predict the possible future of societies, *The Third Wave* implied that change was inevitable and that preparation for a more international society was essential. Three is the leitmotif throughout the text. The chapter outlines a number of historical links in comparative studies and international education, including lifelong education, and examines three currently neglected ideas – 'memes' intelligence and new forms of electronic communications – which will become important in the future of education. Two, perhaps sardonic, comments are apposite; first a quote of Samuel Beckett's, 'in the future everything will turn out alright unless something foreseen turns up' and, second, that of a former colleague who was often heard to say that if you are venturing into the realms of futurolog

hen make sure that your predictions are far enough into the future that no one can
disprove them.

'Threeness' and complexity[2]

Toffler's 1980 book began with the idea that the rise of agriculture was the first
turning point in human social development. This wave started about 10,000 years
ago and started to attenuate around 1650–1750. The Industrial Revolution was the
second breakthrough; this continued until about 1950 in the USA, and continues
still in many parts of the world. However, from about the 1950s the third wave of
global change has become apparent whilst ripples from the first two waves continue
to affect us. The British townscapes and countryside amply demonstrate this
inherited historical turbulence. Many core values in education are directed at
helping us to understand these realities of history and social development. Humans
living in the third wave of social change have created a new 'info- or techno-
sphere':

> Third Wave people ... are more at ease in the midst of this bombardment of
> blips – the ninety-second news-clip intercut with a thirty-second commercial, a
> fragment of song and lyric, a headline, a cartoon, a collage, a newsletter item, a
> computer print-out ... Rather than trying to stuff the new modular data into
> the standard Second Wave categories or frameworks, they learn to make their
> own, to form their own 'strings' out of the blipped material shot at them by the
> new media. (Toffler, 1980, p. 177).

Toffler was describing American society as he observed it in the 1960s, but it is now
apparent that many of the social characteristics he saw can now be recognized
globally.

Any observant sailor knows that ocean waves synthesize into recognizable
patterns according to the prevailing weather conditions, and that preparation for a
long sea journey entails experiencing three emotional waves: the *anticipation* of the
challenge, the *exhilaration* of getting going and the *reality* of seasickness. Coleridge's fantastic poem *The Rime of the Ancient Mariner* in which, it will be
remembered, the mariner chose 'one of three' of the wedding guests to tell his story
was written whilst walking in the Quantock Hills with William and Dorothy
Wordsworth in 1797. In his darker years, Coleridge was to find out the reality of
seafaring during his voyage to the Mediterranean, suffering seasickness, dejection
and discomfort, but also getting interested in navigation and sail-settings. His
imagination was inspired by the shapes and sights that tall-masted ships afforded
him in the myriad lights and shades of his daily round; he was to use many of these
memories to fuel his writings (Beer, 1974; Holmes, 1999).

An emerging 'third culture' is now detected, consisting of those scientists and
others in the empirical world who, through their work and popular writing, are
taking the place of traditional intellectuals by exploring the deeper meanings of our

lives and making them more understandable. Whilst Einstein had a beautiful sto
to tell about relativity, he was not seen as a 'man of letters', just as major scientis
such as van Neumann, Norbert Weiner and Niels Bohr were excluded from th
literary intellectuals.

C. P. Snow (1993) famously recognized these 'two cultures' in his book of th
title first published in 1959 which many educational systems in the middle of th
twentieth century came to replicate in their curricula and ethos, especially those
the English-speaking world and, Snow argued, most notably England. A short tim
later, in 1963, Snow proposed the 'third culture' arising from the scientif
revolution in which writers such as Dawkins, Gould, Dennett, Penrose, Minsk
Feynman, Pinker and many others have popularized the main ideas encompassed i
nineteenth and twenteeth century new knowledge (Brockman, 1995; Snow
1993).

The political 'third way', Giddens has contended, is a process of not on
countering inequalities in the industrialized societies of today, but also rediscove
ing an effective role for public institutions such as schools. He has questioned, fo
example, the contention that globalization is responsible for *increasing* inequalitie
and quotes American studies that indicate only about 30 per cent in econom
differentiation of male salaries is due to global competition, this being more tha
compensated by the growth of female income (Giddens, 1999).

Diverse lifestyles mean that many people, over their working life, are likely t
experience unemployment, and thus periods of poverty, as well as times of work an
relative affluence. Nevertheless, partly because of these diverse experiences of lif
'third way' economists and sociologists argue that equality of opportunity ha
become of more concern during the 1990s. This is indicated, says Giddens, by th
fact that more people show increased concern for social and educational egalitariar
ism (Giddens, 1999).

Popper, whom Giddens has used to underpin a number of his ideas, wrote abou
a 'world 3' in which he tried to combine values in society with subjective an
objective knowledge. It is difficult to summarize Popper's ideas on this topi
though this rather curious comment is interesting:

> As with our children, so with our theories, and ultimately with all the work w
> do: our products become largely independent of their makers. We may gai
> more knowledge from our children or from our theories than we ever imparte
> to them. This is how we can lift ourselves out of the morass of our ignorance; an
> how we can all contribute to world 3. (Popper, 1976, p. 196)

What came to be known by mathematicians as 'the two-body problem' (such as th
analysis of two connected pendulums) is a situation now amenable to school pupils
For the 'three-body problem' – adding a third pendulum to the system – makes fo
a far more complex, though not random, array of motions of the pendulums. Th
outstanding mathematician, Henri Poincaré, spent several years trying to solve thi
kind of problem and, as we shall see later, his work has had important effects in th
new fields of complexity and chaos some 87 years after his death.

Threeness was a feature of ancient societies and has emerged as a factor in the complexity of contemporary society as we enter the third millennium. Three is the second prime number, divisible only by itself and one. It shares this property with, perhaps, an infinite count of other numbers such as 5, 7, 11, 13, 17, 19, etc. The products of prime numbers, such as 3 × 3, 3 × 5 and 3 × 7, were seen by the early Greeks, such as Pythagoras, to contain magical properties (Duncan, 1999). There are the three ancient tongues (Hebrew, Latin and Greek), the three vowels IOU have two meanings, and there is three-in-one as of the Trinity. Three can be both lucky, and unlucky. And, of course, there is the eternal triangle.

Lifelong learning

Lifelong learning has its roots in adult education, agrarian movements of the seventeenth and eighteenth centuries and the integration of learning with life and work. Robert Owen experimented with communities which combined learning, family, work and religious worship at his famous New Lanark (which lies about 20 miles up the Clyde Valley from Glasgow) almost 200 years ago. As a consequence, Southey was inspired to build an educational community in North America; by degrees these roots of lifelong education led to Dewey's notions of education as an evolutionary and natural growth of knowledge throughout life. The radical educational change of the *folkhøjskole* movement inspired by N. F. S. Grundtvig in Denmark was a real attempt to combine learning with living throughout life to encourage cultural generation and, for Scandinavians at least, national regeneration (Jarvis, 1999).

About the same time that Owen and Southey were experimenting with educational communities, Coleridge was penning the lines of *The Ancient Mariner*, and William Blake crying out against the injustice of the Industrial Revolution. 'Art degraded, imagination denied – war governed nations' was how Blake saw his world, a world dominated by a materialistic ideology in which matter triumphed over the mind and spirit, where the Newtonian universe resulted in 'dark satanic mills' resulting in the 'banishment of the soul' (Hall, 1996).

A hundred years later, Basil Yeaxlee was using Dewey's views in *Democracy and Education* to promote lifelong learning in adult education. Yeaxlee's book was titled *Lifelong Education* and freely discusses the implication of seeing life as a continuous learning process. In the final chapter he quotes H. G. Wells:

> The attainment of the World Republic and the attainment of fully adult life are the general and particular aspects of one and the same reality ... We shall be man in common and immortal in common, and each one of us will develop his (or her) individuality to the utmost, no longer as a separated and conflicted being but as a part and contribution to one continuing whole. (Yeaxlee, 1929, p. 164)

In a sense, discussing lifelong learning in the context of globalization is by no means new. Yeaxlee's book emphasized that the role of each individual was incorporate learning into his or her experiences and interests, and recognize t advantage that accrued to the community – which Yeaxlee tended to interpret ir spiritual framework (Cross-Durant, 1987). Throughout the tradition of continuin and adult education in England (though less so in Scotland and Wales), there h been a tendency to see lifelong learning as genteel education for leisure reserved f those that have 'spare time' (King, 1999). Another important strand of lifelon education in the twentieth century has fed off class wars, recognizing the relatio ship between unemployment and structural social change and recognizing ho professionalism is related to the world of work and skills (Monasta, 1990; Schulle 1990). A very recent report into lifelong learning in Europe titled *Why's the Be Always Stronger Up North?* contends, for example, that schools, colleges ar universities should contest the terrain of lifelong learning with employers, unio and multinationals, who also have a vital interest in the field (Coffield, 1999).

Scandinavia of the 1960s, influenced by Swedish educators such as Torste Husén, started seriously to apply the idea of lifelong education to formal schoolin as well as informal adult education. A recent Swedish teacher education refor proposes training and education that prepares teachers to work in all sectors education. In the UK with the U3A, or University of the Third Age, lifelor learning has become happily established within formal education for older st dents. It is a concept that has become linked, politically and structurally, with tl process of widening access to education at all stages of life and infuses movemen such as work-based learning, problem-based learning and research methods base on evidence-based learning. Given the rich heritage of lifelong education an having now gained a central role in present policy debate, it would be ironic if now became relegated to describing a sector of the formal system (Husén, 1979

Comparative and international studies

One of the early popularizers of comparative studies in education, Michael Sadle anticipated Toffler's metaphor when he said that 'Great tidal movements economic and spiritual change sweep over the world with irresistible force' (Sadle 1964, first published in 1900). Certainly, as exemplified by the development c lifelong education, major educational reforms can occur before and after great soci upheavals such as wars or famine, when social restraints to change can be at the weakest.

The field of comparative and international studies analyses the systematic an contextual changes in education, and uses many of the disciples of the soci sciences and humanities to achieve this. Comparing educational tradition an change is a delicate task, however:

> Educational traditions can be deceptive. Some are old and carved in stone Others are young and appear immutable because the observer has a shor historical memory. Conflicting traditions may compete within a culture. Tradi

tions may be strengthened or weakened by cross-fertilization but the processes by which some imports are welcomed and others rejected are mysterious. Educational traditions are both a source of richness and intransigent obstacles to widely desired change. (McLean, 1995, p. 172)

The uniqueness of national systems of education as expressions of national life and national character has appeared in a new and recent form (for the UK at least) through the concept of education for citizenship. A nineteenth-century observer of international education, K. D. Ushinsky wrote:

Education takes the whole man as he is, with all his national and individual characteristics – his body, soul and mind – and above all addresses itself to a man's character; and character is that very soil in which national characteristics are rooted. (Quoted in Holmes, 1981, p. 25)

This probably pushes the influence of nationalism a little too far in the direction of stereotypification for the modern reader who is likely to have experience of working in or with other cultures and languages. Effective performance in a foreign culture or a multicultural setting requires patience and tackling a learning curve of personal skills that ensure survival.

Whilst one feels 'at home' in one's own culture, living in another continually requires adjustment or dealing with the daily surprises of local habits, idiomatic language, customs and personal feelings (Davies, 1984). It is difficult for *national* curricula to cope with the needs of both minority and majority cultures; they are extraordinarily insensitive to this point. Comparative educationalists were some of the first to design courses in multiculturalism not least because internationalism sensitizes us to different cultures; however, we also have to keep in mind, as the Canadian Matthew Zachariah says, that internationalism and multiculturalism are by no means the same phenomenon (Corner, 1988; Zachariah, 1990).

In everyday life, the number of languages and cultures encountered *seems* to increase. In London and a host of other cities, an evening out might be to see an Elizabethan play at the Globe Theatre, have a meal at a Chinese, Indian or Turkish restaurant with friends who may well originate from several countries and possess a range of languages and cultures, drive home in a car whose parts have been manufactured in four other countries and assembled in a fifth, then sit at home enjoying a 'digestif' whilst watching *Eurotrash*. This kind of experience has been called 'glocalization', or the concentration of global phenomena, i.e. languages, arts, corporate enterprise and cultures, into a locality such as a city or multicultural community.

It has been claimed that, of the current 6000 languages in the world, over half will die out in the coming century, losing vast areas of literature, culture and knowledge (Crystal, 1999). This is likely to occur despite the enormous efforts of educational movements throughout the twentieth century, in the UK and else-where, to maintain the first languages and cultures of 'minorities' (Corner, 1988; Coraer and Bunt-Kokhuis 1991).

The 'heyday' of internationalism and the development of comparative studies

The main writers in comparative studies of education in the 1950s and 1960 include Brickman, Hans, Bereday and many others. This was the heyday of unrestrained internationalism, or so it was perceived at the time. Interest in international studies was intense, and academic mobility was relatively easy.

Over the duration of the three waves of social change identified by Toffler an important human perception has slowly, and almost imperceptibly, occurred. The ancients saw their world at the centre the universe, within the all-embracing celestial sphere. From the sixteenth century the evidence advanced by Copernicus that the sun was the centre of the universe has convinced the great majority of mankind. Increasingly, rocket and satellite technologies of the twentieth century have enabled us to 'stand outside of ourselves' and look at our world from afar individually and collectively we have become – in Schön's terms – 'reflective beings' (Schön, 1983).

This background of a changing perception of human consciousness within a world three culture, coupled with the practical advantages of convenient and cheap travel, allowed international studies to offer a sheen of adventure – even mystery – about discovering the diversity of interpretations of knowledge in other educational perpectives, customs and languages. Writers in comparative studies became increasingly confident of their explanations of the macro-problems to be found in international education and clear in their visions for the future.

Bereday outlined a simple method of four stages to use in comparative studies which he termed description, interpretation, juxtaposition and comparison, and these methodological stages remain a simple way of constructing research in the field today (Bereday, 1964). Nevertheless, just one stage – say the detailed observation and interpretation of teaching and learning in a single classroom – immediately raises the difficulty of generalization from the particular (Stenhouse 1979). Researching information on a modern education system containing thousands of classrooms is an immense task; to undertake the same work in another country and then carry out detailed comparative analyses can occupy the talents of a team of researchers for many years.

Several strategies have been proposed to better cope with these problems. Framework analysis, which discriminates by levels of analysis in the dimensions of geography, demography, society and education is one way to cope with educational complexity (Bray and Thomas, 1995). Because educational boundaries merge into those of history, languages, economic background, family structure, religions and host of other factors, what might be broadly term 'contextual analysis' has been a popular approach to comparative studies. Proponents of case studies thus emphasize the primacy of detailed individual observation and cultural and linguistic context (Bell and Grant, 1977; King 1979). Other important research uses discourse analysis; discourse cartography, as developed by Paulson, tries to catch the process of change more acutely than structural analysis appears to do, and thus enables a more dynamic understanding that postmodernist views seek (Paulson, 1997).

More recently, Watson has brought attention to the continuing growth of the role of multinational organizations, such as the OECD and the World Bank, and the multinational corporations – IBM, BT, Coca-Cola, for example – coupled with the proliferation of the telecommunication and media industries. Relatively few countries are affected by global transnational corporations, which are effectively based in only fourteen OECD countries and three-quarters of whose wealth is confined to Western Europe, Japan and the USA. Further, the top 250 global companies have larger turnovers than the 90 poorest countries' gross domestic products (GDPs) (Watson, 1999). Global development is prominent in tele-communications and financial markets linked through the Internet, environmental and atmospheric change and 'the use of the whole world as a potential production line or for division of labour' (Watson, 1998, p. 15). As alluded to earlier, Giddens, Brockman and others have attempted to track educational, cultural and social change as a global process.

Throughout the use of the above models (and many others) for international studies, other all-pervasive influences, such as post-colonial attitudes and the phenomenon of multiculturalism, have infused international studies and ques-tioned just who might benefit from them. The paradox of cultural relativism, the hegemony of the developed world and the persistence of the North–South economic divide remain. Whilst the number of students studying in other countries con-tinues to increase (there are probably about 65,000 postgraduates world-wide receiving support for studies abroad; Watts, 1999)), this remains a small fraction of those who travel for leisure in order to sample a 'blip', to use Toffler's term, of another culture.

Today's writers on international education are more uncertain about solutions because they recognize the complexities of educational change, and cannot so easily – like many social scientists – fight through the thicket of postmodernism. That need not be because, as is suggested in some contemporary papers, academics in the field of comparative studies are lesser than their predecessors. Perhaps teachers and academics, rather like today's politicians, can no longer expect their views to hold sway without challenge, or that their students and acolytes will step in line when beckoned.

The schoolteacher and college lecturer also recognize this shaky foundation supporting their platform of knowledge and know-how. Unless they are allowed the incentive to view educational change in the context of their own society and others, and transfer these understandings to the school classroom and their pupils, they may well feel (as many seem to) like flotsam and jetsam tossed about in the continual waves of ideas, curricula and management processes that overtake their school. For teachers to appreciate the need for change in teaching and learning, they wish to see and understand the big picture of educational and social change.

In the past findings from comparative research in education have been useful, particularly for teachers and policy-makers, to answer questions such as:

- Has any other country tried out the reforms we are thinking of?
- Are children performing better now than in the past?

- How competitive are we in terms of educational achievement?
- Are we getting value for money?

What comparative educators have been keen to do is to not only try to answer such questions, but also provide interpretations within the all-important national and regional contexts where the research has taken place. This will almost certainly include reference to those 'intransigent obstacles to widely desired change' that McLean has referred to, and may also show that intended reforms in one country have already been tried in another with consequences that can guide policy.

Sometimes unforeseen events, such as the central European 'Velvet Revolution' in 1989, lead to irreversible political, economic and educational changes. Kotásek has compared the explosion of legislation and subsequent strategic decisions on educational reform in ten countries (Bulgaria, the Czech Republic, Estonia, Latvia, Lithuania, Hungary, Poland, Romania, Slovakia and Slovenia). Several trends are indicated: as ideological control of education was reduced, choice and decentralization has increased; and across the central European countries, these changes have been concentrated in two relatively short periods occurring around 1990–1 and 1998–9.

For comparativists the interesting thing about these New European reforms is that they are not the result of clear planning or long-term visions of education, but responses to totally unforeseen political changes (Kotásek, 1999). Vaclev Havel, whose play *Velvet Revolution* tried to anticipate the changes from communism still, apparently, regards the Czech Republic as the 'theatre of the absurd':

> Where does patriotism end and nationalism and chauvinism begin? Where does civic solidarity begin and tribal passion begin? Where does the spontaneous and thoroughly respectable delight in the remarkable athletic achievement of one's fellow citizens end, and the expropriation of someone else's achievement by a mob with no ideas and no personal sense of responsibility begin? (Havel, 1999)

Havel continues to act as a spokesman for the whole of central Europe, pushing for European Union membership, greater integration and an EU constitution.

Memes as cultural artefacts

Young children, within a few years of life, absorb basic literacy and number systems which come to act as part of their educational survival strategy. These basic systems rapidly elaborate into 'meanings', some of them universal, by a process by no means fully understood. Three is a factor of the number 42 (which itself is double Pythagoras's magic number 21) and which, in Douglas Adams's *The Hitch Hiker's Guide to the Galaxy* (Volume One in a Trilogy of Four, as the author would have it), is the answer to the question of life, the universe and everything. It has to be borne in mind that it took Deep Thought's computer software, one of the central 'characters' of the book, 75,000 generations to come to this answer, which is 3 to the power 3 to the power 3 to the power 3 *years*, assuming that we and our children will continue to enjoy an increasing life expectancy! Tim Berners-Lee, the originator of the web, heads W3C (World Wide Web Consortium). The 'third place' can be found at a Starbucks Café, an oasis between work and home.

The number three is a universal, and for the most part, so is its symbol; this statement is more true now than it was in the past. Previous civilizations developed number symbols – Mesopotamian, Egyptian, Mayan, Greek, Latin, Chinese to name a few. Such symbols came from sticks and pebbles for the Mayans, hieroglyphics for the Egyptians and letters of their alphabets for the Greeks and Romans, and characters for the Chinese. These symbols (and combination of symbols) all had various strengths and weaknesses when applied to say, the creation of a calendar, calligraphy or navigation (Duncan, 1999). Modern global number symbols are based on the Hindu system which has evolved, over several thousand years, to those we teach today in early primary, with the important addition of the concepts of zero and minus. This could be seen as a 'meme', albeit a very slowly evolving one – a cultural artefact – a global unit of knowledge.

Memes are cultural artefacts that are copied from one person to another by imitation (Dawkins, 1976). Since that first definition of a meme, coming from the world of evolutionary biology and in some ways analogous to the gene, there has been a considerable growth in the study of memetics. A limited number of writers have tried to apply the idea of memes to the process of learning, in both humans and animals (Meltzoff, 1996).

There is much debate on whether a meme is a 'replicator' or an 'interactor' (or both), and the kind of distinction that is to be drawn between 'imitation' and 'contation'. The latter debate is concerned with the process of how 'memes' are passed on from person to person, or what teachers would normally refer to as the process of learning. The debates in contemporary memetics are quite fascinating in themselves, but for education it would be worth trying to apply memetics to individual and social learning.

Social learning implies learning something from other people by observing, imitating and interacting with them. Individual learning normally implies learning on one's own by reflective thinking, reading a book or working on a computer, possibly through surfing the web. Although teachers intuitively understand the differences between these two learning processes, and set great store by this distinction, it turns out in practice to be extraordinarily difficult to define the boundary between the two.

None the less, such distinctions are important in education because they will substantially affect the ways that teaching and learning are 'technologized' in the future. Bound in with this question are economic and political questions, for example, the recruitment of teachers and their education and training, the quality of teachers, human machine interaction such as teaching through computers and/or the web, or the most effective ways of debating issues in morality and ethics. Let us highlight the implications of emphasizing individual learning over social learning. Imagine a limited cadre of expert teachers maximizing the use of computers and the web to enable themselves to reach out to school pupils across the country. If by

2010 all school pupils will have access to a computer it is a small step to extend this idea to all people – in reality moving from school-based learning to open lifelong learning. Extending the idea to global learning (and incorporating all primary language translations – quite a challenge), then it is possible to imagine the instantaneous transmission of a kind of world curriculum. Does this have any sense in reality, and would such a scenario increase or decrease the diversity and richness of knowledge across the world?

Memetics is a hotly disputed field, especially by social scientists (Aunger, 1999). Blackmore points out that memetic learning cannot include some kinds of learning such as the formation of cognitive maps, emotional states and perceptions which are formed predominately though social learning. She does suggest, however, that all forms of cultural behaviours could be passed on through imitative, instructed and collaborative learning, and these are all forms of learning potentially possible through the World Wide Web (Blackmore, 1998).

> Human beings are fundamentally unique not because they are especially clever, not because they have big brains or language, but because they are capable of extensive and generalised *imitation*. (Blackmore, 1998, p. 5)

The development of learning through the union of the new electronic communications and people. It is 30 years since the start of the practical development of the World Wide Web and ten years since the first development of a global process of communication. These developments hold immense attraction for the banking, retail and communications fields, and thus directly or indirectly, for education. As for radio and television communications, there are likely to be mixed blessings.

Developing global intelligence

Intelligence is a highly contested area of education. We have been familiar with logico-mathematical intelligence and linguistic intelligence for some considerable time. Basic literacy and numeracy have become the global keys which are able to unlock the benefits of education for all people, anywhere and of any age. Kamens, Benevot and others have argued this is how to recognize the fundamental elements of a primary global curriculum. For many, the extent to which it was deemed that they exhibited these two kinds of intelligences, triggered the decisions as to the kind of education to which they could be most suited.

In 1983, Howard Gardner stirred up what had become a relatively stale debate centring around the nature–nurture question by suggesting that there were five other discrete intelligences including the musical, the spatial, the bodily-kinaesthetic, the intrapersonal and the interpersonal. Subsequently, he added classificatory intelligence and spiritual intelligence, though he was not too sure of the latter (Gardner, 1983). What Gardner succeeded in doing was to make what had become a relatively unattractive theory appear interesting again. To teachers, the possibilities that children may be blessed with different intelligences to different degrees seemed much more manageable than the rather cut and dried measurements of normalized intelligence test scores. They were able to look more carefully at children and examine their own assumptions about potential and achievement.

Gardner (1983, pp. 59–64) also established criteria of an intelligence:

- the potential isolation of the area by brain damage;
- the existence of it in idiots, savants and other exceptional individuals;
- an identifiable core operation/set of operations;
- a distinctive developmental history, along with a definable set of expert 'end-state' performances;
- evolutionary history plausibility;
- support from experimental psychological tasks;
- support from psychometric findings; and
- susceptibility to encoding in a symbol system.

One of the attractive aspects of the theory is that much weight is placed on the arts, applying cognitive measures to them as much as to the sciences and mathematics (Gardner, 1993). Perversely, the arts (and often history) are quite deliberately portrayed in terms of magic and mystery. Just as Keats regretted the 'unweaving of the rainbow' by Newton through his demonstrating that 'white' light was made up of a rainbow of colours and therefore took mystery from nature, so, it is sometimes argued, the arts require a kind of abstract, mysterious quality that goes beyond just everyday creativity (Dawkins, 1998).

Can Gardner's intelligences be shown to exist? White has put forward a logical argument to show that this cannot be demonstrated one way or the other, but he does believe that schools based on the notion of multiple intelligence, and there are 'MI schools' in North America and some in the UK, are likely to be more aware of all the range of abilities in which children have potential (White, 1998). One particular criticism of the theory is that what are normally referred to as talents are difficult to distinguish from Gardner's 'intelligences', encouraging more attention to be paid of late to the processes of teaching and learning in classrooms.

The public popularity of Gardner's writings has tended to obscure other modern theories of intelligence. Anderson, for example, distinguishes intelligence based on physiological processes and higher-order skills like judgement and reasoning. Sternberg's Triarchic Theory posits meta, performance and knowledge-acquisition components, and endeavours to bring together diverse aspects of intelligence found in the real world (Anderson, 1992; Sternberg, 1988).

Extelligence, language and cultural rituals

Most learning in practice, wherever it takes place, remains a limiting way for developing human potential, as individuals, as a community or globally. We now have computers, the very machines that allowed the complexities of Poincaré's equations to be turned into diagrams so beautiful and natural that we are able to discern trees, flowers, leaves, maps and many other everyday objects in them. When computers are connected to the Internet and everything else that is connected to i is taken into account – laboratories, libraries, millions of individuals with their ow point of view and expertise – this is 'the greatest organized source of informatio that has ever existed on this planet' (Stewart and Cohen, 1997, p. 244).

Stewart and Cohen call this information source 'extelligence-space' or simpl 'extelligence'. Intelligence deals in understanding: extelligence deals in informa tion and primarily depends on two aspects of intelligence – language and cultura rituals. Language grows though 'ontic (or ontological) dumping', and cultura rituals provide the new ideas and words that become embedded in language. Mor prosaically, and referring back to an earlier quote, this is 'the process of liftin ourselves out of the morass of ignorance' that Popper required for his World 3.

Combining the ideas of extelligence-space and memetic theory, it is possible t imagine a continuous transmission of learning and culture via a global electroni web allowing an extremely rapid spread of memes and the process of *imitation* Humans are exceptional at learning by imitation and moving between individua and social modes of learning throughout their cultural evolution, includin language. In postmodern language, a continuous narrative of knowledge woul have been established through an interactive global atmosphere of discourse According to Berners-Lee, the World Wide Web was an attempt to create a random association between 'absolutely anything and absolutely anything (Naughton, 1999). There are those whose faith in the web leads them to claim th possibility that new 'electronic learning' could enable absolutely anyone to lear absolutely anything, absolutely anywhere.

Comparative studies for the future

Some would say that the basic issues facing international education are not new. Gary Theisen, in his 1997 address to the American Comparative and Internationa Education Society said:

> I fully recognize that the only thing 'new' in life may be the inventive formulae for retelling old fables. The issues defining modern states, whether they be political, economic, or educational, are well travelled friends who would scoff at our preoccupation with the advent of the new millennium and the embedded hope for new beginnings. (Theisen, 1997, p. 397)

Broadfoot has likened comparative education to jade stone, which was a cultural artefact, used for working tools as well as decoration by both the Maoris and Chinese. The subtle qualities of jade are similar to those of comparative education, where the cultural context of schools and the deeper understandings of 'conflicting traditions' in different countries and societies need to be teased out (Broadfoot, 1999). Studies in comparative education should not lose sight of their roots in historical and cultural analysis (Watson, 1998).

In common with the social sciences the tensions in comparative education between the interpretative and positivist research traditions are always present, and because education is such a human activity, a '*pre*-modern' rather than a '*post*-modern' view forms a constant backlash to what are perceived as rationalist assumptions. Some argue against 'the current international obsession with measurement that underpins the assumption that it is possible to describe, compare and evaluate all the different aspects of educational activity' and reject many of the quantitative attempts to compare education performance (Broadfoot, 1999, p. 222). It is certainly true that the hardest part of any research is the interpretation of the data. However, the same author goes on:

> As even the natural sciences come to terms with the implications of chaos theory so the impetus to reject traditional Western models of rationality and to replace them with the more relativist perspectives of postmodernism is growing. (*Ibid.*, p. 226)

Brockman, in developing his ideas of the third culture, would propose that such views (and they are certainly those held by many writers in education) are uninformed. The above statement ignores the fact that ideas of uncertainty and chaos have been perplexing scientific rational thinking for a long time. Chaos, as is now commonly known, was developed in an early mathematical form by Henri Poincaré over 100 years ago through his work on dynamical systems, in his day called 'qualitative theory of differential equations' which he worked on trying to solve the three-body problem – how do you describe the motion of three bodies in space if you know their starting points?

Although Poincaré worked for three years on the three-body problem and made good progress, he gave up when he came across a kind of motion that looked as if it had no structure. This apparent random motion was worked on by many people over the intervening years to the extent that we have now become familiar with the beautiful patterns developed by Lorentz attractors and Mandelbrot sets (Bragg, 1998, p. 194).

So, far from science 'just beginning to come to terms with chaos', it can be more justifiably argued that natural philosophy, or science, begat chaos and it was scientists such as Birkhoff, Lorentz and Mandelbrot who developed the field to the level of understanding we have today (Gleik, 1990). In the 1980s fractals, natural examples of which are leaves and ferns, became an organizing principle in the study of polymers and in problems of nuclear reactor safety. Hollywood uses fractals in the creation of realistic landscapes, earthly and extraterrestrial. Poincaré would have been pleased at these artistic applications, as he strongly argued against seeing mathematics as totally subject to classical logic and preferred to see problems in a holistic way: 'A scientist worthy of the name, above all a mathematician, experiences in his work the same impression as an artist; his pleasure is as great and of the same nature' (Poincaré, quoted in Bell, 1986, p. 526). Bell describes Poincaré as 'the last universalist', the last person able to grasp the whole range of knowledge across the sciences and the arts of the day.

By no means all scientists believe that rationality rules over all knowledge (after all, many of them hold religious beliefs). Roger Penrose has argued that mathematical understanding itself relies on 'non-computational activity' of the brain or mind, though adds that this does not imply that mental faculties are beyond what can be achieved computationally, that is quantitatively (Penrose, 1994). Francis Crick does push rationality as far as you can go when he says:

> The Astonishing Hypothesis is that 'you', your joys and your sorrows, your memories and your ambitions, your sense of personal identity and free will, are in fact no more than the behaviour of a vast assembly of nerve cells and their associated molecules. (Crick, 1994, p. 3)

So comparative education has to recognize a more public understanding of the sciences and social sciences, whilst continuing to argue the vital importance of knowledge in context.

Conclusion

Being intellectually adventurous is more scary than bungey jumping or paragliding, and sometimes carries the same adrenaline rush. Teachers know well the satisfying feeling of working within a well-established secure area of knowledge. Intellectuals and researchers (who are for the most part also teachers) come to the realization that the new idea of today which refutes established knowledge will itself be refuted tomorrow.

Whilst comparative and international education uses big ideas, it is rooted in precise observation of the particular. It will continue to have a role in informing government policy, as governments will continue to have a vital interest in their educational systems for the foreseeable future. Private organizations and corporations, especially those in communications, have realized the powerful commercial value of electronic media and the access it gives them to the educational global market.

What is the agenda for comparative and international education for the future? Conventionally, it will continue to interpret and compare educational traditions, grow its roots in historical and cultural analysis, analyse the macro-problems of education by identifying global themes, emphasise the *context* of education through the international perspective of languages, gender, ethnicity and multiculturalism, and ask direct and simple questions such as, Who educates? Who learns? When?

But there are also new tasks for the future which must include providing purposeful and practical goals for advising governmental education reforms; investigating the role of public and private agencies in education, multinational organizations and corporations; analysing changing structures and forces such as private education, partnerships, electronic information systems such as the web; and reviewing new theories of learning arising from the social and natural sciences that will impact on global and international education. That is an agenda which will keep everyone busy for a while.

Notes

1. This chapter is based on an Inaugural Lecture titled 'Every third wave: developing global intelligence in education' given by the author at Middlesex University in November 1999.
2. Increasing number is normally associated with increasing complexity which is a main argument used throughout this chapter. However, this is not always the case; Bayesian mathematics uses a simple idea that the more often something happens (such as the sun rising in the morning) the more likely it will happen in the future. As with Poincaré's analyses, computers have enabled recent applications of Bayesian statistics to pattern recognition in several fields of human behaviour.

References

Adams, D. (1979) *The Hitch Hiker's Guide to the Galaxy*. London: Pan.

Anderson, M. (1992) *Intelligence and Development: A Cognitive Theory*. Oxford: Blackwell.

Aunger, R. (1999) '*Do Memes Account for Culture?*' Conference report, Cambridge. King's College. http://www.cus.cam.ac.uk

Beer, J. (1974) *Coleridge: Poems*. London: Dent.

Bell, E. T. (1986) *Men of Mathematics*. New York: Simon and Schuster.

Bell, R. and Grant, N. (1977) *Patterns of Education in the British Isles*. London: Allen and Unwin.

Bereday, G. Z. F. (1964) *Comparative Method in Education*. New York: Rinehart and Winston.

Blackmore, S. (1998) 'Imitation and the definition of a meme'. *Journal of Memetics*, 2(2), 6.

Bragg, M. (1998) *On Giant's Shoulders*. London: Hodder and Stoughton.

Bray, M. and Thomas, M. (1995) 'Level of comparison in education studies'. *Harvard Educational Review*, 65, 472–90.

Broadfoot, P. (1999) 'Stones from other Hills may serve to polish the jade of this one: towards a neo-comparative "learnology" of education'. *Compare*, 29 (3), 217–31.

Brockman, J. (1995) *The Third Culture*. New York: Simon and Schuster.

Coffield, F. (1999) *Why's the Beer Always Stronger Up North?* Studies of Lifelong Learning in Europe. Bristol: Policy Press.

Corner, T. (1988) 'The maritime and border regions of Western Europe'. *Comparative Education*, 24 (2), 229–45.

Corner, T. and Bunt-Kokhuis, S. (1991) *The Space Between Words*. Tilburg: Tilburg University Press.

Crick, F. (1994) *The Astonishing Hypothesis*. London: Simon and Schuster.

Cross-Durrant, A. (1987) 'Basil Yeaxlee and the origins of lifelong education', in P. Jarvis (ed.) *Twentieth Century Thinkers in Adult Education*. London: Routledge.

Crystal, D. (1999) 'The death of language'. *Prospect*, November.

Davies, A. (1984) 'The interaction of language and culture', in T. Corner (ed.) *Education in Multicultural Societies*. London: Routledge.

Dawkins, R. (1976) *The Selfish Gene*. Oxford: Oxford University Press.

Dawkins, R. (1998) *Unweaving the Rainbow*. Harmondsworth: Penguin.

Duncan, D. E. (1999) *The Calendar*. London: Fourth Estate.

Gardner, H. (1983) *Frames of Mind*. London: Heinemann.

Gardner, H. (1993) *Frames of Mind: The Theory in Practice*. New York: Basic Books.

Giddens, A. (1999) 'Social change in Britain'. The 10th ESRC Annual Lecture.

Gleick, J. (1990) *Chaos*. London: Sphere Books.

Hall, E. (1996) *In Defence of Genius*. Arts Council Annual Lecture. Halifax: Dean Clough.

Havel, V. (1999) 'The first laugh'. Speech at the Central European University, Budapest.

Holmes, B. (1981) *Comparative Education: Some Considerations of Method*. London: Unwin.

Holmes, R. (1999) *Coleridge: Darker Reflections*. London: HarperCollins.

Husén, T. (1979) *The School in Question*. Oxford: Oxford University Press.

Jarvis, P. (1999) 'Global trends in lifelong learning and the response of the universities'. *Comparative Education*, 35 (2), 249–57.

King, E. (1979) *Education for Uncertainty*. London: Sage.

King, E. (1999) 'Transformation'. *Comparative Education*, 35 (2), 109–17.

Kotásek, J. (1999) 'The problems of reforming teacher education'. Keynote address at the 24th ATEE Annual Conference, Leipzig.

McLean, M. (1995) *Educational Traditions Compared*. London: David Fulton.

Meltzoff, A. (1996) 'The human infant as imitative generalist', in C. Heyes and B. Galef (eds) *Social Learning in Animals: The Roots of Culture*. San Diego: Academic Press.

Monasta, A. (1990) 'Education, employment and work organisations', in T. Corner (ed.) *Learning Opportunities for Adults*. London: Croom Helm.

Naughton, J. (1999) *A Brief History of the Future*. London: Weidenfeld and Nicholson.

Paulson, R. G. (1997) 'Mapping visual culture in comparative education discourse'. *Compare*, 27 (2), 117–52.

Peurose, R. (1994) *Shadows of the Mind: A Search for the Missing Science of Consciousness*. New York: Oxford University Press.

Popper, K. (1976) *Unended Quest: An Intellectual Autobiography*. London: Fontana.

Sadler, M. (1964) 'How can we learn anything of value from the practical study of foreign systems of education?' *Comparative Education Review*, 7 (2), 307–14.

Schön, D. (1983) *The Reflective Practitioner*. New York: Basic Books.

Schuller, T. (1990) 'Paid educational leave: idée passée or future benefit?', in T. Corner (ed.) *Learning Opportunities for Adults*. London: Croom Helm.

Snow, C. P. (1993) *The Two Cultures*. Cambridge: Cambridge University Press.

Stenhouse, L. (1979) 'Case study in comparative education: particularity and generalisation'. *Comparative Education*, 15 (1), 5–10.

Sternberg, R. J. (1988) *The Triarchic Mind: A New Theory of Human Intelligence*. New York: Viking.

Stewart, I. and Cohen, J. (1997) *Figments of Reality: the Evolution of the Curious Mind*. Cambridge: Cambridge University Press.

Theisen, G. (1997) 'The new ABCs of comparative and international education'. *Comparative Education Review*, 41 (4), 397–412.

Toffler, A. (1970) *Future Shock*. London: Pan.

Toffler, A. (1980) *The Third Wave*. London: Pan.

Watson, K. (1998) 'Memories, models and mapping: the impact of geopolitical changes on comparative studies in education'. *Compare*, 28 (1), 5–31.

Watson, K. (1999) 'Comparative educational research: the need for re- conceptualisation and fresh insights'. *Compare*, 29 (3), 233–48.

Watts, N. (ed.) (1999) *The International Postgraduate: Challenges to British Higher Education*. London: UK Council for Graduate Education.

White, J. (1998) *Do Howard Gardner's Multiple Intelligences Add Up?* London: Institute of Education, University of London.

Yeaxlee, B. (1929) *Lifelong Education*. London: Cassell.

Zachariah, M. (1990) 'For a committed internationalism in the comparative study of cultures'. *Compare*, 20 (1), 83–7.

Name Index

Subject Index